ID0396946

GANGSTERS

GANGSTERS

Fifty Years of Madness, Drugs,
and Death on the Streets of America

LEWIS YABLONSKY

NEW YORK UNIVERSITY PRESS
New York and London

NEW YORK UNIVERSITY PRESS
New York and London

© 1997 by New York University

Library of Congress Cataloging-in-Publication Data
Yablonsky, Lewis.
Gangsters : fifty years of madness, drugs, and death on the
streets of America / Lewis Yablonsky.
p.   cm.
Includes bibliographical references and index.
Contents: The current gang problem—Gangs in the 20th century—
Gang characteristics—Black and chicano gangs : in and out of
prison—Why gangs kill : the sociopath factor—Some effective
interventions—The therapeutic community approach to gangs—
Varied theoretical viewpoints—The violent gang as a near-group—
Joining a positive gang : a plan for treating gangsters in a
therapeutic community.
ISBN 0-8147-9679-6 (cloth : alk paper)
1. Gangs—United States.   2. Gangs—United States—Prevention.
I. Title.
HV6439.U5Y3   1997
302.3'4—dc20   96-35713
                         CIP

New York University Press books are printed on acid-free paper,
and their binding materials are chosen for strength and durability.

Manufactured in the United States of America

10 9 8 7 6 5 4 3 2 1

Contents

o o o o o o o o o o

Acknowledgments

○　○　○　○　○　○　○　○　○　○

M Y PERSONAL AND PROFESSIONAL understanding of gangs has been influenced by many people. My brilliant and beloved son Mitch, a Los Angeles County probation officer, supported me throughout the travails of researching and writing this book, and pointed me in many useful directions for the acquisition of data. I am deeply grateful to my dear friends Norman Herman, Ben Krentzman, and Vince Jeffries, who listened with a feigned attentiveness that often bordered on sincerity to all of the good and bad concepts on gangs that I bounced off of them over the past several years, and on many occasions they contributed to my knowledge on the subject.

The L.A. County Probation Department was a vital source of data for my book. Barry Nidorf, Chief Probation Officer, paved the way for many of my interviews, and also provided me with an insightful analysis of the probation department's methodology for preventing, treating, and controlling gangs. Two probation officers, Jim Gallipeau, a thirty-year-veteran of the gang wars in South Central L.A. and Brad Carson, whose knowledge is based on his gang prevention efforts in Venice, helped me considerably in developing my overall perspective on gangs. I am also grateful to Ken Bell of the Los Angeles County district attorney's office and Peter Shutan of the Los Angeles city attorney's office for providing me with their valuable insights into the L.A. gang problem.

My dear friends and colleagues in the Amity Therapeutic Community provided me with a considerable amount of data on gangs in a variety of ways. The support of Amity's directors, Betty Fleishman, Naya Arbiter, and Rod Mullen, facilitated my entry into two of Amity's landmark prison programs — the California Department of Correction's Amity Right Turn Project in the R. J. Donavan San Diego Prison and the short-lived, but innovative, therapeutic community project in the Beaumont Texas Prison. Many Amity people helped me with my book personally and professionally. Notable in this positive gang of people was Elaine Abraham, Sheila Giddings, Fred Tent, Ernie Logan, Rachel Curtis, and Raymond Adame. Two special contributors to this project were two former L.A. Crips, my good friends Alex Pipkin and Demitrius McGee. My dear friend and colleague Zev Putterman, one of the most brilliant and intelligent ex-junkies on the planet, also contributed enormously to my viewpoint on several aspects of the gang problem.

Over the past forty-five years, several hundred active and former gangsters, in and out of prison, provided valuable data for the book. The platitude, "without their help, this book would not have been written" is literally true. I am most grateful for their cooperation in individual and group interviews, and their responses to questionnaires. Lena Lindsey and Jake Smotherman assisted me in the administration of the questionnaires.

My colleagues at Texas A & M University — Commerce, welcomed me into the Department of Sociology and Criminal Justice at a pivotal juncture in my sociological career and provided a pleasant and productive intellectual environment for the completion of this book. My special thanks go to Drs. Mathew Kanjirathinkal, Bill Thompson, Rock Clinton, and R. N. Singh and to President Jerry Morris. Randy McBroom, Jackie Harred, and Gregg Williford helped to analyze my gang questionnaires and contributed enormously to this aspect of the book.

Finally, and of importance, the enthusiastic acceptance of this project by New York University Press Editor-in-Chief Niko Pfund, and the excellent editorial suggestions of my editor, Tim Bartlett, proved to be of enormous help in the development and completion of this book.

Introduction

○ ○ ○ ○ ○ ○ ○ ○ ○ ○

If you want to truly understand something — try to change it.

— KURT LEWIN

STREET GANGS IN AMERICA prior to the end of World War I were relatively nonviolent when compared to contemporary violent gangs. In the first half of the twentieth century, the behavior of juvenile gangs was marked by a sense of camaraderie, a territorial imperative, some fistfights, and random acts of delinquency. Over the past fifty years, in the post–World War II period, gang-related acts of madness, drugs, and death on the streets have increasingly become a serious national problem. This gang problem, involving drugs and senseless violence, has turned into a nightmare for citizens and police in almost every city, large and small, in America.

In October 1995, a family car with several children in it took a wrong turn and drove into a Los Angeles gang's territory on a dead-end street. The gang's hair-trigger proclivity for violence exploded. Believing their territory had been invaded, they sprung into action and opened fire on the car with a hail of bullets from automatic weapons that killed a three-year-old girl with a bullet in her head and wounded several members of the hapless victim's family. Most regrettably, this is not an isolated incident in the contemporary violent gang's pattern of senseless homicidal activities. Although they mainly kill each other, innocent victims often wind up in the cross fire of lethal gang violence.

I have been engaged, personally and professionally, in an effort to understand and change the bizarre and senseless violence of gangs for almost fifty years. My personal introduction to the phenomenon of senseless gang violence happened as an eight-year-old victim. My family lived in the area of a black ghetto in Newark, New Jersey, and I grew up in the swirl of violence and rage that dominated our neighborhood. I attended Miller Street School, a dominantly black school, whose only claim to fame was that Sarah Vaughn, who later became a famous jazz singer, was an alumna.

At Miller I was in the white minority, and I was referred to as an "ofay" or "fayboy" (meaning white boy) by the black gangs that dominated the school. During those years, from age eight to twelve, I was victimized many times by the school's black gangs for what I considered at that time rational and irrational motives. The rational approach was a form of protection called "tech-taking" that involved the extortion of fifteen to twenty cents a week — big money for a kid in those days. The "protection" was that you wouldn't be assaulted if you paid up.

The irrational assaults were related to my being an "ofay." As a white minority, I was periodically assaulted for no special reason — other than what I later found out as a sociologist was reverse prejudice. In those days, violence seldom, if ever, involved any lethal weapons. Most fighting was done one-on-one with fists, although on occasion it was group-on-one. In these early ganglike situations, my response involved rolling with the punches and getting a few punches in here and there as I was being knocked down. Some fairness prevailed when I was allowed to fight one-on-one with an adversary. There were a few occasions when I actually won in a fair fight.

Later on in my teenage years, I attended and graduated from one of Newark's dominantly black high schools, South Side High. (South Side High was renamed, Malcolm X-Shabazz High School in the 1970s when it became an almost totally African American high school.) In the early 1940s, the school was self-segregated, with black students hanging out on one side of the school and whites on the other. I often integrated the black area of the school, largely because I was interested and entertained by male black students who played "the dozens." This was a verbal game, where a number of kids would encircle two main actors, who would verbally spar with each other by spontaneously creating nasty rhymes, which usually attacked the opponent's mother. (A one liner I recall was, "Fucked your Ma in an alleyway, when I got through, she thought she was Cab Calloway.") The adversary would counter with what was called "a backhap." If his retort was strong, the group would chant, "Man what a strong backhap!" Retrospectively, I believe the dozens was really the earliest form of what is now hailed as the new musical form known as "gangsta rap."

My interest in the dozens, unfortunately contributed to a memorably violent situation in which I was seriously assaulted by a black gang. The high school dozen players were minor leaguers. One black classmate and friend of mine told me, "Man if you dig these guys, you should check out the cats on Prince Street."

The corner of Prince and Kinney Streets was the center for older more expert dozen players. One afternoon, after enjoying several hours of their fascinating impromptu entertainment on the corner of Prince and Kinney Streets, I headed home. I apparently was in the wrong place at the wrong time. Several blocks from Prince and Kinney, four young black men came walking toward me with a belligerent demeanor. They crowded me off the sidewalk. As I tried to get out of their way, one of them greeted me with the puzzling query, "Hey you ofay motherfucker, what did you say about my mother?" Being stupid and nervous at the time, I started to answer the question with something to the effect of, "I never met your mother." This was, of course, completely beside the point to my attackers.

The next thing I knew, after receiving a punch right on the jaw, I was down on the ground in a fetal position trying hard to avoid kicks to my head and body. The beating continued ferociously for several minutes, after which, bloody and bowed, I wandered home. To this day, I still think about the senselessness and the raging ferocity of my undeserved beating by this gang. That event, plus other social factors in my teenage years in Newark, caused me to carry a switchblade knife for protection until I was almost eighteen. In my early years, the platitude that "some of my best friends are juvenile delinquents" certainly applied to me.

Another valuable experience that further introduced me into the world of gangs, delinquency, and social problems before I acquired any formal education on the subject was a job I had with my father. His occupation for most of his life was driving a laundry truck that picked up laundry in the poorest section of Newark. This almost completely African American neighborhood was — and to a large extent remains — socioeconomically, a third world country. People sent out their laundry because they had no available facilities for washing their clothes.

During my adolescent years when I helped my father on his truck, I delivered laundry to poor people, some living in cellars with orange crates for furniture and mattresses on the floor. Experiencing these situations directly, spending time informally talking with our clients when I delivered their laundry, and observing children growing up under these conditions were among my most emotionally affecting and profound sociology lessons.

My two brothers, Morris and Joe, also helped my father with his difficult job. In addition to helping him deliver laundry, an important aspect of our job was, in effect, being security guards in a crime-ridden and often violent neighborhood. Without our presence, laundry would be stolen from the truck. One day, in an unguarded moment, someone did steal the truck with a load of laundry on it.

Our work presented my family with some tough firsthand experiences and insights into the causes of crime, criminological issues, and victimology. This might possibly explain why I became a criminologist and my brother Joe served as an FBI agent for thirty years. At the peak of his career, he was Special Agent in Charge of the Las Vegas, Nevada, office and in this capacity went up against the mob that controlled Nevada casinos. Joe and I over the years have shared a considerable amount of data and theories on both adult and youth gangs. Many of his insights on gang behavior, derived from these discussions, are woven into this book.

These observations of social problems and early gang-related experiences during my adolescence strongly motivated me to attempt to understand the social and psychological nature of gang violence in American society. Consequently, in my early adult years, after a three-year-tour of duty in the Navy during World War II, I completed an undergraduate degree under the GI Bill at Rutgers University and went on to graduate studies at New York University, where I completed my masters and doctorate in sociology and criminology.

During my NYU graduate student days, I worked as a group supervisor for two years in a juvenile detention center attached to the juvenile court facility in Newark. Many of the youths incarcerated in this jail were gangsters from my old neighborhood. Many of them, with some affection, remembered me and identified me as the "laundry man" who had been in their homes. Intimately knowing something about their earlier life experiences provided me some insights into the social background that led to their delinquent behavior and incarceration.

My position in the juvenile jail as a group supervisor enabled me to learn more about the phenomenon of gangs and delinquency. I spent many hours informally talking with and researching the gang kids in custody. During those years I learned a great deal about their motivation for participating in gangs, gang violence, and the structure of gangs. My work in the detention center was most valuable in providing the data for writing several papers on the structure and function of gangs for several graduate courses in sociology and psychology that I was taking at that time at NYU.

After I acquired my masters, I became a research associate for three years on the Highfield Project, a residential treatment program for delinquents referred by the courts. Part of my function on the research project involved interviewing delinquent youths in the Highfield's institution and their family and friends in the community with regard to their "before and after" personality and behavioral changes that might have resulted from their participation in the project. Many of the boys in the project were involved with gangs. Through my observations of their group interaction sessions, interviews with them individually, and interviews with their families, I was able to learn a great deal about the roots and social psychology of their violent gang behavior.

My first major, direct, and in-depth research into the structure and function of gangs was implemented in a period from 1953 to 1958 on the Upper West Side of Manhattan in a large area infested with gangs and gang violence. This five-year-period of firsthand research with violent gangs was part of a job I acquired in 1953 as director of the Crime Prevention Program of a community organization known as Morningside Heights, Inc. The project was sponsored and funded by thirteen educational, religious, and medical institutions, including Columbia University, and was supported by the New York Police Department.

Prior to my activating the New York project, I felt it would be useful to directly explore other programs for delinquents and gangs. In this regard, I was fortunate to be able to spend several weeks in 1953 in Chicago with a number of pioneers in the field of delinquency, including Clifford Shaw, Henry Mckay, and Sol Alinsky. All of these sociologists from the "Chicago School" and others were helpful to me in charting my plans for working with gangs in New York.

In my gang research, I had a strategic and understandable position vis-à-vis the gang youths in the area as the director of the Morningside Heights project. They had a good reason for understanding our work. To them we were not simply poking around in their lives for some vague research reason. Our agency was attempting to do something concrete to prevent and control the crime and delinquency of the area through various social, recreational, and family projects that we developed. The residents, comprised of almost a half million people from every possible ethnic, racial, religious, class, and economic background, also had an awareness of our efforts, and many people in the area cooperated with our project.

The overall crime picture included robbery, burglary, homicide, drug addiction, and assault. Many of these crimes were perpetrated by young gangsters, and consequently, the violent gangs in the area were considered a basic problem. When I first began to implement various projects, my preventive work with about seventy-five gangs in the neighborhood was highlighted by a lack of substantial knowledge about them. That knowledge was necessary to develop effective methods of gang control. It was this limitation and the apparent lack of effective methods available to other professional and social agencies in New York engaged in gang work that spurred my intensive gang research at that time. If I was going to develop an effective program for the prevention and control of gang violence, it was necessary for me to understand the gang's organization and motivation for violence.

I conducted many interviews, questionnaires, gang discussions, agency conferences, and talks with the Police Youth Squad, police commanders, and other officials. These interactions were not designed for research purposes alone; they were part of the project's day-to-day activity. We developed a virtual database of gang information through our work with this program.

My relationship to the delinquent youths in the neighborhood was similar to that of an anthropologist engaged in fieldwork. During the five-year period I directed the project, I lived and worked in the area. I bonded with many gangsters. It became natural for them to hang out in my office and under certain circumstances to visit my home. Phone calls and contacts at all hours from gang boys with special problems, youths in jail, citizen volunteers with emergency gang-war problems, or the police became part of my daily routine.

In addition to some of the more formal methods of questionnaires and focus groups that was part of my research design, my daily communications with the people and conditions I was trying to change was a significant element of my overall research into gangs. I learned firsthand what Dr. Kurt Lewin meant by his assertion that attempting to produce change in people was an intrinsic element in learning about the overt and underlying dynamics of their behavior.

My relationship with the gang youths in the neighborhood was a two-way street. My concern with their motives and activities led to their concern with mine. Many long, philosophical afternoons and evenings were spent with gangsters in my office or on the corner discussing life. Much was learned on both sides about the world. The essence and meaning of gang behavior and its violence were often more clearly revealed in these discussions than in the many formal research methods I utilized during this five-year period.

During this period, as part of my work, I directed a parolee project for gangsters released into the area in an Upper West Side courtroom that was available in the evenings. I often brought guest lecturers into our group therapy. These included former parolees who had been in gangs and were now successful law-abiding citizens. At one of our sessions I managed to involve former middleweight boxing champion Rocky Graziano. Rocky had in his earlier years been involved in gangs and had done time in the New York City Riker's Island prison. Most of the parolees in my group had recently been released from Riker's Island, and they were anxious to hear Rocky's "lecture" on how he had changed his life from gangster to celebrity. (This metamorphosis was vividly depicted in the book and later the film *Somebody Up There Likes Me,* starring Paul Newman as Rocky Graziano.)

That night the premier sportswriter of that era, Jimmy Cannon, heard about Graziano's appearance and joined the group. He accurately and eloquently reported the dynamics of this one gang-parolee session the following day in his nationally syndicated column in the *New York Post.* His analysis captured the flavor of the 1950s and the young gangsters of that period.

> They were ex-cons who came voluntarily last night to a courtroom in Upper Manhattan magistrates court There would be a talk by Rocky Graziano who had been in prison. And Lewis Yablonsky, who is concerned with their anguish, would preside. He is the director of the crime prevention program of a philanthropic organization. . . .
>
> They liked Graziano. They sat, somber and slightly hostile, before he started his monologue. They were still defendants because that's what they were the last time they were in a courtroom. . . . You felt their anxiety as Yablonsky explained how important sports are. . . . Losers do a lot of looking before they find a guy who listens to them because he's interested. "We ran a baseball league," Yablonsky explained in his solemn young man's way. "Six gangs, we didn't have any gang wars. We had a 10-team basketball league. It was tremendous. They got interested, Sports — a gimmick. It gets them into a good relationship with a good adult. A man they respect."
>
> There was one kid I felt had made it all the way. He wore a one-buttoned jazzy coat. I'd bet on him. He had the drug habit and had shaken it. You had to be touched by his fierce pride. He stood up there when Yablonsky solicited questions and told them the ring was out of his nose.

. . . He explained how he had dug in for kicks but he was asking, asking, asking. He was telling but also wondering and going back over it and attempting to put it together. Why, why, why? They wanted to know and Yablonsky was trying to give it to them in his educated way. Not talking down to them but using the language of the streets. . . .

"You go in for sports?" I asked the kid in the one-buttoned jacket. "Stick ball in the streets," he replied. "In the summer." "What about basketball?" "The winter's for dances," the kid said. Of course, summer's for stickball and winter's for dances. But the seasons don't change in the can [prison]. That's what Yablonsky told them in his way. And so did Graziano.[1]

In addition to the data I gleaned from groups like the parolee group, another important source on gangs was my facilitation of about twenty "emergency" gang-war peace conferences. Local gangs trusted us and were free to use our offices and meeting rooms to discuss their problems. I was allowed to listen to and participate in discussions related to the real and imaginary threats of attack by other gangs. Some of the gang-war and peace meetings consisted of harangues about enemy gangs, plans for attack, elaborate means of defense, and counting real and imaginary members and brother gangs. Emotional heat was always high, and many deep feelings, bordering on paranoia, were freely expressed.

I had considerable trust from many gang youths, and because of this, I was allowed to tape-record many of these informal sessions. One reason for their permitting tape recordings was their desire to hear themselves on playback. Their egos seemed to be nourished by hearing their own voices on the tape recorder. Increasingly, they permitted me to influence their emergency meetings, and in some cases, I succeeded in intervening to control their postmeeting violent behavior.

These recordings were a source of invaluable information since the boys were very spontaneous and open in these discussions. In the gang-war discussions, they appeared to be freer than when other, more formal research devices were employed. (Some of these audiotapes, and my viewpoint on gangs, were later used in a CBS network broadcast on violent gangs narrated by Edward R. Murrow that I helped to produce in the role of a consultant to CBS. A part of this broadcast, involving the analysis of a gang murder, appears in chapter 2.)

As indicated, in my early research into the phenomenon of gangs in New York, I utilized a variety of approaches. These included (1) in-depth interviews with gangsters, individually and in groups, both in the project's office and on the street; (2) tape recordings of field notes; (3) written questionnaires; (4) employing two former gang leaders as paid interviewers; (5) various therapy groups; (6) unanticipated data from an unusual diary kept by a gang leader; and (7) a number of other research methods.

My five years of gang research became the basis for my NYU doctoral dissertation. And my thesis was the foundation for writing my first book on gangs, *The Violent Gang.* [2] Since these earlier experiences and publications, I have updated and vigorously continued my research on gangs. Notable, in this regard, has been my group-therapy work as a licensed therapist with adolescents in several southern California psychiatric hospitals. In thousands of intensive group psychotherapy sessions in these hospitals over a span of twenty years, I have learned a great deal about the social and psychological dynamics of adolescents involved in gangs and the context of their family background. In this process, in my groups there were a number of gang youths referred by the courts. All of these youngsters have contributed enormously to my understanding of youth collectivities and gangs. Many of my research findings derived from this therapeutic work are incorporated into this book.

For this volume, over the past five years I have further developed my research into gang behavior. This has included a number of intensive interviews with Los Angeles County probation officers, the district attorney's office, and Los Angeles City police officers who work directly with gangs.

My special work since 1990, as a group therapist in the Amity Therapeutic Community projects in the R. J. Donovan California Prison and a prison in Beaumont, Texas, with incarcerated gang members, has produced a considerable amount of data about gangs and how we can resocialize gang members into law-abiding, productive citizens. In my prison work, I gathered considerable relevant data from gangsters about their gangs through my directing regular psychodrama and group therapy sessions, individual interviews, special gang focus groups, and the use of written questionnaires.

In brief, all of my personal experiences and my forty-five years as a criminologist and social psychologist researching and directing therapeutic projects with young gangsters and gangs are encompassed in this book.

In my analysis I will use terms that are consistent with my research findings on gangs. For example, I will not refer to a youth as a "gang member"; I prefer using the term "gangster." The term "member" connotes a more precise and definitive participation in a social group than my research reveals about adolescents and young adults who participate in violent gangs. The violent gangs that are the focus of my research are more loosely organized than most socially defined groups, and the youths who involve themselves in violent gangs participate at different levels of intensity. Some youths, at different times, participate more or less actively than other youths in their gang's varied violent and delinquent activities. Consequently, rather than use the term "member," I find it is more appropriate and accurate to use the term "gangster" in referring to the youths and young adults who participate in violent gangs.

There are many groups in the panorama of collectivities that are referred to as gangs in American society. These include the notorious adult organized-crime gangs referred to as "the Mob," "La Cosa Nostra," or "the Mafia." There are gangs in the United States comprised of a variety of racial and ethnic backgrounds, including African American gangs, Mexican American gangs, Asian gangs, and Jamaican gangs. There are also other diverse collectivities labeled as gangs, including the so-called Aryan Nation, white skinhead gangs, female gangs, motorcycle gangs, and many other collectivities that sometime participate in illegal activities.

Based on my research, black and Chicano male gangs in the age range of twelve to twenty-eight comprise the largest in numbers and produce the most significant social problems in cities, large and small, throughout America. Consequently, although other gangs will be peripherally referred to, black and Chicano gangs are the focus of this analysis.

One of the enigmas about violent youth gangs, which is by no means fully answered in this book, is related to the question, What is it about American society that produces these unique and lethal collectivities? Although there are some semblances of youth gangs in other countries where I have worked, including Europe and Japan, somehow the United States has the dubious honor of spawning the most senselessly violent gangs. This raises a significant question that is difficult to understand and demands further cross-cultural research.

Another factor that I believe is important to note is that in researching and writing this book I have focused on the more violent gangs. My research and that of others over the years indicates that not all gangs in the hood or the barrio are comprised of maniacal sociopaths hell-bent on murdering their real and imagined enemies. There are more coherent social gangs in many neighborhoods that fit the prototype of earlier groups that provided camaraderie and solidarity for their cohesive membership. The emphasis in my analysis has been on the more lethal sociopathic gangsters and their gang structure.

In my description of the reality and the brutal nature of violent gangsters, it may appear that I have limited compassion for the youths caught up in this senseless violence. I have to admit that I, like most law-abiding citizens, find their delinquent and senseless violent behavior reprehensible. In my extensive travels through "gangdom," however, I have also had the positive experience of observing the fact that, given a chance in an effective treatment program, many youths seemingly trapped in the violent gang world can change their behavior in most positive ways and facilitate positive change in their community. Individuals who started down the delinquent/ criminal path have turned their life around and become valuable citizens. As was true in the early part of my life, some of my best, most interesting, and most valued friends are ex-gangsters, ex-junkies, and ex-criminals.

The book is essentially divided into four parts. Part 1 deals with the history and causal context of gangs, the harsh realities of gang violence, and the dire consequences of the gang phenomenon. Part 2 analyzes various characteristics of contemporary gangs. Part 3 presents traditional methods for preventing and controlling gang violence and the therapeutic community approach that has proven successful in treating criminals/addicts and gangsters in prison and in the community. Part 4 reviews and analyzes notable gang theories and presents a projected plan for treating gangsters in a therapeutic community.

The treatment approaches I propose comprise the most important parts of the book. My efforts toward focusing on a solution are generated not only by my intellect but by my heartfelt and sympathetic emotions about the human waste and destructiveness that violent gangs produce. On a personal and professional level with regard to this difficult social problem, my work with prisoners is the most deeply affecting emotional situation in my life.

Perhaps I can explain my strong feelings on this subject more specifically by describing the following scenario that I observe every time I enter a large California prison to direct group psychotherapy and psychodrama sessions with the men in custody. After being searched and checked out at the front gate of this prison of around five thousand men, I have to walk almost a mile through several depressing "big yards" to the therapeutic community cellblock where two hundred prisoners in the program reside. As I pass through these big yards, I can't help observing hundreds of prisoners along the way. They are usually engaged in the typical negative prison activities, including small, secretive groups discussing crimes they have committed or will commit, or individuals simply strutting around displaying their absurd macho posturing.

Most of these young men are intelligent black and Chicano individuals between the ages of eighteen to thirty who are wasting away in the cold storage of prison life. My heartfelt and emotional reaction is that the current prison system (which includes the recent politically hysterical three-strikes laws) destroys the valuable human potential that exists in these unfortunate men. All of them, even the worst sociopath, has a spark of motivation and compassion in him, and if given a chance through a humanistic treatment program, this positive spark could be ignited into a flame that would lead him into a law-abiding and satisfying lifestyle. Their plight, which is characteristic of the approximately 1.6 million prisoners incarcerated in the United States, motivates me to attempt to understand the causes of this regrettable situation and to develop methodologies for their effective treatment.

I am hopeful that some of the insights and possible solutions I have presented in the book can be developed and implemented for resocializing youths who participate in gangs. I wholeheartedly agree with the often ridiculed comment attributed to the founder of Boy's Town, Father Flanagan, that "there is no such thing as a bad boy." It is my firm belief that all of these young men, including the toughest sociopathic gangsters, can with the proper humanistic treatment be salvaged from a life of self- and other-destructive behavior into responsible law-abiding citizens who can lead happy and productive lives that would benefit them and the larger society.

GANGSTERS

PART ONE

GANGS: NOW & THEN

1.

The Current Gang Problem

o o o o o o o o o o

ON ANY GIVEN EVENING, along with the weather report and sports scores, the TV evening news in large and small cities throughout America present the horrendous toll of assaults and deaths that result from gang violence. The incidence of gang violence has escalated, and the patterns of gang violence have become increasingly lethal in the past fifty years.

Contemporary gangs differ significantly from gangs of the past with regard to several significant factors:

1. *Gun Firepower.* Today's gangs have access to and pack more lethal weapons than at any time in the history of America.
2. *Intraracial Violence.* In the first half of the twentieth century, minority gangs tended to band together and fight gangs from different racial and ethnic backgrounds. Today's gangs, especially black and Chicano gangs participate in internecine warfare with black on black and Chicano on Chicano violence.
3. *The Use and Commerce of Drugs.* In the past fifty years there has been a marked increase in the involvement of gangsters in the use and dealing of drugs.
4. *The Multipurpose Gang.* In the past gangs tended to have more simple functions for its participants. Youths joined gangs for a sense of belonging

and to "protect" their territory. Today's gangs provide more deviant opportunities for their participants — including violent activities, drug use, the commerce of drugs, and the possibility for participating in the illegal activities of organized burglary and robbery.

Since there are diverse definitions of the term "gang," before analyzing each of these factors in more depth, it is useful to clearly define my perception of the contemporary gang. The contemporary violent drug gang incorporates the following basic characteristics and activities:

1. All gangs have a name and a territorial neighborhood base, and they maintain a fierce proprietary interest in their neighborhood. They will fight for the territory they claim as their own and will attack any interlopers who come into their "hood" who belong to an enemy gang.
2. Joining a gang often involves a "jumping in" ritual that ranges from informal verbal acceptance to a violent initiation rite, and leaving the gang takes many forms.
3. Delinquent and criminal acts involving burglary and theft are important gang activities for achieving a "rep" (reputation) and status in the gang.
4. Senseless violence, including drive-by shootings and "gangbanging" (fighting other gangs), is a basic gang activity.
5. The commerce of drugs, their use, and violent acts for the maintenance of drug territory are part of the gang configuration.
6. Gangs provides a form of social life and camaraderie that usually involves gambling, getting high, hanging out, and partying.

THE IMPACT OF MORE LETHAL WEAPONS

A significant factor about contemporary gangs compared to earlier gangs is the enormous increase in lethal weapons. During my years in the mid-1950s of researching and working with gangs in New York City, I observed and noted many acts of violence. Most of it involved stabbings and hand-to-hand combat. Manufactured handguns were seldom used in gang warfare, and there were no automatic weapons on the street. Occasionally, a zip gun would be employed in a gang fight. A zip gun, often referred to as a "homemade," would be manufactured by an enterprising gangster in his shop class. This unreliable weapon was comprised of a metal pipe as a barrel, a wooden handle, and a bunch of heavy elastic bands to provide the power to shoot a bullet. When the trigger was pulled on the mishmash of wood, pipe, and elastic bands, the bullet was as likely to shoot the shooter as the intended target. There were very few real guns in the possession of gangbangers in the 1950s.

In recent years, increasingly lethal weaponry like AK 47s and Uzi assault guns have become the gang's weapons of choice for retaliation and drive-by shootings. In the maniacal foray into "enemy territory" of a drive-by, gang-bangers inaccurately spray and kill as many innocent people as the enemy gangsters they are attempting to kill. Various research, including police reports, reveals that only about 50 percent of gang-related murders hit the target of enemy gangsters. The other 50 percent of victims of gangster drive-bys and street violence are innocent children and adults who happen to be in the wrong place at the wrong time.

BLACK-ON-BLACK AND CHICANO-ON-CHICANO VIOLENCE

Despite the fact that they miss their intended targets half the time, gangsters are still shooting at replicas of themselves. One of the mysteries of the contemporary violent gang problem is that black and Chicano gangsters murder gangsters from their same racial and ethnic background. This phenomenon is a social-psychological enigma that I have explored in my research interviews with black and Chicano gangsters in both the community and in prison.

On a number of occasions in my gang prison therapy groups where the gang members were trying to change their behavior, I have sat a black L.A. Crip in a chair directly facing a black L.A. Blood and posed the question, "Why do you guys want to kill each other?" The response is usually a garbled commentary about gang turf or a simple and direct, "I don't know." The gangster's responses are usually cryptic and irrational, and they have no logical explanation.

One of my speculations about the phenomenon of internecine black-on-black or Chicano-on-Chicano gang violence is that there is a hidden fear that generates a reluctance to directly take on the larger white society's power structure. Gangsters who have the feeling that they are an oppressed minority may feel safer venting their rage on each other, in the same way that angry family members too often act out their anger inside their family situation.

Another possible explanation for this curious phenomenon would be the self-hatred theories of the social psychologist Kurt Lewin. Lewin posited the theory that self-hatred anger is often committed against people from the same minority group because they see in these others a hated reflection of their self.

A true authority on gangs is Stanley (Tookie) Williams, who is forty-one and is on death row for murder at San Quentin. Tookie was a cofounder of the L.A. Crips with the notorious South Central L.A. gangster Raymond Washington. Williams is a legendary figure in the world of Los Angeles gangsters, and the 400 gangsters who convened in a hotel ballroom for a gang summit peace meeting in 1993 vociferously cheered him when he addressed them with a videotaped message on a huge television screen from San Quentin. His message condemned urban violence and urged a peace treaty among L.A. gangs. A portion of his message that cogently comments on black-on-black violence was reported in a later interview with a *Los Angeles Times* reporter:

A black youth may participate in a gang because of his need to vent anger, or the need for love, protection, retaliation, a sense of security, recognition, discipline, psychological gain, sex, drugs or a surrogate family. Also a black youth may join a gang because his relative is a member. So that individual gravitates to it automatically, because he grew up into it. But of all the possible reasons for gang participation I can empathize with is a black youth's desperate need for psychological comfort. And gangs provide that by providing a vehicle — gang membership — that allows him to feel that finally that youth really belongs to something, or is a part of something.

In other words, there is a place for a black youth in this country when he joins a gang, as opposed to that youth feeling left out in a white-dominated society. I really believe that's the underlying current for all gang participation. In fact, I believe that need, the need for psychological comfort, cuts through every other reason why gangs are so popular among black youths.

(*Why then do you think so many young black men harm and kill each other?*) I believe the core of it is an embedded sense of self-hate. What I mean by that is, an individual who has been spoon-fed so many derogatory images of his race will, after a period of time, start to believe those images. The images I'm talking about are stereotypes that depict the majority of blacks as being buffoons, functional illiterates, violent and promiscuous, welfare recipients, indolent criminals. . . . Unfortunately, too many black people have been brainwashed into believing these stereotypes. And when an individual gets to believing such things, that individual gets to believing, "Well, hell, if it's true, then I must be just as disgusting as those images that are being depicted." So you end up lashing out at the individuals [other gang members] that you consider to be part of those stereotypes. In desperation, you're trying to obliterate that negative image to rid yourself of this self-hate monster that subconsciously stalks you. In a sense, you're trying to purify yourself, your environment, your race.

(How did you purge your self-hate?) I learned that basically all the negative stereotypes about black people aren't true. Those stereotypes aren't applicable to the whole race. There is no stereotype that can depict a whole race. So, after I studied and learned about the great individuals there are in my race both men and women — I woke up. Plus, I started acknowledging my own abilities to achieve minor things — self-accomplishments like being able to read well, to articulate well, to be disciplined, things of that nature. Nothing spectacular, but still they were self-accomplishments. So my feelings of self-hate gradually changed. It didn't happen overnight, it took some time and effort on my part.

Maturity has something to do with it and the gaining of knowledge. I've been studying a lot since I've been in prison — economics, politics, black history, math, English, philosophy, psychology. And what I've learned has taught me to appeal to logic. If something's counterproductive, I don't want to have anything to do with it. If it's for black betterment, then I'm all for it. Period.[1]

In my view, Williams's observations on the gang phenomenon are most perceptive. It is regrettable that his apparent exceptional intelligence has been wasted through his lifelong involvement with gangs and imprisonment.

FAMILY ISSUES

Most youths who become gangsters have had no positive adult role models in their lives. Although it is not as prevalent in Chicano families, around half of America's black children grow up in a family without the presence of a positive adult male role model. The role models they have are fathers, older brothers, and uncles who have been involved in the drug and gang scene. In too many cases, their adult role models are frequently in and out of prison.

The issue of absentee prisoner fathers as negative role models was dramatically and concisely revealed in a psychodrama session I directed for men attempting to change their criminal lives in a California prison therapeutic community project. The subject in the session was Fernando (not his real name), a fifty-year-old longtime Chicano gangster in and out of prison.

In the process of changing his way of life in a positive direction in the program, Fernando developed a sincere concern for his three teenage sons who had become gangsters, following in his footsteps. The essence of a two-hour psychodrama session I directed with him was that, despite the fact that Fernando had been away from them in prison half of his life, they wanted to emulate their criminal father who was their role model and hero. Fernando, as a result of his change of perspective, now felt helpless and guilty about his negative influence on his sons, and the insights he achieved in his therapy motivated him to try to change their behavior.

In the psychodrama session I directed with him, the sons were role played by several prisoners in the group, who understood from their personal experience how his real sons would react to their father's new perspective on life. Fernando opened the psychodrama session by tearfully telling his "sons" how terrible he felt about the negative influence he had on their lives and how he was now changing his life. To his gangster sons, Fernando had been a hero who had established a strong reputation as a veteran drug dealing and murderous gangster in their barrio. In the psychodrama session, his "sons" were appalled at the new message he was giving them that essentially said "crime doesn't pay." One role-playing convict "son" aptly said, "Man, we got our reputation on the streets from you. We have a rep because we are known as your sons. And now you're punking out on us. You're talking like a pussy."

In the psychodrama, after being rebuked by his "sons" several times for his new viewpoint on life, he was ready to give up and quit the session. The other inmates in the group chastised him and told him, "Hang in there." One sharp member of the group opined, "You know, Fernando, you have been a terrible father and role model for your sons for many years. You're not going to change them overnight. But if you demonstrate a new positive role in here and when you get back to your family and the community — that's the best way to change their behavior."

After he was released from prison, Fernando did change his way of life. When he was paroled, he entered a therapeutic community and later on became a drug counselor. He reconnected with his sons as a positive role model and had a positive affect on them. In a follow-up on Fernando's progress, I met with him and one of his sons about a year after his release from prison. In our discussion, I learned that at least this son was now in a positive relationship with his father and that Fernando was attempting to establish a similar relationship with his other two sons. Fernando's rehabilitation and his impact on his son is, unfortunately, a rare exception. For too many youths growing up in the barrios and hoods without positive male role models, the gang has an irresistible attraction.

Most black youths growing up in the inner city have maternal figures in their family who provides the necessary nurturing for the youths' proper socialization. However, most of the youths who participate in gangs tend to have mothers who are besieged by their own problems. The film *Sugar Hill* opens on a black child who witnesses his mother fixing heroine and then dying from an overdose. This abrupt portrait of the child's socialization dramatically, if melodramatically, reveals the causal context that too often in the real world produces a sociopathic gangster/drug dealer.

Elijah Anderson, an African American social scientist, succinctly delineates how a mother in a fatherless home, besieged by her own problems, can affect the negative socialization of her child. According to Anderson,

> The overwhelming majority of families in the inner city community try to approximate the decent-family model, but there are many others who clearly represent the worst fears of the decent family. Not only are their financial resources extremely limited, but what little they have may easily be misused. The lives of the street-oriented are often marked by disorganization. In the most desperate circumstances people frequently have a limited understanding of priorities and consequences, and so frustrations mount over bills, food, and, at times, drink, cigarettes, and drugs. Some tend toward self-destructive behavior; many street-oriented women are crack-addicted ("on the pipe"), alcoholic, or involved in complicated relationships with men who abuse them.
>
> In addition, the seeming intractability of their situation, caused in large part by the lack of well-paying jobs and the persistence of racial discrimination, has engendered deep-seated bitterness and anger in many of the most desperate and poorest blacks, especially young people. The need both to exercise a measure of control and to lash out at somebody is often reflected in the adults' relations with their children. At the least, the frustrations of persistent poverty shortens the fuse in such people — contributing to a lack of patience with anyone, child or adult who irritates them.[2]

I have observed the fatherless family situation described by Anderson in the many family groups I have directed. Single-parent mothers can be quite violent with their children in an effort to get them to behave. They will scream at them or hit them for the least little infraction, partly out of the frustration and anger they have about their own lives. A youth growing up in this type of family intuitively learns that interpersonal problems are solved by violent behavior, and this in part accounts for their violent gang behavior.

Drug and Violence Factors

Atrocious violence is one way of "putting in work" and rising in the hierarchy of the contemporary gang. Another pattern of significant "work" for a gangster is involved with the commerce of drugs. The gangs I studied and hung out with in the 1950s in New York City had a different connection to drugs than contemporary gangs. In earlier gangs, drug addiction was a side note to the social narcotic of violence that pervaded gang behavior. Most gangsters between the 1950s and the 1980s were not involved in the commerce of drugs.

In the 1950s, heroin was the major drug of gangsters. Rather than consolidating the gang, as occurs in contemporary gangs involved in the drug trade, drug use tended to break up early violent gangs. Their main activity involved gangbanging for kicks, and some measure of camaraderie, and drugs interfered with the effective performance of these tasks.

In the 1950s gang period, I observed that when a gangster started using heroin, he tended to drop out of the gang since his involvement with heroin addiction was an all-consuming activity. Heroin addiction tends to be a loner activity that requires daily forays into the community to commit thefts, burglaries, and muggings for the purpose of supporting an expensive habit. Feeding a heroine habit was a full-time job and didn't allow much time for gangbanging. Several gangs I was researching and working with in the 1950s broke up because a number of the gang's core gangsters became heroin addicts.

The contemporary gangster's role in the business of drug dealing is related to his status in the gang. The L.A. Crips, which incorporate a number of different subgroups or "sets," provide a typical example. In the Crips, the "OGs" (the designation for original gangsters or older gangsters) are usually the prime managers of the gang's commerce of drugs. According to data I acquired from the head of an FBI gang task force, some Crip OGs have a direct connection to importing drugs from South American suppliers. "Gs" (middle-range gangsters still earning their stripes and a reputation) and

"Wannabees" (younger gang member recruits) put in work serving as "mules" (transporting drugs) or selling drugs on the streets directly to consumers.

The OGs, who administer the overall drug-dealing operation, seldom get their hands dirty with the direct violence often necessary to maintain control over a drug business territory. If a dispute arises over their drug business or territory with a rival, they will commission a "hit" (an act of violence and sometimes murder) on the violating rival. The hit is usually carried out by younger gangsters who want to put in some work to acquire a reputation and status in their gang.

In the past decade, OGs, who earn small fortunes from the drug trade, will seldom get involved in senseless, nonprofitable gangbanging. They do on occasion serve as advisors to lower-level Wannabees and Gs involved in emotionally motivated gangbanging and drive-by violence.

In the contemporary violent gang, in a pattern similar to one that existed in earlier gangs, gangsters involved in the drug trade who become addicted are often shunned or dropped by the gang's leaders because they find them unreliable in their lucrative business. As one OG dealer told me, "If a guy starts using too much of the product, he becomes a fuckup, and we can't count on him for anything." In another interview, an OG who had become hooked on crack-cocaine told me, "I really wanted to clean up, not that I didn't love crack, but because it interfered with my business."

There are two patterns of gang violence: one is senseless, nonprofitable gangbanging, fighting another gang over territory that no one owns; the other is related to the drug business. This new pattern involving drugs and gang violence is not exclusive to the West Coast. It has become a phenomenon in almost all cities, large and small, in the United States. A *New York Times* article succinctly described the problem:

> They are a new breed of criminal in New York City: young members of crack-peddling gangs who murder on a whim. And though police officials say they are confident the gangs can be uprooted by methods that have worked before, other law-enforcement experts and social scientists are less optimistic.[3]

Sterling Johnson, Jr., a New York City special narcotics prosecutor, states in the same article,

> These gangs are more violent than anything this city has ever experienced. Crack cocaine has spawned an allied industry of young hit men who kill for the slightest reasons. In 1958 it took only 11 homicides in an outbreak

of gang mayhem with zip guns and knives to stun the city. Recently in northern Manhattan alone, over the last five years, drug gangs have been responsible for as many as 500 gang-related murders, and most of these murders remain unsolved.[4]

Dr. Charles Bahn, a professor of forensic psychology at the John Jay College of Criminal Justice, is among those who believe the drug-oriented violent gangs I have described will be harder to eliminate than their predecessors. Based on his study of more than fifty gang members who have been arrested for murder and other felonies, he concluded: "Previous youth gangs were usually larger and they had a quasi-family role for their members. In these new gangs the social aspect is subordinate to the illegal drug business. There are more of these gangs, they are more antisocial and more ruthless." [5]

This form of drug-related gang violence struck a new chord with an incident in Boston that may be a prelude to a pattern, which now exists with the Mafia in Italy and the drug cartels of Colombia, of murdering troublesome public officials. On September 25, 1995, a forty-two-year-old prosecutor for the Massachusetts attorney general's office, Paul McLaughlin, who was well-known for the prosecution of inner-city gangsters, was gunned down by a young assassin. As McLaughlin was getting into his car, a hooded teenager emerged from the evening shadows, shouted some angry words, and shot him point-blank through his forehead. The hooded killer, who escaped from the scene of the crime, was identified by a witness as a fifteen to sixteen-year-old black teenager. In fact, McLaughlin at the time was in the process of prosecuting several Boston drug gangs. A comment made by a fellow member of the attorney general's office was ominous, "This pattern of assassination of law-enforcement officers, characteristic of Colombian drug lords, has come to America."

In a way, these new "violence-for-profit" drug gangs make more sense than the violent activities of the senseless gangbanger. The dealing of crack-cocaine drugs is a most profitable enterprise. It creates reality-based "turf," or territorial disputes. The enforcement of a profitable street-drug control position involves a more logical brand of violence than the senseless gangbanging violence that has no apparent purpose.

In the summer of 1994, twenty-two gang murders mostly connected to territorial disputes over the drug trade occurred in Venice, California. The murders that took place came close to home. My son, a probation officer who lived in Venice during this period, called me one morning at 3 A.M. to tell me that there was the dead body of a sixteen-year-old youth at his front gate. All of the six sons of the family who lived across the street were in the gang drug business. The dead youth came from this family.

This murder is only one example of a pattern of homicides that plagues Los Angeles and other cities in the United States. My research visits to South Central L.A. revealed for me the impact violent drug gangs have on the ambiance of a community. This area of L.A. could be the set for some B movie about the world after a nuclear apocalypse. The area has become a nightmare landscape inhabited by marauding thugs. Innocent citizens living in the area are held hostage in their home by the nightly violence, and innocent people out on the streets late at night too often wind up as victims. When darkness comes to the hoods of L.A., many law-abiding citizens cower behind locked doors. Shadowy groups of young men pad quietly down the alleyways while police cruisers glide through the streets and the clatter of helicopters fills the sky.

The chilling impact that the violent drug gangs have on a community is cogently presented in a *Los Angeles Times* article that depicts how warring gangs can terrorize a neighborhood:

> In the shadow of commercial high-rises, the residents of a block-long stretch of Shatto Place live with a fear more natural to a place like Sarajevo. Rarely do they let their children play in the street or socialize outside the aging brick buildings that line the short block between Wilshire and 7th Street. Many are afraid to go outside because they, too, live on a battlefront. The 600 block of Shatto Place is controlled by one powerful street gang, and a rival gang's territory is just a block away. All too often, their war over turf and drug profits rages just outside the residents' doorsteps. . . .
>
> Lately, the casualties have escalated. On a Friday evening two weeks ago two young men, one of them a juvenile, were shot to death on the block by rival gang members, and a third victim was murdered in a shooting two days later. The second shooting resulted in yet another death. "It seems like every other day, something happens," said a resident who has lived on the block for three years. Life on the block means being constantly on the alert. One 20-year-old man who grew up on the block and still lives there has developed a survival tactic. Whenever an unfamiliar car drives by, he gets ready to hit the ground. "If a car passes, I just get low. My friend's father got caught in cross-fire a couple of years ago." [6]

A pattern that has taken hold in some violent drug gangs involves transporting their drug empires to other cities. Two cases in point are the L.A. Crips and the prison-based Mexican Mafia. An interview I had with Charles

Parsons, the special agent in charge of the Los Angeles FBI office, and his director of a special task force on gangs revealed that the Crips often send representatives to other cities to enlarge their lucrative drug operations. In 1995 the L.A. FBI Special Task Force on Gangs arrested twenty-two Mexican Mafia gang members. Two of the gangs leaders were in prison at the time. The FBI prosecuted these gangsters under the federal Rico statute, originally promulgated for prosecuting organized crime (RICO stands for "Racketeering Influenced and Corrupt Organizations").

In summary, in the 1990s many violent gangs in New York, Chicago, Miami, Dallas, Cincinnati, and Washington, D.C., have entered the illegal drug business. They are actively spreading drugs and violence to other cities all across the country. In Chicago, where gang membership is now in the thousands, after a lull in the 1970s, the infamous El Rukins gang is under active investigation for drug trafficking. In New York, police are struggling to contain the explosion of drug-related violence. A Miami-based gang called the Untouchables is pushing crack northward to Atlanta, Savannah, and other cities of the Southeast, where the group is known and feared as the Miami Boys. An investigative reports TV documentary on the drug trade shows in detail how gangs have brought drugs from Colombia into a small city like Tyler, Texas.

The gangs' entry into drug trafficking on a major scale may be creating the nation's biggest crime problem in decades. Drug profits are soaring and so is the drug-related homicide rate in cities where the gangs are most entrenched. It is arguable, in fact, that the emergence of drug gangs from coast to coast is very similar to what occurred during the early years of Prohibition, when La Cosa Nostra consolidated its status as an underworld cartel by building on the profits of illicit alcohol.

Today's drug gangs are far more erratically violent than the organized crime of the Mafia or La Cosa Nostra. A Mafia hit was and is more coordinated and focused on solving a "business problem." The new drug gangs that are derived from the gangbanging traditional gang are wilder and more lethal. This random violence is partially related to the younger Wannabee motivation to put in work toward building a reputation and status.

The large increase in violence is also due, as indicated, to the extraordinary availability of military and paramilitary weapons. Because of inadequate gun control laws, law enforcement agencies are relatively helpless in controlling guns on the streets of our cities. Guns like Uzis, AK 47 assault rifles, and AR15 semiautomatics are frequently bought (some even legally in gun shops) by gangsters, who finance their high-tech arsenals with profits from the drug trade. In effect, over the past decade the gun-blasting drug wars dramatized by the *Miami Vice* TV show and in exploitative "action" films are played out in reality on the streets of cities around the country by this new form of violent gang.

The Contemporary Multipurpose Gang

The desire for a rep, the increased lethal nature of gangster violence, and the advent of the dealing and use of crack-cocaine has changed the structure and behavior of contemporary youth gangs. My research with gangs in the 1950s revealed three basic types of youth gangs in the United States, which appeared most persistently around the country up to around 1985: social gangs, delinquent gangs, and violent gangs.

These prototypes seldom appeared in a pure form, however, these different gangs focused on social, delinquent, or violent behavior:

1. The social gang was a group comprised of tough youths who banded together because they found their individual goals of a socially constructive nature could most adequately be achieved through this type of gang pattern in their hood or barrio.
2. The delinquent gang was dominated by delinquent patterns of activities characterized by such direct illegal behavior as drug dealing, stealing, or assault, with monetary profit the essential objective of the gang's activity.
3. The violent gang's activity was dominated by sociopathic themes of gang-banging over turf, spontaneous prestige-seeking violence with a kind of status-oriented emotional gratification as the goal.

Although the aforementioned gang prototypes seldom appeared in a pure form, most gangs had a central characteristic that distinguished them, and most of their behavior revolved around one of these central themes. There were youths who belonged to one or more types during their adolescent years, and some youths belonged to several types of gangs simultaneously. These three types of gangs persist in cities around the United States; however, many of their central activities have merged into a somewhat different type of gang that is now on the urban scene — a type of gang that I would characterize as the "multipurpose gang."

Many youths in the hoods and barrios have become participants in this new form of all-encompassing gang. This has in large part resulted from the commerce and use of crack-cocaine over the past decade. The new typical multipurpose gang tends to encompass all violent gang activities, including gangbanging over territory, some social activities, and delinquent behavior, especially drug dealing.

Predominantly social gangs have virtually disappeared because of the escalation of violence in the neighborhood that emanates from the violent drug gangs and the new "get-tough" government policies that have eliminated funding for the recreational resources and programs that used to exist in many neighborhoods. Recent conservative government policies have virtually eliminated antigang recreation, sports, drug rehabilitation centers, and general welfare programs. Although these social programs never fully eliminated delinquent/criminal gang behavior, they did provide a reasonable form of control and prevention of the problem. Partly because they have no viable socially acceptable alternatives, many youths living in gang-dominated neighborhoods participate in contemporary multipurpose, violent drug gang activity.

The most accurate way to define this new multipurpose contemporary gang is to summarize the earlier presented definition of its basic characteristics and activities. The gang has a distinctive name and a territorial neighborhood base; its participants are involved at different times in various delinquent and criminal acts, including burglary, theft, and violence; the commerce of drugs and their use are a significant part of the gang configuration; and the multipurpose gang also provides a form of social life and camaraderie that includes senseless gangbanging, gambling, drinking, hanging out, and partying.

In his own inimitable fashion, gangleader Kody Scott, an original Crip, described in his book *Monster* some of the characteristics of the multipurpose nature of contemporary gangs as follows:

> The serious banger often finds himself handling several "jobs" in the course of his career. For years I found my position in the set to be manifold. At any given time I was the minister of information, which included such responsibilities as writing on walls declaring who we were and who we wanted to kill, and verbalizing our intent at gangland supremacy on street corners, on buses, in school yards, and at parties; minister of defense, which entailed organizing and overseeing general troop movement and maintaining a highly visible, militarily able contingency of soldiers who could be relied upon for rapid deployment anywhere in the city; teacher of war tactics, which, I guess, would fall under the heading of instructor; and combat soldier and on-the-job trainer.[7]

The so-called Shoreline Crips in Venice, California, are a prototype of this new form of multipurpose violent gang found in Los Angeles and around the country. My research with the Shoreline Crips indicated that they committed both acts of emotional/senseless violence through gangbanging and more rational drug-business violence. Under the same gang banner, gangbangers and drug dealers interacted.

Most Shoreline Crip gangsters participated in old-type territorial disputes with other gangs in the West Side area of L.A. and became involved in senseless violence. They also, however, committed what I would characterize as more rational violence related to "smoking" (killing) someone who attempted to sell drugs in their hood. The hit would usually be ordered by an OG and then committed by a Wannabee or a G who was engaged in seeking a reputation and status in the gang. This combination of rational and irrational violence accounted for over twenty-two drive-bys and "walk-up" (point-blank shooting) murders in the summer of 1994 in the Venice area.

The gang drug-dealing scene in Venice by the Shoreline Crips is typical of the activities of drug gangs around the United States. On almost any day in Venice, one can observe drug dealing on several select corners by Shoreline Crip gangsters. When a police cruiser is in the neighborhood, the dealers are warned by their gang cohort lookouts and scurry into convenient apartments. They soon reappear when the police threat is gone. Their clientele often includes white drug buyers from Beverly Hills and yuppies who drive in from Beverly Hills and the San Fernando Valley to get their weekend supply of drugs.

As long as they behave themselves as good clients by paying the asked-for price, there is no trouble. However, any dissonant behavior is met with retaliatory gang violence. As a case in point of the consumer side of this equation, in my psychodrama group therapy work in an L.A. psychiatric hospital, I had a young lady in my group who had become a gang victim in the Venice area. She was in the hospital for an addiction problem and a traumatic reaction to a gang rape that had been committed on her by Shoreline Crip gangsters. She revealed to me in one of my group therapy sessions that she had gone to Venice in her car to buy her weekly supply of drugs. She was short of money and attempted to haggle with the corner dealer. He pulled her out of her car and, with the aid of some of his "homies" (associates), assaulted and raped her in one of the gang's safe houses.

The Shoreline Crips are a typical multipurpose gang. Their constituency includes the Wannabees, Gs, and OGs. The OGs manage the commerce of drugs in the area. Some of them, as the FBI pointed out, have a direct contact with the Colombian cartels, the major source of American crack-cocaine. The younger Wannabee recruits put in work both in traditional, senseless gangbanging violence with their enemies for the goal of acquiring gang status and reputation and in serving their role-model OG masters in more logical violence related to the commerce of drug dealing. The Gs, or middle-range gangsters, are involved in gangbanging and violence related to the drug trade for fun and profit and as an emotional outlet for the rage that emanates from the dysfunctional conditions in their family and their community.

THE EMOTIONAL CHARACTERISTICS OF GANGSTERS

A significant emotional factor that persists from the time of the early gangs and remains in the new violent-drug-gang equation is the sociopathic reck-lessness of gangster behavior, involving ruthless acts of violence with no concern for their victims and no remorse for their atrocious behavior. The hoods and barrios of America are heavily populated with teenagers and young adults whose poverty and deprivation have contributed to their ruth-less emotional behavior.

Real and imagined territorial disputes remain a constant source of conflict between gangs. Gangbanging over territory is a weird charade played out on the streets of America: gangsters, in fact, own nothing, especially their so-called territory. Many of these disputes are a pretext for acting out rage related to the gangsters' personal emotional problems.

The gangsters' personality problems of low self-esteem and sense of alien-ation drive them to act super tough to compensate for their sense of inferior-ity. It produces what I term the "machismo" or "macho-syndrome." This syndrome is an effort to present themselves as a superman to compensate for their underlying feelings of low self-concept and of being "nobodies" in the larger society.

The macho-syndrome is characteristic of individuals who are so insecure about their masculinity that they behave at the opposite end of the contin-uum in a form of tough supermasculinity. This involves physically, emotion-ally, and verbally posturing as a machismolike superman. In the gangbang-ers' hoods or in any prison big yard, one can observe this extreme tough-guy behavior in action. Males with this syndrome don't simply walk, they move with an unmistakable superman strut. Emotionally and verbally, they are always engaged in proving their machismo. Any comment of disrespect to a gangster that implies femininity, like, "You're a pussy" or "You're a faggot," will quickly produce a violent response.

The gangster's macho-syndrome is an effort at compensating for his failure to succeed in the larger society. Youths with this affliction are usually failures in school and have no viable occupation. Gangsters have created their macho-syndrome stance in part as a reaction to their deeper feelings of alienation and hopelessness about achieving any degree of success in the larger society.

Violent gangsters who feel alienated from the larger society create the gang to provide some sense of belonging to a "family," and a feeling of being somebody in their gang "community." The rage they feel from other sources is often expressed in gangbanging and other forms of senseless violence. The gang they have created outside of the law-abiding society offers them some kind of status in what they perceive is a barren and hopeless world.

On the subject of acquiring status through the gang, I had an interesting interview with a twenty-year-old gangster who was serving life in prison for a vicious murder. He told me how being known by his gang name Killer Ray was a great source of pride to him:

> Man, you don't know what I had to do to get this name. I love it. I put in the work for this name. People calling me Killer shows that they respect me, and they're not going to fuck with me. No one is going to "dis" Killer Ray, cause they know what will happen to them.

The phrase "putting in work" refers to the necessary violence, theft, and other delinquent behavior required to achieve status in the gang. In this context of acquiring a reputation and status in the gang, a gangbanger told me how he put in work at the scene of a gang murder that escalated his status in the gang:

> This dude was on the ground, and he wasn't dead yet. My homies and I were standing over him looking down at him. He was kind of moaning. I put the gun in his mouth and smoked him. My homies never forgot what I did. Everyone talked about it for a long time. After that I was more accepted in the gang and I became known more as someone you don't ever fuck with.

Seeking status in society through illegal means is imbedded in the socio-logical concept of "anomie." In my view, anomie is a most useful theory for explaining the social-psychological raison d'être for the existence of gangs in

American society. Several sociologists, especially Emile Durkheim, Robert Merton, and, more recently, Richard Cloward and Lloyd Ohlin, have theorized about the concept of anomie.[8] The theory posits that there is a disparity that exists between the idealized success goals and the means for achieving these goals in American society. When certain segments of the society accept and desire the society's goals, but because of limited opportunity cannot achieve these goals, they turn to deviant and illegal means for achieving the society's goals. I believe the contemporary gang is, in part, the alternative that has evolved from the status frustration of many minority youths who feel hopeless about achieving success through legitimate means in American society.

In this context, in the barrio or the hood their gang has become for many minority group youths their only achievable source of identity, status, and emotional satisfaction. Ill-trained to participate with any degree of success in the dominant middle-class world of rigid ideas, values, education, and adult demands, they construct their own pseudocommunity — the gang. In their gang, they can set achievable goals that can be realized through violent behavior. Their gang is an idealized empire, part real, part fantasy, that helps them endure the confusion of adolescence and the other emotional problems they confront in their separate and unequal world.

The violent gang becomes a haven for these emotionally needy youths, in part because it provides a vehicle through which they can act out their rage against what they perceive as an unfair and hostile world. They strike back through gang violence at a society they feel has boxed them into hopelessness. The gang for these youths is created as a deviant group for achieving the power, status, and respect that they believe, with some evidence, is denied them in the larger society.

The demands for performance and responsibility in the violent gang are readily adapted to the needs of these emotionally disabled youths. The criteria for membership is vague, yet easily possible when compared to the more demanding requirements of school or a job.

Gangsters often claim that the gang is organized for protection and a feeling of having a family. This is often a hope and a myth rather than a reality. On too many occasions I have seen gangsters ready to snitch and give each other up to the police for some relief of their arrest situation. Their idealized behavioral family values are often quickly abandoned when it is to their personal advantage. Yet it is of emotional importance and solace to the gangster to believe that their gang is a family haven in the hostile world that surrounds them.

The Damien Williams case is one notable example that reflects the mythology of gang members' "hanging tough for their homies" and not snitching on them in order to perpetuate the myth of the gang as a family. Williams, an identified Crip gangster, was convicted of viciously assaulting an innocent truck driver, Reginald Denney, during the 1992 Los Angeles riots. During his trial I was called as an expert witness. The police who drove me to the courthouse told me that Williams, when he was apprehended, confessed to the crime in a taped interview. In the police station he began to cry, admitted his culpability in beating Denney, and expressed his strong motivation to implicate other gangsters who committed violent acts if the police would release him from custody or offer him a plea bargain. Williams's behavior is typical for most gangsters, who profess undying loyalty to their "familial" gang yet in actuality will quickly sell-out their gangster "brothers" if it will serve their own, self-centered needs. (Williams's taped confession was not allowed into evidence in the trial because he had not been properly given the Miranda warning against self-incrimination by the police.)

The youth most susceptible to violent gang membership emerges from a social milieu that trains him inadequately for assuming a more constructive social role in the larger society. In fact, the defective socialization process to which he is subjected fosters a lack of humanistic feelings. At hardly any point is he trained to have feelings of compassion or responsibility for other people, not even for his partners in crime. Most gangsters, even when they are not certifiable sociopaths, at least in terms of their behavior outside of the gang, enact the sociopathic syndrome of senseless violence in their gangbanging behavior.

Gangbanging, the basic activity of one gang fighting another gang, is a standard cultural form for gangsters and reflects the limited compassion that is characteristic of the sociopathic gangster. A gangster can commit horrendous acts of violence in the context of gangbanging, and it is sanctioned by his gang. After a period of participating in a variety of dehumanized acts to achieve and solidify their rep in the gang, they tend to become unfeeling. They become insensitive to the pain of the violence they inflict on their victim. They develop a limited ability to identify or empathize with their victim or have any sense of remorse. Through this gang process of desensitizing their behavior, they become capable of committing spontaneous acts of senseless violence without feeling concern or guilt. I interviewed one gang member who had killed another boy, who gave a classic sociopathic comment that aptly describes this pattern of feeling, "What was I thinking about when I stabbed him? Man, are you crazy? I was thinking about whether to do it again!"

A common response that I have elicited from a number of gangbangers in prison for murder involved the following dialogue:

LY: How do you now feel about the guy you murdered?

G: It's no big deal. He deserved it for dissing (disrespecting) me.

LY: Do you have any regrets?

G: Are you out of your fucking mind? Of course I have regrets. I'm here in the joint doing life!

Leadership in the violent gang is not acquired by a vote from his constituents. Leadership in the violent gang is achieved by continuing acts of the cool, unpredictable violence that is characteristic of gangbanging. One of the violent-gang leader's vital functions for other gang members is that he serves as a role model in the commission of an idealized form of violence. The leader is a shining example for gang followers. The leader has "heart" and will pull a trigger without any overt signs of fear or, most important, regret. As a prototype of the violent gang, the leader is thus an ideal role model. Free-floating violence, pure and unencumbered by social restrictions, rationality, conscience, or regret, characterizes the venerated, typical, heroic gang leader.

The selection of senseless violence by gangsters involves a curious logic. This form of violent behavior requires limited training, courage, personal ability, or even physical strength. As one gang boy commented, "Any kind of gun makes you ten feet tall." Because this pattern of senseless violence is a demonstration of easily achieved power, it is the paramount value of the violent gang.

The very fact that it is senseless rather than rational violence that appeals to gangsters reveals a great deal about the meaning of violence to them. It is an easy, quick, almost magical way of achieving power and prestige. In a single act of unpremeditated intensity, a gangster establishes a sense of his own identity and impresses this existence on others. No special ability is required to commit this brand of violence, not even a plan, and the guilt connected with the senseless violence is minimized by the gang's approval. This is especially true if the violence fulfills the gang's idealized standards of a swift, sudden, and senseless outbreak.

As indicated, gangsters lack the qualifications required for participation in more structured law-abiding organizations. Any youth in the gang's hood is easily accepted into the group. If qualifications for participation in the violent gang were more demanding, most gangsters, especially the more sociopathic leaders, would be unable to participate. The violent gang is thus a human collectivity where even the most emotionally and socially deficient and rejected youth is accepted and is able to acquire some success and status.

One aspect of the gangster's senseless violence is related to a concept I have termed "existential validation," or the validation of one's existence. This syndrome basically relates to the gangster's emotional alienation from human feeling or meaning. In contrast to the gangster, most people have a sense of identity and existence in their everyday activities. They do not require daily, intense, outrageous emotional excitement to know they are alive, that they exist. The sociopathic gangster, however, desires this kind of emotional excitement and intensity on a continuing basis. Their sense of boredom, and the feeling of an underlying insecurity about their masculinity, requires increasingly heavier dosages of bizarre and extreme violent behavior to validate the fact that they really exist and that they have some power in life.

Extreme, violent behavior is one activity that gives the sociopathic gangster a glimmer of feeling. Existential validation through violence (or other extremist bizarre behavior involving sex or drugs) gives many of these emotionally dead youths some feeling. As one gang killer told me, "When I stabbed him once, it felt good. I did it again and again because it made me feel alive."

Too often, erroneously, gang violence is attributed by the police and the media, from their more logical viewpoint, as being related to a more rational explanation of gang vengeance or retaliation. In fact, many acts defined as gang violence are really the individualistic behavior of a violent sociopath who may or may not have a strong gang affiliation. In this context, the term "gang-related" violence has come into vogue and is used almost daily in urban newspapers. Often this label has nothing to do with an actual gang homicide.

A media-identified gang-related murder may simply mean that a psychotic or sociopathic murderer, who has some peripheral gang affiliation, has committed a pathologically based, senseless act of homicide. As previously indicated, many victims of so-called gang-related murders (about 50 percent) are ordinary citizens of all ages who happen to innocently and tragically find themselves in the line of fire. The emotionally disordered sociopath who committed the murder may later claim a gang affiliation to mask his psychosis and give it a cloak of immunity. Many murders characterized as gang related, therefore, may have very little connection to gang retaliation and more to do with a disturbed sociopath's paranoia. The murderer's self-identification as a gang member gives the emotionally disturbed killer a cloak of immunity from being considered just plain crazy. Being perceived as a gangster fighting for his home boys and their territory is more likely to be considered a more rational and valorous act than being a crazy person carrying out a senseless act of murder.

Psychotics usually act out their pathology alone; the violent gang is comprised of a group of pathological individuals acting in concert. When a sociopathic gangster commits a senseless act of violence on his own, it is viewed as being pathological. However, the same act perpetrated with others, as, for example, in a drive-by murder, gives this maniacal activity a patina of rationality.

A brief appraisal of collective behavior patterns gives some clue to this element of group legitimization and sanction for bizarre and pathological group action. Kurt and Gladys Lang make this point in a discussion of crowd behavior. They assert that certain aspects of a group situation help to make pathological acts and emotions acceptable. They write: "The principle that expressions of impulses and sentiments are validated by the social support they attract extends to collective expressions generally. The mere fact that an idea is held by a multitude of people tends to give it credence." [9] In the violent gang, when all the gangsters "go crazy together," as in gang warfare, their behavior tends, at least in the viewpoint of some people, to have greater rationality. Gang "legitimacy" therefore partially derives from the fact that group behavior, however irrational, is generally not considered as pathological as the solo act of an individual.

In this context of emotionally disordered behavior, many gangsters who commit gang-related murders, in my view, are pathological and have suicidal personalities. Most gangsters have low self-esteem, and this is reflected in their suicidal tendencies. They continually place themselves in the line of deadly gunfire that may come from an enemy gang or a police bullet.

Father Gregory Boyle, the director of a gang-prevention program in the East L.A. parish of his Dolores Mission Church, sees gangbanging in the same way I do, as a form of pathological and suicidal behavior. In an article, "Hope Is the Only Antidote," he comments,

The week before Christmas, I had to bury the 40th young person killed by what is still a plague in my Eastside community. I've grown weary of saying that gangbanging is the urban poor's version of teen-age suicide. The violence that has us in its grip has always indicated larger problems: poverty, unemployment, racism, the great disparity between the haves and have-nots, dysfunctional families and above all, despair. And for our neglect in addressing these problems as we ought, it shouldn't surprise us that their symptomatic manifestations have only worsened. This week, I will bury a homeboy who, unable to find his way clear to imagine a future — put a gun to his temple and ended his life. This desperate act of an 18-year-old sidestepped the inner city's more acceptable mode of suicide — the irrational battlefield of a gang war. He chose instead to make explicit the wish for death long implicit among our youth.[10]

Committing suicide explicitly reveals the manifestation of an inner emotional pathology. As indicated, being a gangster is a more highly desirable pathological syndrome than many other patterns that are viewed with greater opprobrium in society. The person who is in a position to accept the gang front for his pathology is not generally considered as crazy as someone who babbles a verbal word salad. Even more advantageous is the fact that as a gangbanger he has found an acceptable macho public role in his own community that is to some extent validated in the violent larger society.

THE GANG IN A VIOLENT SOCIETY

In the socioeconomically depressed ghettos and barrios of most American cities, violent gangs are perceived by civic-minded people and law enforcement leaders as a cancer that must be eliminated from their community. At the same time, in contrast to this viewpoint, there is a mass and varied audience for the glorification of gangster violence in film, songs, and verse in the larger society. These diverse viewpoints reveal how the gangster image is both denounced and romanticized in contemporary American society.

Historically, American culture and folklore have eulogized "heroic killers." In the Old West, Jesse James, Billy the Kid, and others became idolized killers. In the Roaring Twenties, Al Capone, who was responsible for ordering the murder of at least a hundred men and of killing some of them himself, became for many American citizens a popular and admired public figure. John Dillinger and Bonnie and Clyde became the gangster icons of the 1930s. In more recent years, Benny "Bugsy" Siegal, Sam Giancana, and various other Mafiosi have became venerated gangsters to many people in books and films.

In contemporary society, a large segment of the population both black and white seem to adore murderous sociopathic film heros. Stallone, Willis, Norris, Schwarzenegger, and others reflect this public worship of the heroic sociopathic killer who, against impossible odds, wins by indiscriminately murdering dozens if not hundreds of their enemies in a two-hour movie. The validation of this mad macho-syndrome is affirmed by billion-dollar box office receipts at movie theaters, not only in America, but around the world. In this context, young gangsters can see themselves as heroic figures protecting their turf by fighting and sometimes killing their real and imagined enemies.

The worship of the killer as a "hero" and the tacit acceptance of acompassionate behavior in the mass media by many people in the larger society tends to accord some credence to the violent gang's sociopathic activities. The general public seems to enjoy the brutal, revolting, and senseless sociopathic violence that is presented by film and TV stars and perceive it as exciting entertainment. In contrast with my viewpoint and that of many other like-minded citizens, violence, murder, and mayhem on the big screen earn millions of dollars because it is supported and "enjoyed" by large segments of the population.

Most violent behavior is stigmatized and thought of as sick, mad, or pathological. The violent gang's behavior is too often perceived by the gangster and his community as heroic activity. The community's covert aggrandizement of this mad behavior to a certain extent reinforces the violent gang as a desirable, stigma-free collectivity for sociopathic youths.

In recent years murder on the big screen has become more democratic. Young black actors now emulate the white film sociopaths and romanticize the violent gang in such violent films as *Menace To Society*, *South Central*, *New Jack City*, and *Blood In-Blood Out*. In a bizarre way, this glorification of gangster life provides young wannabee gangsters with an acceptable and desirable role to be sought and achieved in American society.

In another "art form," the pseudopoetry of gangsta rap, "poets" like Ice T and Snoop Doggy Dog, using lyrics with brutal sexist phrases about "hos" and "bitches" and glorifying murders, sell in the millions. The murderous cop killers of gangsta rap are perceived by devotees of this music as heroic figures who when they step out into their hood are always under attack and must kill or be killed. The line between advocating gang murder in gangsta rap and in real life was crossed by Snoop Doggy Dog when Snoop and his bodyguard, who were in their car at the time, killed a youth they considered to be an enemy in a gang-related homicide in Long Beach, California. The prosecution, in their final arguments, characterized the homicide as a pure and simple drive-by gang murder. Despite the prosecution's viewpoint, Snoop, whose real name is Calvin Broadus, and his bodyguard were acquitted of the crime because there was evidence that the victim had a gun on his person. The defense lawyers made the case that the homicide was perpetrated in an act of self-defense.

In a convoluted way, gangsta rap is au courant in both the black ghetto and the affluent white world. The admiration of the gangsta hero is embraced not only by black and Chicano youths, but by many affluent white adolescents who buy the records, listen to the eardrum pounding music on their radios, and watch the videos on MTV. A featured article in the venerable *New Yorker* magazine described how gangsta rap and poetry readings are being commingled in presentations in a large number of New York City nightclubs. As evidenced by the large audiences of a cross section of the population that are reported to attend these presentations, it can be concluded that the gangsta phenomenon has been accepted and integrated into the pop culture of the larger society.[11]

Another possible clue to the legitimation of gang violence may be its uncomfortable closeness to the behavior of the chronically insane warfare that exists on an international level in "rational" societies. The crazy machinations of the violent gang and its "military structure" are bizarre replicas of current patterns of international violence and warfare. One can legitimately raise the question, Was the brutal warfare and genocide perpetrated by Adolph Hitler on the world, the Vietnam War, or the warfare and "ethnic-cleansing" genocide that has taken place in the European Balkans any more or less pathological or senseless than the violent gang's violence? The sociocultural institution of war pervades all societies, and to some extent it provides the context for the madness of violent gang warfare.

The unique American violent gang and its mad bloodletting has emerged in the fertile soil of a society that has in this past century developed violence into an art form. It may be difficult to argue that the media, especially TV and films — where senseless, brutal murders occur with great frequency — is the cause of the violent gangs in our midst. However, no one can deny that the multiple-murder, blow-'em-up, and shoot-'em-up films that dominate the large and small screens of America and the continuing senseless international warfare of nations has some connection to the proliferation and continuance of the pathological violent gang problem.

2.

Gangs in the Twentieth Century

o   o   o   o   o   o   o   o   o   o

T HERE HAVE BEEN FOUR periods of American juvenile gangsters, violence, and gang warfare in the twentieth century:

1. The first fifty years were characterized by a benign period of youth camaraderie, a concern with territorial control, various acts of delinquency, and violence — largely involving fistfights and knife assaults.
2. The second identifiable period was in the post–World War II era, in the 1950s up to the mid-1960s, and showed a shift toward violence related to territorial disputes acted-out in more severe forms, stabbings now and an occasional murder using a gun.
3. The third identifiable period saw a hiatus in gangs, gang violence, and warfare during the late 1960s through the early 1980s, partly as a consequence of various quasi-political groups like the Black Panthers and the Brown Berets. These groups and others included many black and Chicano youths who might have participated in gangbanging violence into relatively positive efforts for social change through political activities.
4. The contemporary violent gang problem is entwined with the business of drugs, involves drive-by murders using high-powered, lethal automatic weapons, and has resulted in extreme violence.

Gangs, 1900–1950

The historical documentation of any subject is at best an imprecise discipline. In looking back on the history of gangs, I am dependent on the writing of a few individuals from the past who had the time and inclination to research and write about gangs. Despite this, an analysis of violent gangs in America from an earlier era provides a useful context for understanding the contemporary gang.

EARLY ADULT GANGS

Juvenile gangs emerged over the years from a mold created by early adult gangs. The earliest reports of adult gangs in America appear around the turn of the century on the Lower East Side of New York City. The phenomenon was chronicled in a colorful book by Herbert Asbury called *Gangs of New York*. [1]

These early gangs had such names as the Dusters, the Pug Uglies, the Dead Rabbits, and the notorious Five Points gangs. According to Asbury, the Five Points gangs and the Bowery gangs carried out their grudges against each other with constant warfare. Scarcely a week passed without a half dozen conflicts. On one occasion, led by the Dead Rabbits and the Pug Uglies, all of the gangs of the Five Points began their celebration of the Fourth of July with a raid on the clubhouse building of the Bowery Boys and the Atlantic Guards gangs. There was furious fighting, but the Bowery gangsters triumphed and drove their enemies back to their own neighborhood. In the melee, a few metropolitan policemen who tried to interfere with the gang warfare were badly beaten. There were apparently no guns or knives used. The warfare took the form of fistfighting and the use of a few bats.

The gangs of this era were territorial, and this factor may have set the precedent for the enormous value placed on turf, hood, and barrio by contemporary youth gangs. Another factor in the early adult gangs that may have set a precedent for today's gangs was a disrespect and antipathy toward the police. If anything, the gangs of that era were more hostile toward "the coppers" (so-called because of their copper badges) than contemporary gangs. Disrespect for the police, therefore, as representatives of the larger society who were intruding on gang turf, began at the turn of the century.

Asbury describes how the police ineffectually responded to an early gang fight:

A lone policeman, with more courage than judgment, tried to club his way through the mass of struggling men and arrest the ringleaders, but he was knocked down, his clothing stripped from his body, and he was fearfully beaten with his own nightstick. He crawled through the plunging mob to the sidewalk, and, naked except for a pair of cotton drawers, ran to the Metropolitan headquarters in White street, where he gasped out the alarm and collapsed. A squad of policemen was dispatched to stop the rioting, but when they marched bravely up Center street the gangs made common cause against them, and they were compelled to retreat after a bloody encounter in which several policemen were injured.[2]

These early gang wars bear some resemblance to current gang battles: they were territorially divided, and gang members didn't shrink from violence in their encounters. However, the extent to which battles involved large numbers of adult citizens, no guns, and the lack of police control shows an apparent difference from modern gang wars. The formal police framework of control and direct gang suppression is, of course, stronger today. Another significant differential between these early gangs and today's gangs is the absence of the lucrative commerce of drugs. Also, these early gang wars were not nearly as lethal as today's conflicts, largely because of the absence of today's prevalence of guns and automatic weapons in the hands of the combatants.

There are also data that seem to suggest that the current violent gangs have a more pathological "membership" than the earlier forms. The early gangs appeared to be socially acceptable group structures, at least within the norms and values of the neighborhood in which they existed. Although most of the public may have considered the gang's behavior deviant, it was normal in the particular neighborhood in which it occurred. Senseless, unprovoked gangbanging for kicks and ego gratification did not seem to be part of the early gangs' pattern. However, the criminal social fabric of illegal liquor sales, theft, and particularly politics was closely integrated with the gang activity of that era.

CAPONE-TYPE GANGS OF THE 1920S AND ORGANIZED CRIME

A new era of adult gang violence was ushered in by the bootleg gangs of the Roaring Twenties. In a way they set the precedent for today's gangs and their involvement in the commerce of illegal drugs. The deviant gangster culture and its practice of drive-by murders was created and developed in this violent era in America, as was its romanticization.

In carrying out research for a biography I wrote about the movie actor George Raft, I interviewed Howard Hawks, who directed the original *Scarface*, one of the best films on 1920s gangster behavior.[3] Hawks's film was largely based on the criminal gang exploits of Al Capone. This was the first film that depicted the newly invented drive-by gangster murders of that era. Hawks told me that in doing research for this film he interviewed gangsters from Chicago, members of the Capone mob who had actually carried out drive-by murders in the 1920s. The gangster drive-by, a unique American invention, was created and developed by Al Capone. Hawks informed me,

> Originally I had one drive-by murder scene in *Scarface*. This opened the film. When my producer Howard Hughes saw this, at that time, strange vehicle method for murder, he asked me how prevalent this practice was in gangland. I told him it was used as a standard practice for killing enemy gangsters. Hughes then told me, "Put more of those dramatic drive-by scenes in the movie."

These early bootleg gangs, although illegal, were not alien to the society in which they existed. Despite their bloody intergang and intragang murders, they maintained a close affiliation with the political, social, and economic conditions of the times. The gangsters of the twenties were the henchmen of political maneuverers and some of the big businessmen of that period. Gangsters were used in management-labor conflicts and to control liquor sales, prostitution, and gambling.

Violence was used as an instrument of establishing and maintaining these somewhat socially accepted business ventures. Capone called these enterprises "the legitimate rackets," and his self-concept was that of a businessman providing needed services for his community. Many community leaders, politicians, and citizens supported these early gangs.

The pre-Prohibition gangs of New York were usually classified by their national, religious, or racial background. They were principally made up of newly arrived groups like the Irish, Italians, and Jews. Irish gangs controlled the West Side, and the East Side belonged to the Italian and the Jewish gangs. The Lower East Side of Manhattan in the first twenty years of the century was the breeding ground for many gunmen and racketeers. In a subtle way, through movies and news reports, the Vito Genoveses, Lucky Lucianos, Bugsy Siegels, Meyer Lanskys, and Frank Costellos that emerged in those days became the role models for today's gangsters.

Italy's major criminal export to America in this period was the "mafia," or "crime syndicate." Its early form in the United States was the secret order of the Unione Siciliane, often referred to as the Black Hand. This early form of La Cosa Nostra originated in this country through a leader known as Ignazio (Lupo the Wolf). The Unione had several local bosses until Joe "the Boss" Masseria took charge in the 1920s. The Unione at that time was not restricted to gangsters. Among its members were some men of respectable reputations and occupations. Occasionally the doors to membership were opened to non-Italians such as a lawyers who performed the helpful job of acquitting some Unione gangster in the courts.

The early form of joining a gang allegedly involved a ritual of initiation that included an ancient rite of scratching the wrist of the initiate and the wrists of the members, after which an exchange of blood was effected by laying the wounds one on the other, thus making them all blood brothers. Many people have seen this ritual aggrandized in such films as *The Godfather* and *Goodfellas*. This was an early form of what today's gangbangers call the jumping-in ritual, but being jumped-in is a more bloody procedure since the worthy initiate is often brutally beaten by his homie gangsters.

As part of the normal business of the various illicit enterprises conducted by the gangs of the twenties, homicide was employed as a logical, important, and normal activity for the enforcement of gang rules. Several thousand gangsters died in New York and Chicago in the bootleg liquor wars of the 1920s over disputes related to the operation of the illegal liquor business. Sometimes, but not as often as today's gangs, the drive-bys killed innocent victims.

The murder of a bootlegger became a daily event. Rumrunners and hijackers were pistol-whipped and machine gunned. They were taken for rides on the front seats of sedans, garroted from behind, and at times had their brains blown out with a bullet to the back of the head by fellow mobsters they thought were their pals. They were lined up in pairs in front of warehouse walls in lonely alleys and shot down by enemy-gang firing squads. They were slugged into unconsciousness and placed in burlap sacks with their hands, feet, and necks so roped that they would strangle themselves as they writhed. Charred bodies were found in bombed automobiles. Bootleggers and sometimes their molls were pinioned with wire and dropped alive into the East River. Others were encased in cement and tossed overboard from rum boats in the harbor. In a way, gang murders of this early era were more inventive than today's gangsters.

Life was cheap and murder was easy in the bootleg industry; the early gangsters who fought their way to the top were endowed with savagery and shrewdness. The killings were carried out to consolidate gang territory for greater illicit profit. Murders were not usually committed for emotional reasons but were part of cold and calculated gang business practices. In some cases, former gang friends killed their friends with a comment like, "Listen Charlie, I like you, this is nothing personal — it's just business." And often the victim would quietly cooperate with his own demise by saying, "I understand."

The form of these gang-war murders was different than today's violent gang murders, however, the lethal results were similar. Although contemporary gangs engaged in the commerce of drugs carry out hits against rivals who invade their territory, their violence is not as precise as the earlier form of gang murders. The enforcers of the earlier gangs killed in a businesslike fashion. Their personal kicks and distorted ego gratifications, unlike modern gangs, was secondary to their professional demands.

This early type of calculated murder by a violent gangster is depicted in the career of the infamous mob hitman Abe "Kid Twist" Reles. Reles admitted committing over eighty murders in the normal course of his work as an agent of New York's Murder, Inc., a division of the Meyer Lansky/Bugsy Siegal gang. According to all reports, the murders that Reles committed had an unemotional quality. Reles claimed that he never committed a murder out of passion, excitement, jealousy, personal revenge, or any of the usual motives. He killed impersonally and solely for business considerations.

Early gangsters, like Reles, were not allowed to kill on their own initiative. Murders were ordered by the leaders at the top on behalf of the welfare of the organization. A member of the mob who would dare kill on his own initiative or for his personal passion or profit would often be executed. Organized crime murders were a business matter organized by the chiefs in conference and carried out in a disciplined and efficient way.

When Prohibition was abolished, the early criminal gangs with their great wealth earned from bootlegging and other illegal enterprises entered into more legitimate rackets. They developed quasi-legitimate businesses by controlling unions, government building contracts, refuse removal services, and extortion from legitimate businesses. They eliminated competition through violence. They were exposed in the 1950s and 1960s by the Senate Kefauver committee and later on by Attorney General Robert Kennedy's war on organized crime.

The mob to this day earns billions of dollars from racketeering, extortion, the commerce of drugs, and other illegal enterprises. A large source of mob money for investment in illegal and to some extent legal business activities has come from the mob's hidden ownership of Las Vegas casinos. The gambling business, legal in Nevada, has produced billions of dollars legally and through money-skimming activities from the casinos of mob owned or controlled hotels.

These billions have been funneled into the coffers of organized crime bosses and troops. Along the way over the past fifty years, the mob's activities and internecine conflicts have resulted in thousands of murders; there are hundred of unmarked graves in the deserts of Nevada. A semifictionalized version of these gang activities appeared in the film *Casino*. These murders, for business and profit, parallel some of the murders committed in the past ten years by the new form of the violent-drug gangs fighting over drug territory on the streets of America.

Many contemporary gang murders have a drug business motivation, however, the emotion-driven gangbanging form of territorial protection violence remains a part of the violence committed by today's gangs. Most of the contemporary gangster drive-by murders, in contrast to the 1920's drive-bys, are motivated by an emotional paranoid revenge factor, either real or imagined, rather than for drug business purposes. They typically involve a group of gangsters, high on drugs or alcohol, who are full of rage at the world and go on a senseless murderous foray into what they perceive is enemy territory. After announcing their presence with the verbal gang sign of "Hey cuz," they may blow away with an Uzi or an AK 47 several children or older family members having a picnic in their backyard along with their intended enemy gangsters.

PRE-1950 YOUTH GANGS

Contemporary violent youth gangs have a historical precedent not only in adult gangs but also in earlier forms of youth groups. The term "youth gang" has been used for a variety of diverse youth groupings significantly different from the current violent drug gangs. The generic term "gang" to describe youth collectivities in the early part of the twentieth century has been applied to collections of youths organized to go fishing, to play baseball, to steal cars, or to commit homicide.

One of the earliest applications of the term "gang" to youth groups was made by Henry D. Sheldon in 1898. He classified gangs, according to their activities, as (1) secret clubs, (2) predatory organizations, (3) social clubs, (4) industrial associations, (5) philanthropic associations, (6) literary and musical organizations, and (7) athletic clubs. He maintained at the time that, among boys' clubs, "the athletic clubs are immensely the most popular, with predatory organizations a poor second." [4]

An early description and use of the term "gang" was presented in J. Adams Puffer's publication entitled "Boy Gangs." [5] Puffer's gangs were essentially boys' clubs and athletic teams. He described one early gang's activity as follows:

> We met out in the woods back of an old barn on Spring Street. Met every day if we did not get work. Any fellow could bring in a fellow if others approved. Put a fellow out for spying or telling anything about the club. Tell him we didn't want him and then if he didn't take the hint force him out. We played ball; went swimming, fishing, and shooting. Each of us had a rifle. Meet (at night) and tell stories of what we had done during the day. . . . The purpose of club was to steal; most anything we could get our hands on; fruit from fruit stands; ice cream at picnics, and rob stores. . . . Especially noteworthy is the desire of the gang for a local habitation, its own special street corner, its club room, its shanty in the woods. [6]

Early youth gang researchers and writers seldom used any complex theoretical categories for describing the gangs they studied. Essentially they relied on descriptive appraisals — presenting the gang, so to speak, as is, based on their firsthand observations. More recent students of gang behavior have utilized more abstract analyses, including computerized statistical analyses.

THE CHICAGO SCHOOL'S GANGS

A pioneer group of delinquency and gang researchers emerged in the late 1930s and 1940s in and around the University of Chicago. Building on the theories and research of such sociologists as W. I. Thomas, Florian Znaniecki, George Herbert Mead, and Ernest Burgess, the Chicago School pioneers contributed enormously to creating a foundation for our current understanding of gangs and delinquency. These pioneers in the field included Frederic Thrasher, Frank Tannenbaum, Clifford Shaw, and Henry McKay. These researchers used a form of participant-observation that relied heavily on firsthand qualitative research data collected directly from the boys in their gangs. Their causation theories were essentially based on the social context of the slum and poverty. Their research and writing was heavily based on case-history material and personal documents obtained from offenders in both institutions and the open community.

As I indicated in the Introduction, in 1953 I was hired to become the director of the Morningside Heights, Inc., project in New York. I made it a condition of my employment that I spend two weeks in Chicago to meet with several of the Chicago School researchers. I was honored and privileged to spend the two weeks touring the South Side of Chicago and various gang projects with such luminaries in the field as Clifford Shaw and Henry McKay. Through their auspices I was able to visit and meet many people involved in Chicago gangs and gang projects. Moreover, through a variety of intensive discussions with Shaw and McKay, I was able to directly learn about their viewpoints on gangs and delinquency. Following is a summary of their perspectives based on my firsthand discussions with these pioneers and a review of the literature.

Frederic Thrasher produced the first extensive sociological study of gangs in Chicago based on his research on the South Side of Chicago. His findings were presented in a now classic volume entitled *The Gang.*[7] Gangs, according to Thrasher, involved youths "with esprit de corps, solidarity, morale, group awareness, and attachment to a local territory." Thrasher presented detailed descriptions of many diverse types of gangs to illustrate his material. A typical "tough" gang observed by Thrasher was the so-called Murderers gang:

> Shortly after the race riots of 1919, residents in the vicinity south of the stock yards were startled one morning by a number of placards bearing the inscription "The Murderers, 10,000 Strong, 48th & Ada." The placards brought attention to a gang of thirty Polish boys who hung out in a district known as the Bush.[8]

Thrasher described the activities of another typical gang as follows:

> Every morning they would get together at their corner or in their shack near by to "chew the rag" and talk over the events of the day. The new members who were taken in from time to time were congenial spirits who had shown ability to elude the police or gameness in a fight. . . . Most of them were habitual truants, and they acknowledged their commitments to the parental school [house of detention] with great pride. Many of them had been in the juvenile detention home and the jail. Their records were a matter of considerable prestige in the group.[9]

Frank Tannenbaum described the phases of gradation and graduation into larger and more serious crimes by members of the early Chicago delinquent gangs.[10] The older gang boys, with more experience, were more involved in crime; they stole as a source of income. According to Tannenbaum, gang youths went from stealing to shoplifting, and from that to "rolling bums." Then came pickpocketing, car stealing, holdups, and sometimes murder. All of the escalations of crime were carried out in connection with other members of the gang.

The Chicago School in its analysis of the causes for gangs gave heavy weight to family disorganization. They perceived the family, as we do today, as not performing its proper function for youths who participated in gangs. According to Tannenbaum,

> The family, by its internal weakness, may have been a contributory factor. The father or mother or an older brother may have been delinquent, or there may have been a sharp conflict of opinions and attitudes in the family, or constant bickering and incompatibility between the parents, or the father may have been dead and the mother forced away from home so that the children were left unsupervised.[11]

Another basic assumption of the Chicago School researchers and theorists was that delinquency was a normal activity in poor slum neighborhoods and that most offenses (about 95 percent) were committed in association with others in a gang. They perceived the gang as a basic primary group necessary for self-sustenance, and all outsiders, including the police, were targets for hostility and aggression.

The theories and research of the early Chicago School have had a lasting impact on the sociological image of delinquency in general and the gang in particular. Their conceptualizations may be summarized in the following propositions: (1) The youth begins his delinquent career on a thin line of malicious and mischievous play and then becomes more concretely involved in delinquent gang activity. (2) The natural conflict of a youth with the community and its conflicting set of norms and values drives him further into gang activity. (3) The gang emerges as a result of the failure of community forces, particularly the family, to properly integrate many youths into the more constructive, law-abiding society. (4) Loyalty and esprit de corps are strong mobilizing forces in the delinquent gangs, and it becomes a cohesive entity. (5) The gang becomes a kind of street-corner family for youth who are detached and disassociated from and in conflict with the law-abiding community. (6) The gang in this context becomes a school for crime that provides both the opportunity, the training, and the motivation for a criminal career in association with others. (7) A youth enmeshed in the delinquent gang as a primary group gets driven further into a delinquent career by the negative effect of society's institutionalized patterns for dealing with the gang youth and his problems. A youth thus moves up in the delinquency hierarchy, and as a result of his criminal associations and training, becomes in his later years a recalcitrant criminal.

STREET-CORNER SOCIETY

The Chicago School had the impact of spurring other studies of street gangs. William F. Whyte reported on a major participant-observation study he carried out in Boston in the mid-1930s.[12] To institute his research, Whyte moved into the Italian neighborhood of a large eastern city near Boston, which he called "Cornerville." He learned Italian and "hung out" with a group known as the Norton Street Gang. For three years he participated in the activities of the gang, developed friendly relations with the leaders, and with their cooperation, studied the group's structure.

A primary factor about the Norton Street Gang was that it was a product of the Depression. Most of the members were in their twenties and normally would have been working if jobs had been available. The gang, according to Whyte, emerged because the boys could accomplish more together than separately. The gang gave its members a feeling of solidarity, or belonging. They participated in constructive activities, engaged in athletics, helped each other financially, and discussed mutual problems. Unlike today's gangs, the Norton Street Gang was a cooperative group, beneficial to its membership.

Whyte's comments on gang leadership further supports an image of the Norton Street Gang as a constructive organization: "The leader is the one who acts when the situation requires action. He is more resourceful than his followers. Past events have shown that his ideas were right. In this sense 'right' simply means satisfactory to the members. The leader is respected for his fair-mindedness." [13]

This nostalgic image of leadership in the earlier gangs tends to persist in the analysis of contemporary gangs by some researchers, and it is an erroneous assumption. Today's violent/drug gang leaders are not wise, fair-minded, judicious leaders who are helpful to their associates. They tend to be exploitative, egocentric sociopaths with a hair-trigger potential for sudden, swift, and senseless violence. In brief, earlier gangs were social gangs and bear little resemblance to today's violent gang.

THE 1950 YOUTH GANG ERA

In the period soon after the end of World War II, a different type of gang emerged in urban areas around the United States, especially in Los Angeles, Chicago, and New York. These gangs were less cohesive than earlier gangs, had less of an emphasis on camaraderie among participants, and were clearly more violent.

THE NEW YORK CITY YOUTH BOARD

In response to a large breakout of gang violence in the post–World War II period in New York City, then Mayor Robert Wagner created a special social organization, the New York City Youth Board, for preventing and controlling gangs. So-called detached gang workers were sent into the streets to deal with the fighting gangs of that era. The Youth Board produced a useful methodology for controlling gangs, and their efforts produced a significant amount of research data about the gangs of the 1950s.

In a series of manuals based on their work, the Youth Board developed a concept of the gang that became an accepted diagnostic image for many similar programs in urban areas throughout the country. In one manual they described the violent gangs of that period as follows:

> The gangs with which we worked were surprisingly well organized, on both a formal and informal level. Each club was divided into several divisions, usually on the basis of age. As the boys grew older they "graduated" from one division to another — a feeding process which insured the continued life of each gang. Each division had its own officers including a president, vice-president, and war counsellor. [14]

An appraisal of several Youth Board publications reveals a conceptual perspective on gangs that in many ways resembled the Chicago School viewpoint. According to the Youth Board, the gangs they worked with possessed the following characteristics: (1) Gang behavior is normal behavior for youths; (2) all gangs have a high degree of cohesion, esprit de corps, and organization; (3) gang size or membership is measurable; (4) the gang's role patterns are clearly defined; (5) gangs possess a consistent set of norms and expectations clearly understood by all members; (6) all gangs have a group of clearly defined leaders who are respected by gang members, distinctly specified, and vested with a direct flow of authority; and (7) gangs have a coherent organization for gang warfare.

The Youth Board's image of the 1950s "bopping gang" was apparently greatly influenced by the earlier work on gangs described by Thrasher, Shaw, McKay, and Whyte. My own work and research with gangs in the Morningside Heights project, especially in terms of gang organization, revealed a departure from this perspective of gangs as cohesive entities.

THE MORNINGSIDE HEIGHTS GANG PROJECT

Based on my research and direct work with about seventy-five gangs from 1953 to 1959 on the Upper West Side of Manhattan and into Harlem and my review of other gang research and reports during that era from around the United States, I concluded that there were three basic types of gangs. The basic norms, behavior patterns, and personality characteristics of the membership tend to distinguish each gang type. It is useful to delineate the structure and function of these three gang types since they still exist, in a modified form, in the 1990s.

Social Gangs

This form of gang was a relatively permanent organization that typically centered its activities around a specific stable location such as a hangout, candy store, or clubhouse. All members were intimately known to one another, and there was a sense of comradeship and a "we" feeling. Members belonged in a clear-cut way. Some wore club jackets or sweaters with an insignia, which identified the members to the external community.

Most of their activities were socially oriented and required a degree of responsible social interaction in the group. Their activities included organized athletic participation, personal discussions, organizing dances, and other socially acceptable activities characteristic of adolescence. Membership was not based on self-protection (as in the violent gang) or on social athletic prowess (as in a pure athletic team), but on feelings of mutual attraction and a level of camaraderie.

This type of gang seldom participated in delinquent behavior, gang warfare, and petty thievery, except under unusual conditions. They became involved in minor gang clashes, but only under great pressure. The social gang had considerable permanence. Its members grew up together on the same block and often developed permanent lifelong friendships that continued when they left the "corner" and moved on into their adult life. The social gangs of the 1950s were a natural part of the community, and many youths of that era belonged to the community centers that were part of the neighborhood.

The Delinquent Gang

The delinquent gangs I observed in the 1950s were primarily organized to carry out various illegal acts. The "social interaction" part of the gang's behavior was a secondary factor. Prominent among the delinquent gang's behavior pattern was the commerce of drugs (especially heroin), burglary, petty thievery, mugging, assault for purposes of profit (not simply kicks), and other illegal acts directed at monetary gain (or "raising bread"). These gangs were generally tightly organized cliques that could steal with maximum effectiveness. In recent years some gang researchers have termed the delinquent gang as "corporate, or entrepreneurial gangs." In the past decade, the most prevalent form of this type of gang is involved in the drug trade.

In summary, the delinquent gang was comprised of a cohesive group of emotionally stable youths socialized into illegal patterns of behavior. Violence was employed as a means toward the end of acquiring material and financial profit. In contemporary gangs, delinquent gang cliques of this type are often referred to as "crews" that operate within the framework of the larger multipurpose violent gang. Wannabees and middle-range gangsters doing work in the gang often become part of a delinquent gang crew to earn a reputation and status in the overall violent gang.

The Violent Gang

My research in the 1950s focused on the violent gangs of that era. This type of gangbanger or warfare-oriented gang was the primary gang of the 1950s and continues to exist into the 1990s within the more encompassing multipurpose gang form. In contrast with other gang types, the violent gang was primarily organized for emotional gratification and violent activities.

My perspective on the gangsters of that era was that they were displaced persons — suspicious, fearful, and, unlike the earlier gang youths, without close bonds of camaraderie with their cohorts. The violent gangs of the 1950s had an impermanence and a shifting membership. The gang's possibilities for hollow glory, its limited expectations of any responsibility on the part of its members, was all-inviting to youths who had difficulty fitting into the larger society.

A primary function of the violent gang in the 1950s was to provide a

excited about the project. They were still at a loss about how to proceed. Together we developed a workable questionnaire that they followed in their interviews.

The gang-boy respondents had mixed reactions to Duke and Pedro as researchers. Some boys cooperated fully with them, others felt they were informants for the cops, and some reacted with hostility. On one occasion Duke arrived at my office, displayed some obviously fresh lacerations on his face, and claimed he had been beaten and robbed of ten filled-out question-naires by six unidentified enemy gangsters. He believed that his assailants were, from his paranoid viewpoint, "Dragon gang agents." (The Dragons were an enemy gang.) The details of the "robbery" were incoherent, and I was never able clearly to ascertain what had actually happened. Despite the incident Duke was not deterred from his work. He requested more blank questionnaires and went back into the field.

In addition to discussing the questionnaires with Duke and Pedro, on several occasions I used a role-playing device to attempt assessing their interview technique. Their approach seemed to vary between a polite request for information at one extreme and a threatening, "You fill it out or I'll beat the shit out of you." Though their interview technique was forceful, they had a talent for getting information. They interviewed fifty-one youths whom they identified as core Balkan gang members.

My appraisal of the fifty-one questionnaires with Duke's and Pedro's help revealed pertinent information about how the Balkan organization viewed itself. Of the fifty-one individuals who claimed membership and identity in the Balkan gang, most lived in the area of Balkan turf. They were core gang members known on a face-to-face basis by Duke.

The fifty-one responses to the question, "How many members are there in the Balkans?" varied within a range of eighty to a thousand. About twenty boys reported between four hundred and six hundred. Most Balkans admitted that they did not know all the other Balkan gang members. Some youths indicated no knowledge of the number of members in the gang. Another typical vague response on membership was: "It's about a few hun-dred or a thousand — lots of divisions." With reference to alliances or brother gangs, there was also no consensual reply. The boys expressed varied esti-mates of names, numbers, and size of "brother gang" divisions, indicating that almost each member perceived the overall gang on an individualistic basis.

There was general agreement (forty-eight out of fifty-one responses) that fighting and defense were the main gang activities, with sports and dances listed next in frequency. Most Balkans joined for defense or, as one stated, "Because I like to fight." Most members did not know how the gang began; several indicated, "Because Duke and Pedro started it," and the balance commented in various ways that it began for protection from being jumped by other gangs.

In response to the question, "What do you think of the Dragons?" (their archenemy at that time), the general response consisted of terse profanities. Their estimate of the Dragons' strength ran from about a hundred youths and five divisions to five thousand youths and fifty divisions.

Almost every Balkan seemed to have his own unique image of the gang. The wide variations of response tended to refute the widely held image of the violent gangs as the more cohesive, tightly organized group described by some researchers in the pre-1950 period of gangs in America.

The imagined large gang size was in part a pseudomembership dreamed up by Duke and others and perpetuated by the core gang members' needs to be part of a vast fighting army that included an affiliation with brother gangs.

The research carried out by Duke and Pedro supplemented and supported my views by revealing the Balkans were a partial pseudocommunity that, despite its guiding fictions (or perhaps because of them), was valuable to its members by providing them with a sense of belonging to a large powerful "Balkan Empire" and that helped to boost their personal feelings of power.

The following summary, based on my research analysis of the Balkans and other gangs in the 1950s, is an analysis of the characteristics of the violent gangs of that era.

Joining most violent gangs was a relatively easy process. The main criterion for membership was a proclivity toward violent behavior. A youth could voluntarily join by approaching the assumed gang leader and requesting membership. The leader practically always accepted the applicant since a large membership helped to strengthen him and his gang's prestige. There was a mythology built up around initiation rites, such as the requirement that a potential member steal something or assault someone, but these entrance demands were seldom enforced.

Gang membership had little formal or permanent character. There was little precise definition of role behavior in the gang. A youth could terminate belonging by simply drifting away from the gang's activities. These nondefined characteristics of membership reflected the degree of responsibility and lack of clarity of the gang member's role in the violent gang of that era.

Gang leaders were essentially self-appointed. They attempted to satisfy their emotional needs through the manipulation of other youths into aggressive action and by committing acts of violence themselves. Gang leaders were the more permanent and core members of the gang. The leaders were often glorified by gang members as a reflection of their own aspirations.

Gang leaders conjured up vast networks of gang alliances (some real, some imagined) to fulfill their own needs and the needs of their gang's members for power. Gang members wanted to believe their leaders' assertions that their gang controlled vast networks of gang alliances that could be called on for gang warfare and defense purposes.

Many gangsters of that period seemed to manifest paranoid delusions of persecution and grandeur. In some cases they were attempting to compensate and adjust serious personality disorders through acting in the role of powerful but sham leaders. Their wild dreams of glory served their pathological needs and those of other participants in the gang.

THE REAL WEST SIDE STORY: WHO KILLED MICHAEL FARMER?

The play and, later, the movie *West Side Story* has become a significant theatrical part of American culture. This entertaining drama presents a highly romanticized viewpoint on gangs that from my perspective was almost totally inconsistent with reality. There was a typical gang murder around the time that *West Side Story* was on Broadway that revealed the true story about the gangs of that era.

This particular violent gang murder dramatized the reality and became a flashpoint for illuminating the gang as a significant social problem. The incident involved the brutal gang murder of Michael Farmer, a fifteen-year-old polio victim, by a gang that called themselves the Egyptian Kings. Farmer was stabbed to death on the night of July 30, 1957, in Highbridge Park on the Upper West Side of Manhattan. The story of this unfortunate event hit the headlines of newspapers in New York City and around the country.

At that time, I had been working with the Kings (apparently not very effectively) and knew the key gangsters involved in the murder. I intensively chronicled this particular gang murder, partly because Edward R. Murrow, one of the icons and originators of documentary news broadcasting in the United States, became interested in this high-profile gang incident and my work with gangs in New York. In my collaboration with Murrow and Jay McMullen, one of Murrow's producers, I spent several months interviewing the boys and helped in the production of a CBS network documentary on the event entitled *Who Killed Michael Farmer?* My tapes and commentary provided the foundation of the program.

The Kings we interviewed most intensely were the younger gangsters in the case who had already been tried and sentenced as delinquents to a state reformatory. They were willing to talk openly about the murder because I knew most of these boys from my past work with them, they trusted me, and they would not receive any more time for their crime. They spoke candidly about their participation in the murder. Following is a presentation of the events leading up to this typical 1950s gang murder, and the aftermath, as derived from my book *The Violent Gang*.

The Kings Murder

On the night of July 30, 1957, a fifteen-year-old boy, partially crippled by polio, was beaten and stabbed to death in a New York City park. His best friend was critically injured by stab wounds inflicted with a bread knife in the same attack. The motives for this crime fit no simple category. No money was taken. No direct personal revenge was involved. According to all reports, the victims did not personally know their assailants, nor did the youths who committed the homicide know their victims.

It was a hot muggy summer night in New York. A casual observer of the boys huddled in discussion in a tenement hallway near the corner of 135th Street and Broadway would detect nothing unusual about this gathering. They talked excitedly, calling each other by nicknames: Magician, Little King, Louie, Big Man were familiar names. One youth clutched a long brown paper bag in his hand. It contained a machete. Another had a razor-point five-inch-long knife tucked away in his clothes. Still another held a harmless-appearing chain used normally to hold a dog on a leash. This chain had a heavy metal ball on the end.

Part of the discussion revolved around the previous evening when several members of the Kings gang had been chased out of the Highbridge Park pool by the Jesters, an Irish-American gang that controlled this pool in their territory. One boy said, "Anybody who doesn't swing out will have to tangle with me when we get back." They were not talking about enemy gang members; they were referring to their own boys. One boy put it this way:

We say before we went up to get it on. Anyone who don't swing out is gonna get it when we come back. They got to pass through a line; they got about fifteen boys over here, and fifteen boys over there, and you know, in a straight line, like that. They got to pass through there and they all got belts in their hand. So you know you will get the shit beat out of you when you get back, if you don't get someone in the enemy gang.

Another boy described how the other gang had called him a "Spick" when they chased him from the pool:

They kept on callin' me a Spick. They kept on saying, "You dirty Spick, get out of here." Every time I go in the pool, they said the same thing to me. I don't bother them, 'cause, you know, I don't want to get into no trouble with them, but one day five of them beat me up.

This boy was Puerto Rican. The Kings, however, had a mixed background. Although predominantly Puerto Rican and black, a number of gang members came from other ethnic groups. They were generally representative of the neighborhood population. Some Kings used racial or ethnic discrimination as a reason for "calling on the rumble" with the white Jesters.

Two of the Kings claimed the Jesters had guns. As they described it:

One guy, the Jester president, said, "I'm gonna burn you." So he pulled out a gun; it looked like a .45, but we weren't too sure. He put the gun up to my head. Another Jester pulled out a sawed-off rifle, and pointed it at us. Somehow we got away.

A Jester I interviewed gave a different version of the King's story:

There was about fifteen of them in the pool, and they [the Kings] started hollerin' things out, like, you know, names and your gonna be wasted and all this kind of shit. The next day about thirty-five guys from the Kings came up to our turf and they smacked one of our guys on the head with a bat. He went to the hospital and got eight stitches.

The Kings that night were joined by a brother gang, the Dragons. The administrator of this consolidation was a "man" (or at least he was twenty-six years old) named Frankie Cruz. He was better known to the gang boys in this area of the Upper West Side as Frankie Loco. Loco (who today would be labeled an "OG") was a twenty-four-hours-a day, 1950s gang leader. He was always giving advice on gang organization, telling gang boys when and with whom to fight. Most of the time he was discussing nonexistent enemies conjured up in his paranoid fantasy world.

Loco traveled up and down the West Side, as one gang boy told me, "talkin', talkin', talkin', and stirring up gang trouble." Loco at one time was under psychiatric observation at the Bellevue psychiatric hospital. He had a scar across the top of his head — the result of a childhood battle. Loco's favorite topic was blood. The only job he ever had was cleaning up the blood in an operating room at a city hospital. He liked his work.

That night Loco had helped to provoke the gang's action. At the Egyptian Kings' murder trial he was mentioned by almost all the defendants on trial for first-degree murder as their advisor. On the night of the homicide he was nowhere around. Loco was primarily a "consultant" and was not with the group swaggering up Broadway that night from 135th Street to 152nd Street.

On the way up Broadway, the gang leader with the machete under his arm met an old friend on his way to a movie. This gang youth was not resistant to joining the Kings heading up to a fight. A violent rumble for him was more attractive than going to a movie. He commented, "When they asked me if I wanted to go to a fight, I couldn't say, 'No.' I mean I could say, 'No,' but for old-time's sake, I said, 'Yes.' " This boy, who went to the fight by chance, later took an active role in killing Michael Farmer. "He got up and I knocked him down and then I stabbed him a few times so he would stay down."

Trial Judge Irwin Davidson based on courtroom testimony, summarized his reflections on the gang's mood that night prior to the homicide:

> There were around seventy-five gang boys in the Kings. They had been assured that reinforcements were arriving from other parts of the city. During the long — and, as it turned out, fruitless — wait at a candy store for their allies, some of the boys had begun to drift away. The seventy-five boys dwindled down to eighteen. I wondered where the police had been. Surely there had been patrol cars in the neighborhood. The boys had sticks, knives, and a machete wrapped in paper. Any passerby could have seen that they were there for no good reason.

A police station was one block away from the corner where the boys met. Citizens in cars and on foot passed this gang buildup for almost two hours; however, gangs blended into most New York City neighborhoods. At about 10:00 P.M. eighteen members of the gang headed north toward Highbridge Park. In one hour, Michael Farmer would be dead.

The walk from 152nd Street and Broadway to Highbridge Park is about twenty New York City blocks. The route passes slum tenements, modern apartment buildings, and old residential homes abandoned to deterioration. A police station was on the way.

In our later interviews the boys revealed some of their thoughts on the way to the murder: "Nobody's gonna steal my rep." "I felt kinda cold inside." "They'll get me later if I don't swing out at somebody." "Tonight I'm going to kill some mother fucker."

They convened at 10:15 P.M. in Stitt Park, a small park that faces Stitt School about seven blocks from Highbridge Pool. The boys discussed a plan of action, then sent out "scouts" to patrol the neighborhood "to see how many Jesters were around." There is some evidence of other boys hanging around in the park; however, they were not necessarily Jesters. But to the scouts everybody looked like an enemy gang member. By this time they were ready to swing out at anyone.

Highbridge Pool is rather large. An American flag waves high over the pool. In a city like New York, with its few available recreation opportunities, the pool was a treasured spot for cooling off in the hot summer. The Kings and Dragons entered the bushy area surrounding the pool in twos and threes to avoid attention. Staked out around the pool, they were, in their own words, "ready to jump anyone who came along."

Michael Farmer and a friend, Roger McShane, were at this time in the Farmer apartment about a block from the park, listening to rock 'n' roll records.

MRS. FARMER: They stayed in his room playin' these new records that they had bought and Michael came out to the kitchen just as I asked my husband what time it was, to set the clock. It was then five after ten. He asked for a glass of milk and as he walked from the kitchen, he said, "I'm going to walk Roger home." *(Sighs.)* That was the last time I saw him.

Youngsters in the area were warned to stay out of the park at night when the pool was closed but not drained. However, it was usual for some of the local boys to slip through a break in the gate entrance and sneak an evening swim. The slightly curved footpath that enters the park at Amsterdam Avenue and 174th Street is about a one-minute walk to the high concrete stairway entrance to Highbridge Pool. It was Michael Farmer's last walk.

MC SHANE: It was 10:30 when we entered the park; we saw couples on the benches, in the back of the pool, and they all stared at us, and I guess they must 'ave saw the gang there — I don't think they were fifty or sixty feet away. When we reached the front of the stairs, we looked up and there was two of their gang members on top of the stairs. They were two smaller ones, and they had garrison belts wrapped around their hands. They didn't say nothin'. I saw the main body of the gang slowly walk out of the bushes.

1ST KING: He couldn't run, cause we were all around him. So then I said, "You're a Jester," and he said, "Yeah," and I punched him in the face. And then somebody hit him with a bat over the head.

2ND KING: I didn't wanna hit him, at first. Then I kicked him twice. He was layin' on the ground, lookin' up at us. I kicked him on the jaw, or some place; then I kicked him in the stomach. That was the least I could do, was kick him.

2ND KING: I was aimin' to hit him, but there were so many guys on him. I saw the knife go into the guy. Another guy kept hittin' him with a machete. Magician grabbed him, turned him around and stabbed him in the back. I was stunned. I couldn't do nothin'. And then Magician told me "You're gonna hit him again with that bat or I'll stab you." So I hit him with the bat. When Magician stabbed him, the guy fell. He started to stand up and I knocked him down. Then he was down on the ground, everybody was kickin' him, stompin' him, punchin' him, stabbin' him. He tried to get back up and I knocked him down again. Then another guy stabbed him again in the back with a bread knife.

4TH KING: I just went like that, and I stabbed him with the bread knife. You know, I was drunk, so I just stabbed him. *(Laughs.)* He was screamin' like a dog.

5TH KING: The guy that stabbed him in the back with the bread knife told me later that when he took the knife out of his back, he said, "Thank you" to the guy he stabbed.

MC SHANE: They got up fast right after they stabbed me. And I just lay there on my stomach. As they walked away they . . . this other big kid came down with a machete or some large knife, and he wanted to stab me with it. And they told him, "No, come on. We got him. We messed him up already. Come on." They took off up the hill. I got up and staggered into the street and managed to get a cab. I got in and told the cab driver to take me to the Medical Center, and get my friend. Then I blacked out.

The coroner's report reveals the intensity of the violence committed on Michael Farmer:

> I found a fifteen-year-old white boy, five feet and a half inches in length, scale weight 138 pounds. The face showing a hemorrhage beneath the skin. . . . There was an ecchymosis [blood erupted into other body tissue] of the outer aspect of the right eye, with a superimposed superficial abrasion. . . . There was an incised wound made with a very sharp implement . . . situated over the bridge of the nose and [extending] . . . over the right eyebrow.

He had found wounds and abrasions on the knuckles and hands of the body. This showed that Michael Farmer had raised his hands to defend himself against the torrential blows being inflicted on him. On the left side was another penetrating stab wound, lower and more deadly. This one went through the entire back into the pleural cavity, and severed a vein and a nerve. This wound, four inches deep, caused Farmer's death.

Roger McShane was on the critical list at the Presbyterian Medical Center. Michael Farmer's parents were notified the same evening of his death.

MR. FARMER: The sergeant from the 34th Precinct called us, and asked who I was, and was I the father of Michael Farmer. I said I was, and he said, "Well, your boy is in Mother Cabrini Hospital, in serious condition." I identified myself further as a fireman in this area, and he said, "Oh, I'll come down and give you a lift down to the hospital." So this sergeant drove us down to the hospital; as we walked in, the officer who was on duty there called the sergeant, and he said the boy had died fifteen minutes earlier.

MRS. FARMER: The sister in the hospital took us downstairs to identify the body. He had an expression on his face as though he was just calling for help.

After the stabbing the gang scattered and fled. The gang members reported their postkilling reactions in various ways. One boy went home, had a glass of milk, went to bed, but couldn't sleep. "I couldn't sleep that night or nuthin' 'cause I used to fall asleep for about half an hour. Wake up again during the middle of the night. My mother said, 'What was the matter with you? Looks like something was wrong.' I said, 'nothin'.' "

Another gang member said,

> First I went to the river to throw my knife away and then I went home. I couldn't sleep. I was in bed. My mother kept on askin' me where was I and I told her that I was in the movies. I was worried about them two boys. If they would die . . . I knew I was gonna get caught.

This boy was more concerned with getting caught and locked up than remorseful over his violent act. In a later interview with him in a reformatory I asked him, "How do you feel about this all now? Are you sorry that you killed Farmer?" His response was, "Are you crazy, man?" Of course, I'm sorry. Who wants to be locked up!"

Unlike most of today's gang murders, which end up buried in the newspapers because they are so common, back then there were banner headlines about the homicide, shocking many residents of New York City on their way to work the following morning.

A large number of detectives worked through the night to piece the crime together. By dawn they began to round up the gang. One gang boy in the paddy wagon, on his way to police headquarters, told me about what he considered police brutality:

> I had on a new suit that I just got out of the cleaners. This detective kept calling me a murderer — "You're going to get the electric chair." Then he started wipin' his feet on my suit! I yelled, "Cut it out." But he kept on doin' it. I thought to myself, if I had a gun I would have killed them all!

When the gang was arraigned in court, Mr. Farmer, the victim's father noted: "To me they are all savage monsters. My boy didn't have a chance. They stood around sneering at me. They didn't show any remorse. They should be put away for life — or better yet executed. They executed my son for no reason."

One mother of one of the killers gave covert approval to her son's participation in the murder. This even shocked a tough gang member who related the incident to me:

> When she sees him she says to him with a smile on her face, "How did it feel when you stabbed Farmer? It was good?" You know, jokin' around with the kid. So we told her, "You know what your son did? He stabbed Farmer in the back." She just went like that, and shrugged her shoulders. Then we didn't pay any more attention to her, because ya know, you don't like to see a mother actin' like that with a son who committed a murder.

Within twenty-four hours, the eighteen youths involved in the crime were apprehended and arraigned. The eleven younger members of the gang, age fifteen or under, were adjudicated in Children's Court and committed to various state reformatories for indeterminate sentences.

The older group of seven, ranging in age from fifteen to eighteen, were indicted and tried for first-degree murder in an unprecedented trial lasting ninety-three days and involving twenty-seven trial lawyers for the defense. An all-male jury rendered a guilty verdict. Three of the adult gang members were released immediately based on time served because it was determined that they were not actively involved in the murder. Two were sentenced to twenty years to life imprisonment. One was sentenced to seven-and-one-half to fifteen years and the other was sentenced to five to fifteen years.

The 1957 Egyptian Kings "walk-by" gang murder of Michael Farmer, although clearly tragic, seems almost benign when compared to the brutal drive-by gang assassinations of the 1990s. Although there are some changes in the structure of contemporary gangs, two factors mark the major differentiation between earlier violent gangs and today's violent gangs: the intensified commerce of drugs and the violence that surrounds the drug business, and the enormous increase in the availability of lethal automatic weapons that are used in gang murders.

PART TWO

THE CONTEMPORARY GANG

○ ○ ○ ○ ○ ○ ○ ○ ○ ○ ○

3.

Gang Characteristics

o o o o o o o o o o

T HE OVERT RATIONALE FOR gang violence and murder committed by the violent gangs of the past was based on territorial conflicts, a sense of being disrespected by another gang, and revenge. These
earlier justifications for violence clearly remain in place for gangs in the
1990s, however, the combination of gangbanging, drive-bys, the drug business, and more lethal guns account for the escalation of murderous violence
by contemporary gangs. Another change in contemporary gangs is found in
the different ways in which gangsters participate in the multipurpose violent
gang from different statuses in their gang's hierarchy.

WANNABEES, GS, AND OGS

In Webster's dictionary, the word "member" is defined as "a distinct part of a
whole . . . any of the persons constituting an organization or a group." The
two key words in this definition that deserve analysis with reference to gangs
are "distinct" and "group." In my view, violent gangs are neither fully distinct
nor clearly defined groups. (This concept of the violent gang as an inchoate
near-group will be fully analyzed and defined in chapter 9.)

With the exception of a number of so-called corporate or entrepreneurial drug gangs, involving a small cohesive group of individuals engaged in the commerce of drugs, my research into contemporary gangs reveals that most gangs have an incoherent or inchoate form when compared to more socially acceptable groups. This is due in part to the emotionally unstable condition of most of the youths and young men who participate in violent gangs.

Gangs are often in a state of transition or flux. Their structure has a degree of coherence and some duration in time; however, they are not usually cohesive, clearly defined groups. Because of this inchoate nature of most gangs, membership in a gang is a concept that is different from membership in more normal groups. Although there are some membership-defining factors — such as wearing a certain color (for instance, in Los Angeles, blue for Crip gangs, red for Blood gangs) — and core members can identify each other, more marginal members in most gangs are not clearly known to each other, and there is an impermanent quality about the structure of the violent gang.

Given these factors, in my analysis of gang organization, the term "member" has a different connotation than the use of this term for normative social groups. The term "gangster" is a clearer, more precise way of defining the fact that the individual is a participant on some level in gang activity. Therefore, in my overall analysis, the term "gangster" will be used rather than "gang member."

Gangsters in a gang do have different statuses in the hierarchal organization, and some gangsters are more committed and are more involved participants in their gang than others. Gangs, then and now, have always had some kind of hierarchal form. In the 1950s era, there were individuals who could be identified by their age as so-called midgets, juniors, and senior gang members. In today's gangs, in a parallel way, gangsters can be identified on three levels, related partly to age but mainly to the amount of violent and delinquent work they have put in to "earn their stripes," their reputation or status in the gang.

I have observed three general gang statuses: (1) WBs, or Wannabees, are youths from about age nine to thirteen who are aggressively seeking roles and status in the gang. (2) Gs are active gangbanger gangsters from about age thirteen to twenty-five who already have achieved acceptance in the gang. The term encompasses the "soldiers" who form the core of the gang. Gs comprise around 80 percent of the gangsters in the contemporary multi-purpose violent gang. Gs have established a role in the gang that can at any point in their participation involve all gang activities including gangbanging, delinquency, and drugs. (3) OG refers to older gangsters or original gangsters. These in some cases are founders of the gang. OG status is accorded to gangsters who have achieved a permanent status in their gang, even when they are semiretired or not active participants.

OGs range in age from eighteen up. In Chicano gangs the phrase "veterano" is sometimes used to identify an OG. OGs have already established their high status in the gang. They have put in their work and have earned their stripes by virtue of a number of years of violent and delinquent/criminal behavior. For OGs, their longevity in the gang and the amount and intensity of work they have put in almost automatically accords them a reputation, respect, and consequently, leadership status. In brief, OGs are the founders of the gang or have come up through the ranks in the gang and have occupied a variety of statuses along the way.

The terms WBs, Gs, and OGs are often used by gangsters in referring to their colleagues, however, they are not always used by them in a precise way to define other participants in their gang. The more common reference used by one gangster about another is "homeboy," "homie," or "homes." This defines the other as being in his "set," or gang. The term "homeboy" is used in a number of ways, for example, "He's one of my homeboys" or the greeting, "Szup (what's up) homes?," the latter meaning "what's happening?" or "what's going on?"

Wannabees can be loosely compared to corporate trainees. They are young gangsters in training. They are putting in work committing acts of often wanton and bizarre violence and delinquency in order to get attention and to obtain a reputation and status in the gang. In some cases, WBs are older, but aspiring gangsters who want to be in the gang, but who have some mental deficiency or physical inadequacy. Their participation in the gang often remains at the WB level, yet they have gained acceptance at this level.

WBs hang around older members in their hangouts and are perceived as kids aspiring to become big-time Gs. For some, they are simply following in their father's, uncles', or older brothers' footsteps. When they see their role-model Gs and older gangsters dealing drugs — at times holding large wads of cash — they are motivated to move up in the hierarchy in order to acquire a piece of the action. The older, heroic role models they aspire to become may be on the corner selling drugs, simply hanging out, or in and out of prison.

WBs observe the crap games and "fooling around" behavior, and they sometimes see teasing and wrestling activity burst into serious violent behavior in the older gangsters they attempt to emulate. They are inspired by and pay close attention to the fact that some of the older Gs have money, fine-looking "old ladies" (girlfriends), and drive new big cars.

Sometimes WBs form a small clique or subgroup within the larger gang. For example a subgroup within the Shoreline Crips of Venice, California, called themselves the "Insane Baby Crips." This set was comprised of around fifteen trainees on their way up the ladder of gang success. Most of them were putting in work, had been to court and juvenile hall several times, and almost all of them were on probation.

School is too demanding for most WBs, so they play hookey most of the time and hang out with their pals. On the rare occasion when they do go to school, they caricature their older gang heroes by acting tough and modeling a swaggering gangster walk. By words, attitude, and threatening stance, they tell other kids at school who might get contentious, "Don't fuck with me. I'm a Crip (a Blood, a V-13, or an 18th Street) gangster."

WBs have arrived when a gun is placed in their hand, and they are invited to go on a foray, or drive-by, into another gang area. They are well aware of when a war with an enemy gang is going down, and they help where they can. They see the weaponry of their gang, and when they are nearing "graduation" to G status, they may acquire a gun of their own as a significant status symbol. Wannabees in the corporate world are out of the mail room when they get an office cubicle or acquire a personal computer: in the gang, acquiring your own gun indicates that you are on your way up the status ladder of the gang.

At an early age WBs begin to smoke marijuana and drink like the Gs and OGs they admire. In the gang's drug commerce, WBs often play a significant role as mules, delivering drugs for OG gangster dealers. Gs are aware that a kid carrying drugs will only go to juvenile court if busted by the police and receive a lighter sentence than an older gangster. If a WB is arrested with drugs, it becomes a mark of achievement positively recognized in the gang.

A *Time* magazine article presented a colorful prototype of a New York youth I would characterize as a WB intent on climbing the status ladder to becoming a G or an OG.

Baby Love sits on the stoop, rolling the largest, fattest joint in the world. He wastes little: in go twigs, seeds, everything, until it seems as big as a torpedo. Other joints are tucked over each ear, and more are secreted in plastic bags under his hat. It is Friday night, the night to get high, get drunk and strut. Baby Love's entire wrecking crew (his homies) are here, sprawled over cars, squatting on the side walk, jiving. . . . "We be in the streets hanging out an' getting high," says Baby Love. He is a very skinny, very small, a very lethal 13-year-old. His eyes are slate gray, flashing to blue when he laughs. Mischief is etched across his face as a bittersweet smile. Like his crew, he is dressed in mugger's uniform; designer jeans, T shirt and $45 Pumas, the starched laces neatly untied. A wolf in expensive sneakers.[1]

The article further notes that Baby Love lives in Brooklyn's dangerous, gang-infested Bedford Stuyvesant section, one of the oldest black ghettos in the United States. The police precinct he lives in has the highest murder rate in the city. Baby Love is trapped in a hopeless situation. He can barely read or write since he seldom goes to school. He is almost always stoned and on probation for stealing.

He lives on the fourth floor of a crumbling tenement with his aunt and sleeps on a stained mattress in a small room he shares with his cousins. He was thirteen when he first saw a man blown away with a shotgun. He carries a .25 automatic for protection like most of his homies. His mother, Rose, is a thirty-one-year-old crack addict who winds in and out of jail. His father, whom he seldom knew as a child except when being beaten by him, is also an addict, doing time in prison for dealing drugs. Baby Love is New York's WB prototype. He resembles the two eleven- and twelve-year-old Chicago youngsters who threw a five-year-old to his death from a Chicago high-rise housing project and the Venice Insane Baby Crips described earlier. WBs like Baby Love can be found in every city in the United States.

The common characteristics of WBs are they seldom go to school; they come from dysfunctional families in which too often their parents are crack-heads or alcoholics, who discipline them sporadically and often abuse them sexually, physically, and emotionally; they are putting in work in a twenty-four-hours-a-day tour of violence, robbery, and theft; they smoke dope and drink daily; and they are often mules for OG drug dealers. WBs are putting in all of this work with the goal of becoming like one of their G or OG heroic role models.

The process of graduating out of WB status to become a full-fledged G is cogently described by Monster Kody Scott. As a young WB he had partici-pated in a Crip raid on an enemy gang and had apparently killed one enemy with several shots from his gun in the presence of his older homies. After the event, in a kind of gang victory celebration, he became a full-fledged G

through the auspices of his OG mentor. He described his ceremonial graduation into full G status in the following way:

> Back in the shack we smoked more pot and drank more beer. I was the
> center of attention for my acts of aggression. "Man, did you see this little
> muthafucka out there?" Fly said to Huck with an air of disbelief.
>
> "Yeah, I saw him, I knew he was gonna be down, I knew it and — " Lep
> then said, "Shut up, man, just shut the fuck up, cause he can still tell on
> all of us." Silence rang heavy in my ears, and I knew I had to respond to
> Lep's reaction. "If I get caught, I'll ride the beef, I ain't no snitch." . . .
> Tray Ball announced my full membership and congratulations were given
> from all. It was the proudest moment in my life. Tray Ball told me to stay
> after the others had left. I milled around, still high from battle, and
> thought of nothing else but putting in work for the set.
>
> "Check this out" Tray Ball said. "You got potential, 'cause Bangin' ain't
> no part-time thang, it's fulltime, it's a career. It's bein' down when ain't
> nobody else down, and being caught and not tellin'. Killin' and not caring,
> and dying without fear. It's love for your set and hate for enemy. You hear
> what I'm sayin'?" "Yeah, yeah, I hear you," I said. And I had heard him
> and never forgot nothing he said from that point on. Also from that point
> on Tray Ball became my mentor, friend, confidant, and closest comrade.
> He allowed me acts of aggression that made my name soar.[2]

Gs and OGs comprise the core of the gang and participate in all of the
gang's multipurpose activities. After a sufficient period of time (including
prison time) and work, they achieve an OG status, which as indicated, is a
position of respect for someone who has earned their bones or stripes by
virtue of the fact that they have proven their commitment to the gang
through years of violent and criminal acts in and out of prison. In terms of
the Mafia model, OGs are "men of respect," the John Gottis of the violent
gang.

A select and small number of OGs, perhaps the most intelligent gangsters,
begin to see gangbanging and senseless violence as a waste of their time and
decide to make some real money in their gangster role. These OGs, who
are often especially violent and cunningly intelligent, move up to become
notorious, vicious, and wealthy drug kingpins.

PACHO

One OG in this genre who made it to the top was Pacho (not his real name).
Pacho, when I met him, was thirty-six. His career as a gangster began at the

age of eleven, when, along with his homeboys, he formed a rat pack that rolled drunks for their cash. Another activity involved the stealing of car radios and other random burglaries. When he rose to what I would term G status at around the age of fifteen, he had established a reputation for violence throughout his barrio.

Pacho had a well-deserved reputation for exploding into senseless violence. In his periodic violent outbursts, he would kick and stab his enemies. On several occasions an ambulance had to be called to bring his victims to the hospital. His reputation spread through the barrio as a "loco vato." He was described by one of his homies in the following way: "No one fucks with Pacho. He is a crazy mother-fucker and he will kill you." In fact Pacho had killed several enemy gang members both in drive-bys and face-to-face.

In one murder that he had committed in a drive-by spray of bullets, he killed an enemy gangster. For this homicide, at the age of sixteen he was sentenced to the California Youth Authority. Because of his violent behavior in custody, he wound up in an adult prison in the California system. Here, he became integrated into the Mexican Mafia and rose to become a leader in the core of the gang at the age of twenty. (The Mexican Mafia, self-named "M," will be described in more detail in chapter 4.)

When released from prison, through a shrewd intelligence and a variety of violent acts, Pacho rose to the top of the drug-gang hierarchy. One incident in particular reveals his ruthlessness and his relation to the Gs who were part of his empire. Another gangster, whom I will call Ramon, attempted to deal drugs in Pacho's territory. According to an informed source, "Pacho put out a contract on Ramon. Several Gs took on the hit. He was shot to death. The police found Ramon nude on a vacant lot with a large cucumber sticking out of his ass. His prick and his balls had been cut off and stuck in his mouth."

During the period of five years when he was at the top of his game as an OG, Pacho earned several million dollars, owned several homes, and became a legendary gangster in his community. His downfall came when he was convicted of involvement in one of the murders he had personally committed. He is now in prison serving a life sentence. Because of his homicidal proclivities, and because he has the power to set up a hit on other prisoners incarcerated anywhere in the California system, he is incarcerated in maximum security in the Pelican Bay prison of the California Department of Corrections.

Pelican Bay is the end of the line for the most violent offenders in the

California system, and one of the highest security facilities in the United States. Only the most violent prisoner of the some 140,000 offenders incarcerated in California are sent to Pelican Bay, where they do their time in solitary confinement around twenty hours a day. (Monster Kody Scott has been housed in Pelican Bay.)

Pacho's rise to a top leader in his gang is achieved by very few Gs. However, his reputation is legendary in his community. Many WBs and Gs know his story and have been motivated to achieve his position in the gangster hierarchy. Pacho's life and lifestyle regrettably serves as the role model for too many youngsters growing up in the barrios and ghettos of cities throughout America. Some American youths aspire to become president, others aspire to become another Pacho.

GANGSTERS — A GENERAL ANALYSIS

SOME GANGSTER MYTHS

The role of gangster, at whatever status level, involves a number of general rights, duties, and obligations. These include, but are not limited to, such general rules and expectations as joining has a clear-cut ritual involved; thou shalt not snitch on another gang member; do not allow the gang's territory to be violated by any other gang; if a homie is harmed, you have to retaliate against the enemy gang; the gang is your most important "family"; your homies love you; you only leave in a box, or in Chicano gang terms, you're in the gang *por vida* — for life; when the gang is under attack by another gang, you will fight; all authorities, certainly including the police, are your enemy.

More often than not these codes and expectations for behavior are followed; however, given the sociopathic personality characteristics of many gangsters they often pick and chose between behaviors that will satisfy their egocentric needs at any given time. Consequently, a considerable amount of gang mythology is contradicted by the reality of gang behavior.

For example, regarding the myth of "standing up for a homie," I have seen many a gangster in a police station and prison ready to snitch on "the dude I love" if it would help his case or enable him to get cut loose. As previously indicated, a notable example of a gang member pleading for mercy at the expense of his homies is the case of Damien Williams, the gangster who was convicted of a felony for beating truck driver, Reginald

Denney, during the 1992 Los Angeles riots. Williams had a reputation among his homies as a stand-up gangster, yet he was ready to snitch on anyone the police wanted. According to a police officer who was present at Williams's interrogation, Williams commented, "I'll tell you anything you want to know about who was there with me if you will only let me go home."

Along these same lines, in the violent gang there is a myth of gang members being family. Around 70 percent of the respondents to my questionnaire referred to their gang as family, or familia. Here again, over the years, I have seen innumerable cases of internecine gang family violence where one homie kills another for no special reason.

On this point, in one notable case, I had inside information about a gang-crew robbery that resulted in a sixteen-year-old WB being killed after the robbery by an OG who had masterminded the robbery. The youngster had participated in the robbery, but had performed poorly during the armed holdup. Later the "loving" OG, in a fit of anger killed him for his poor performance.

I have noted many cases of homies committing violent acts on brother gangsters that explode the myth of the gang's solidarity. Sociopathic gangsters kill irrationally, and this can include their homies. The gangsters' violent behavior toward their homies gives new meaning to "with friends like this, who needs enemies?"

LEVELS OF PARTICIPATION: MARGINAL AND CORE GANGSTERS

A general misconception about gangsters is that they are all similar in their participation in the gang's activities. Some individuals are very marginal gangsters and have a limited participation in a gang, even though they appear to be gangsters by their demeanor and the way they dress. Yet the general public, the press, and police agencies tend to perceive all youths who live in a gang's hood as being gangsters. For example, in police sweeps, they often arrest youths who are not core gangsters but present the stereotypical appearance of gangsters.

In some respects each gangster has his own special motive for participation in a violent gang, and this can affect the intensity of his gang affiliation. The gangster's degree of emotional involvement in the gang is indicated by his level of participation, which may be either core or marginal.

WBs, Gs, and even OGs at different times and for varied reasons have varying involvement in gang activity. Some of the factors that impinge on the intensity of a gangster's participation in a gang include the emotional heat of the moment; the problems and conflict he may have with his parents and family; and at times, the effects of arrest, the courts, and incarceration.

Marginal Gangsters

A marginal gangster may appear at gang-war discussions and battles at those times when he has a temporary need for violent behavior. A case in point involved a youth who went along on the night of a gang murder because "I just had a fight with my old man and I was mad at everybody." My interview with this individual revealed that he had fought with his father the night of the murder over some money he had stolen from him. His father threw him down a flight of stairs. This marginal gangster that night was angry and battered. When he arrived on the corner and heard that a drive-by was about to take place, he was emotionally primed for violent action. In the emotional heat of the random drive-by, he shot and killed an elderly man who was having a family gathering in his backyard.

Some youths who may be included in the category of marginal gangsters are sociopathic individuals who live in a gang hood and are ready to fight anyone, anytime. They seek out violence or provoke it simply as they describe it, "for kicks or action." They participate in violent gang activity because for them the gang provides a convenient and easily accessible opportunity for acting out an enormous rage that emanates from other situations in their life.

Some youths who are, in fact, marginal gangsters become defined as full gangsters through identification by official agencies, especially the police. If they happen to be on the scene and hanging out with the gang, even if they are marginal participants, they tend to be identified as gangsters by the police because of their race, ethnicity, or the way they dress.

The stereotypical appearance of gangster dress and demeanor is often responsible for a youth remaining on the gangster/prisoner criminal justice treadmill, even after they attempt to quit the gang. This was brought home to me by an event in one of my criminology classes. A female student told me about her cousin, a Chicano gangster for most of his life, who had recently been released from a state prison where he had served three years for participating in a drive-by shooting. She told me that he had been home for a month, had quit his gang, was working, and going straight. He was interested in her criminology studies and was willing to talk to our class.

I was taken aback when this reformed gangster arrived at our classroom in the typical gangster uniform, which included the baggy pants, long shirt tails, and the stereotypical prison gangster macho-shuffle. His lecture was in two parts. The first part was a very sincere and believable talk about how he had given up gang life because it would only get him back in prison or dead.

The second part was a vituperative angry diatribe against the police. Part of his hysterical attack was the comment, "These motherfuckin cops won't let me alone. They are always harassing me. The other night I was picked up for just standing on the corner." His harangue was vicious and nonstop.

When he came to the end of his talk, after some questions from several students, I purposely provoked him by saying, "If you don't want to be hassled by the police, why don't you change the way you dress?" He turned on me and went into the stereotypical speech I had heard hundreds of times from gangsters, "No motherfucker is going to tell me what to do." Of course, he was right. Nobody in a free society should dictate the way he should dress. Yet, despite his positive efforts at going straight, this facet of his self-image was self-destructive and could easily become a factor in his being arrested and once again entering the criminal justice system.

My student informed me about a month later that her cousin had been picked up by the police, his parole had been revoked, and he was back in prison. I do not know all of the details of his arrest, but according to his cousin, he had done nothing criminally wrong except continuing to maintain his gangster image. Apparently he had given up the violent/criminal aspects of gangster life, and yet remained addicted to the patina of the gangster appearance.

To marginal gangsters the term "gang-related violence" has a special meaning. The designation "gang related" has appeared in the press and police reports when the police or the media suspect that a violent incident is related to gang activity. In many cases, behavior that may have no relationship to a gang is identified as "gang related" by the police and the press.

The following case illustrates this issue more specifically. In my earlier research, a youth from the neighborhood, who I knew had no affiliation in any way with the Egyptian Kings' gang murder of Michael Farmer was arrested and identified as one of the participants in the crime. During his interrogation by the police at the police station, he was accused of lying about his gang affiliation. According to his story, which I believed, the evening of the fight he had nothing else to do, heard about the impending foray by the Kings on Highbridge Park, and decided that he would "make the scene just to see what was happening." His voyeurism resulted in his arrest. He was, however, later released because there was no evidence that he had participated in the murder.

Another example of a marginal gangster in a so-called gang war incident who was identified as a core gangster is the following incident. A psychologically disturbed youth (this fifteen-year-old boy had been in the county hospital's psychiatric ward on several occasions) manifested his emotional disorder by stabbing another boy in the hood. When arrested and questioned about committing the offense, he continually maintained that he had carried out his assault against his victim (who was not a gangster) because "we had to get even with the bastards." He rationalized his individual paranoid act of assault by claiming to be a member of a gang getting even with someone from a rival gang that was "out to get him." The youth and his victim were not gangsters. However, the incident was identified as a gang-related assault.

In some cases, such formerly common psychotic syndromes as believing oneself to be Napoleon, God, or Christ, and similar powerful paranoid patterns so common over the years, have been replaced on city streets by a gangster rationale of some youths who have no gang affiliation. This rationale for their individualistic, emotionally disturbed behavior is too often mistakenly accepted at face value by gang workers, the police, and the press, thus according gangster status to a pathological individual.

Research data indicates that most youths living in a violent-gang infested hood do not becomes gangsters or participate in the gang even as marginal gangsters. Many youths from the same difficult gang neighborhood have the strong personal and familial emotional resources to resist violent-gang coercion. As one youth who lived in a violent-gang hood told me,

> Man, I don't need to always be beating up on people to prove I'm a big man. They know I can take any of them. . . . When they come on to me with their gang bullshit — I just tell them to fuck off. And I have enough good friends in the hood who will back me if I need them.

Core Gangsters

In my view, the most sociopathic youths in a hood or barrio tend to be core gangsters, the less pathological youths tend to be more marginal participants in the gang, and the emotionally healthy youths in a hood do not become gangsters. Unlike participation in more defined social groups, the amorphous quality of violent-gang organization provides the possibility for the sociopathic gangster to perceive the gang, especially its size, in his own particular way and to utilize it for adjusting a variety of his individual problems. The gang, in this context, provides a sociopathic core gangster a functional entity that can provide a cloak of immunity for his senseless, often insane behavior.

The core category includes both the Gs and OG leaders. These youths are the most dedicated and involved gangsters. They daily see each other face-to-face and live in close proximity to each other in their geographically defined neighborhood. Sometimes they live in the same housing project. They hang around the same location, play together, fight among themselves, worry together, and plan gang-war strategy.

The solidarity of the core gangsters is much greater than that of the outer ring of more marginal gang participants. Gang involvement and their gang constitutes their primary world. Any ego strength, position in the world, and any status or pleasure that they enjoy are tied to gang activity. Their turf and activities, particularly the gang's violence, give meaning to their existence. The core gangster is easy to identify by his intense degree of around-the-clock involvement, participation, and his paranoid gangster code of ethics.

Some paranoid core gangsters have delusions of being persecuted by enemy gangs. Rather than accepting responsibility for their own feelings of extreme hostility, they tend to project the blame for their violent tendencies onto real and imagined gang enemies. The core gangster assumes a role that is supported, if not aggrandized, in his hood, and his violent behavior is highly approved of by his gangster cohorts, rather than stigmatized with a pathological label. Status in a violent gang is a more highly desirable pathological syndrome than many other social roles that are viewed with greater opprobrium. The person who is in a position to accept the core gangster "face" for his pathology is not generally considered crazy, even when his behavior is clearly bizarre and pathological.

The incoherent, changeable nature of the multipurpose violent gang enables the core gangster to define an individualized emotional interpretation for his activity and participation in the gang. For example, some gangsters perceive the gang as organized for protection and that the main role of a G is to gangbang — how, when, with whom, and for what reason he is to fight are seldom clear, and answers often vary from one participant to another. There appears to be no clear consensus of role expectation in the violent gang, and this conveniently enables each gangster to project his own definition onto the meaning of "membership."

Despite the different degrees of participation (core and marginal) and the individualized interpretations of gangsters, a unifying bond among gangsters is their shared belief that through the gang they acquire prestige and status. It is also quite clear that the vagueness that surrounds the delineation of gang membership and organization enables the core gangster to satisfy many varied emotional needs. Many core gangsters act out violence as part of their emotional disturbance; however, others use violence to enjoy a feeling of belonging to a "family" albeit a pathological family. The violent gang provides a sense of power and status for an individual with an underlying sense of low self-esteem and no status in the larger society.

Gang violence, including murder, plays an important role in the gang's activities and has a special social psychological meaning to the core gangster. Core gangsters who participated in a gang murder gave different reasons for their participation in homicide. Following are some of the varied rationales given by different gangsters for their participation in the homicide:

> I didn't want to be like . . . you know, different from the other guys. Like, they shot him, I shot him. I didn't want to show myself as a punk or a pussy. I had to do this to belong to the gang.

> Momentarily I started to thinking about it inside; then I have my mind made up, I'm not going to be in no gang. Then I go on inside. Something comes up, here come all my friends coming to me. Like I said before, I'm intelligent and so forth. They be coming to me — they talk to me about what they gonna do. Like, "Man, we'll go out here and kill this dude." They kept on talking like that and I said, "Man, I just gotta go with you." Myself, I don't want to go, but when they start tallkin' about what they gonna do, I say, "No, he isn't gonna take over my rep. I ain't gonna let him be known more than me." And I go ahead just for selfishness.

> It makes you feel like a big shot. You know, some guys think they're big shots and all that. They think, you know, they got the power to do everything they feel like doing. They say, "I'm gonna shoot a guy," and then another guy says, "You wouldn't do that." Then, when we go on a drive-by, he finds out what I can do. After I killed this dude, people respected me for what I've done. When I walk down the street my homeboys say, "There goes a cold killer."

In summary, the violent gang provides youths with low self-esteem and a sense of hopelessness about achieving any meaningful role in the larger society with a degree of status in their community. Because they feel rejected and alienated from the larger society, in their natural search for a feeling of belonging, these youths have carved out the entity of the gang as their community. In the gang, they can achieve various statuses open to them. On the gang status-ladder, at first they are wannabees. If they participate effectively, through delinquent and violent activity, they can achieve the status of Gs. And over a period of time, if they participate in the gang with notable delinquent and violent acts, they can achieve the venerable and respected role of OG or veterano in the only community in the larger society where they feel accepted, their gang.

4.

Black and Chicano Gangs:
In and Out of Prison

○ ○ ○ ○ ○ ○ ○ ○ ○ ○

T HERE ARE VARIOUS TYPES and forms of gangs in the United States. Throughout the country, there are white gangs in urban and suburban areas, motorcycle gangs, white skinhead racist gangs, Ku Klux Klan gangs, various Asian gangs, Jamaican gangs, South American gangs, a small number of independent female gangs that are unconnected to male gangs, and other groups that could be characterized as gangs. Many of these aforementioned gang-type collectivities are responsible for acts of atrocious racism, violence, and crime. These other gangs, however, are not nearly as prevalent (and in my view, they are another order of data, with different characteristics) as black and Chicano male gangs. My estimate is that 90 percent of the gang problem in urban areas throughout the United States is represented by violent black and Chicano male gangs. Given all of these factors, I have focused my research and analysis in this book on these two types of gangs.

Black gangs are established and function in some form in the hoods of almost all American cities across the United States. For the obvious reasons of migration and immigration and the proximity of many Southwest cities to the Mexican border, a larger number of Chicano or Hispanic gangs are found in the Southwest.

Some Characteristics of Chicano
and Black Gangs

Chicano gangs are somewhat different than black gangs and yet both types have many similarities. Chicano gangs tend to go back several generations in the more stable barrios like Los Angeles, El Paso, or San Antonio in the Southwest. Growing up in a barrio, therefore, tends to present a youngster with gang role models and a history of gangs. In contrast, black gangs tend to be more transient.

My research reveals that another notable difference between these two types of gangs is related to their family backgrounds. Most Chicano gangsters tend to be socialized in more cohesive, albeit dysfunctional, families. Black gangsters are more likely to be raised in dysfunctional families with divorced or absentee fathers. Many black gangsters, because their parents are separated or divorced, live with their grandparents or are out on their own at an early age.

In terms of the commerce and use of drugs, Chicano gangs over the years have become heavily involved with marijuana and heroin, although more recently crack-cocaine has come onto their scene. Black gangsters in the past were very involved with heroine, most recently they are persistent users of marijuana and alcohol and are greatly involved in dealing and using crack-cocaine. Black and Chicano gangs are very similar with regard to their participation in the basic violent gang activities of violent drive-bys, gang-banging, delinquency, drugs, and crime.

Chicano Gangs

Diego Vigil, in his excellent book *Barrio Gangs*, describes Chicano gangs that are present not only in California, but in cities throughout the South-west. He notes that Chicano gangs are made up largely of young males from thirteen to twenty-five years of age. According to Vigil the Chicano gang is a response to the pressure of street life and serves to give some barrio youths a feeling of "familial support, goals and directives, and sanctions and guides."[1]

Vigil states that most Chicano gang youths activities are similar to that found in any neighborhood where adolescents congregate. "They talk, joke, plan social events, and exchange stories of adventure and love. Their alcohol consumption and drug use shows some parallels with that of other American adolescents. Yet it is their other, violent, socially disruptive activities that distinguish gang members from most adolescents. Reflecting the tendency among adolescents to develop new modes of dress and speech, Chicano gang members have adopted a distinctive street style of dress, speech, gestures, tattoos, and graffiti."[2]

The gang's style is called "cholo," a centuries-old term referring to Latin American Indians who are partially acculturated to Hispanic-based cultures. The term when applied to Chicano gangsters reflects the cultural transition of Mexican Americans in the southwestern United States, and it is a process strongly affected by underclass forces and street requisites. Many of the cholo customs are related to an identification with the gang, although many nongang members in a barrio copy the style. Vigil confirms my finding about gangs in his observation that there is a wide difference among members in degree of commitment to the gang and that youths with the most problematic lives tend to become the most core participants in the Chicano gang.

Joan Moore, like Vigil, produced some significant contributions to the understanding of Chicano gangs in her book *Homeboys.*[3] She perceives Chicano gangs as fiercely territorial. The gang's major concerns are protecting their territory by fighting for it when they deem it necessary and using drugs, especially heroin.

According to Moore, all Chicano gangs are fighting gangs, and most if not all use drugs; in fact, the gang is the principal context for both the use and marketing of heroine. She notes that the Chicano youth gang is a specialized structure of the barrio and has its own set of values, norms, traditions, and concepts of status and honor. The gang "klika" ("clique" or "set") usually involves a lifelong membership and a basic reference group for some, but not all members of the gang. A meaningful source of cohesiveness is related to fighting for their barrio. During adulthood, the Chicano gangster's primary loyalty may be reinforced by confrontations with racism and his experiences in various custodial institutions.

CULTURE CONFLICT AND CHICANO GANGS

In general, as a partial consequence of being in a minority position in a new community, immigrant parents often have difficulty providing effective socialization for their children. In this context, many sociologists have pointed out how this problem of culture conflict, the conflict of transferring norms from one society to another, can lead to delinquent behavior and the formation of gangs by the children of immigrants.

The factor of culture conflict is significant in the formation of Chicano gangs. Many children of Mexican immigrant families are affected by language differences between home and school. The lower socioeconomic status of their parents and their families' poorer living conditions also affect youths. They turn to the gang for a status and recognition not accorded them through their families in the larger society.

The immigrant parents of potential Chicano gangsters are consumed with making it economically and socially in the new land and the family structure is often severely affect in the process. This was true of the early Jewish, Irish, and Italian gangs on the Lower East Side of New York and of black gangs in New York, Detroit, and Chicago when their families were newly arrived from the South. In recent years, many Asian youths have also created gangs in an effort to cope with the cultural conflict they and their families confront in the new society.

The context of such social factors as culture and language conflict, lower socioeconomic status and poorer living conditions as compared to families in the larger society, and to some degree discrimination and prejudice has spurred the formation of Hispanic gangs on both coasts. In the Southwest, there are, as indicated, many barrio gangs; and on the East Coast, especially in New York, the factor of culture-conflict has created many Puerto Rican gangs.

JOSE: THE HISTORY OF A HISPANIC GANGSTER

The following portrait of a Puerto Rican youth, based on a number of indepth interviews I had with him, depicts the culture-conflict and socialization process that produced his sociopathic behavior in a New York gang. Jose (not his real name) became a core member of a gang and was directly involved in a gang murder. Jose's Puerto Rico to New York's experience parallels many Mexican youth's experiences related to their families emigration from Mexico to the southwest area of the United States.

Jose's first reaction to New York City when he arrived with his family at the age of eight was to the climate and dirt. "It was always summer in Puerto Rico," was one comment he made to me on the difference between Puerto Rico and New York City. Although he had lived in a rundown slum called La Perla in San Juan, it was heaven compared to the slum he now lived in on Manhattan's Upper West Side. Jose could step out of his shack on the island into sunlight and find the countryside not far from his home, and he could daily meet and greet many friends and neighbors. In New York City, when he left his overcrowded roach- and rat-infested tenement, where two to three families sometimes lived in one apartment, he entered a hostile world of indifferent strangers.

On the island Jose and his family had a positive identity. Although they were poor, the Perez family had honor and dignity typical of their Spanish background. The Perez name meant something, and Jose sought to live up to it. His family and friends identified him as an individual, and he had a position in his community, even though he was a child. Everyone in the huddle of shacks where he lived knew everyone else and had some feelings of concern and caring about one another.

When he first arrived in New York, Jose sometimes dreamed with fondness about distant pleasant evenings of the past in Puerto Rico with his family. They would go to a park near their home in the evenings. The children would play, and the adults would sit around and discuss the day's events. Children and adults at these times even talked to each other. In Puerto Rico Jose had the opportunity to discuss his personal troubles with his parents and the relatives who formed his extended family. It was even pleasant to be criticized since it gave Jose a secure feeling to know someone was concerned. In his former community, not only his own parents, but also relatives and other adults took an interest in children. One man took the boys swimming; a group of older men from a social club formed a baseball league for the younger boys. Jose belonged to a community.

All of this changed in New York. His father, an unskilled worker, found it difficult to get a job that paid a living wage. He worked at menial jobs, earned a minimum salary, and was periodically unemployed. During these periods of unemployment, quarrels and conflict developed between his parents. Overwhelmed with their own problems, the parents sometimes unfairly attacked their children, who were increasingly a burden rather than a joy.

There was no one for Jose to talk to about his feelings. His father began to drink excessively to escape from the immediate realities he could not face. The more he drank, the more violent he became. In his rages, he beat Jose's mother and often attacked Jose for no apparent reason. As senseless violence surrounded him, Jose became indifferent to his family. About his father he said:

> I'll ask him to take me boat riding, or to a ball game. He'll say, "No." He don't go no place. The only place he goes is to the bar. And from the bar, he goes home. Sleep, that's about all he do. I don't talk to my parents a lot of times, there's nothing to talk about. They can't help me.

Family trouble was compounded by the need for Jose's mother to take a menial job to help support the family. This removed her further from the home. Rents were exorbitant. The family was discriminated against, hence barred from moving into certain neighborhoods. Their erratic income was insufficient for a steady monthly rental in a more stable apartment. The family of six continued to live in the two-room, hotel apartment they had originally moved into on a temporary basis. They shared kitchen facilities and an outside toilet with other families and paid a weekly rental because they could not afford a regular monthly apartment rental. Close quarters intensified the family conflict. Jose increasingly resolved his problems outside the home.

In New York he was at first shocked, and later defiant, when he found out he was "different." The first time he was called a "dirty Spick" at school, he became severely upset. This reaction slowly changed under a steady barrage of prejudice to some acceptance of his inferiority, mingled with a constant rage. His responses became increasingly violent; he retaliated and began to attack other children without provocation in anticipation of insults. Because of these factors, he hated school and became a habitual truant.

His newly discovered difference as a now self-defined "Spick" was accentuated by his difficulty in learning and speaking English. His teachers tried, but overwhelmed by a large number of students with various problems, they were of limited help. Their students' personal problems, combined with language difficulties, made teaching most subject matter almost impossible.

The one available school "professional," a guidance counselor for several hundred students, tried to talk to Jose; but by that time Jose was considered a serious behavior problem. His hatred for school became more intense each time he played hookey. He found some solace in marijuana and alcohol, which tended to numb the pain of feeling like a nobody.

He became involved in various acts of theft like purse snatching, which often involved a greater emphasis on violence than on financial gain. His various delinquent acts helped build the necessary requisites for being sent away, first, to a detention facility and, finally, to the state reformatory. Here he joined a gang that gave him protection, a "family," and a certain amount of power, status, and self-respect.

In the reformatory Jose learned explicitly and implicitly from his homies that the two most successful modes of behavior were manipulation and violence. When one did not work, the other one would. Jose found violence and its threat most effective since, as his rep for senseless violence grew, others would respond and comply to his wishes. Jose "naturally" learned to manipulate others and to use violence "properly." Because of his behavior, he was routinely in and out of custody. He didn't mind being locked up because many homies from his street gang were in the institution.

In all his gang involvement, in and out of custody, he never learned to feel affection, to see any signs of it in others, or to trust anyone, not even his family. No one ever taught or modeled these quintessential human feelings. The surrounding hostile and antisocial world that he experienced helped to develop an acompassionate sociopathic personality that became more rigid with each day.

Jose's biological family was of little help to him. Their rules, language, and appearance were old-fashioned; they embarrassed him. Also, his parents and older brothers were busy battling their own enemies. Jose's family was no longer a viable entity for him, and in his search for some semblance of community, the violent gang grew to function as his family.

Jose's role model became an older veterano violent-gang leader called Loco. Although many neighborhood youths thought Loco, as his nickname implied, was crazy. His reputation for sudden violence, using a knife or the gun he always carried, made him greatly feared and respected.

The gang became for Jose a haven and provided a "legitimate" vehicle for expressing his feelings of hatred, disillusionment, and aggression. It also provided an entity most compatible with his unfeeling, manipulative, and now violent personality. Violence was expressed at the right opportunity, or opportunities were created by his participation in the gang. Also the gang helped minimize any feelings of guilt and anxiety about violence that he might have had. Acting out violence with gang compatriots became increasingly satisfying since it increased his prestige in the pseudoworld of his gang. Gang violence gave Jose a feeling of power. He put in his violent work and was rewarded by the respect and reputation that was accorded him as a core gangster as he moved up the status-ladder of his violent gang.

BLACK GANGS

Black gangs represent a large proportion of the violent gangs in large and small cities throughout America. They generally emanate from and are populated by alienated and hostile youths who in many ways experience varied forms of prejudice and discrimination. Because of these factors, they feel a sense of despair and hopelessness about their opportunities for success through the normal pathways to success goals in the larger society. The gang provides them with a pseudocommunity and a sense of power that they do not experience in the institutions of the larger society.

It should be emphasized that the majority of young men who are raised in the black ghettos of America rise above the deleterious social forces that exist in their hood and become hardworking, successful citizens. However, given the complex and horrendous poverty of many black ghettos, those young men who experience the most negative social pressures of their depressed socioeconomic situation create the violent gang as a viable option for success and achievement. In the gang they can achieve a sense of personal power, and it serves as a vehicle through which they can act out their rage about the hopeless situation they experience in their hood. In brief, for these alienated and rebellious youths, the violent gang and its activities becomes a vehicle for expressing their personal feelings of hopelessness and rage; at the same time, their gang provides them with a kind of family and community.

A causal component that fosters violent gangs, which regrettably persists in the black experience in American society, is the breakdown of the family. A disproportionate number of black youths grow up without fathers. And too many black gang youths father children without any responsibility for their proper socialization or welfare. (One of the key factors highlighted in the much heralded 1995 "Million Man March" on Washington was the necessity for black fathers to effectively assume responsibility for their families.)

Another significant part of the black gangster's rage is the very real prejudice and discrimination they experience in American society. Young black men find when they are out of their hood in paranoid white communities that people tend to fear their potential behavior. In general, they find in the work world that they are most likely to be the last hired and the first fired. The police, who represent the larger society's law enforcement in the hood, too often target young black men unfairly in their policing activities. An astounding statistic cited by the National Institute of Justice is that around 30 percent of all young black men are enmeshed in the courts, jails, prisons, and probation or parole of the criminal justice system.

In summary, the general negative elements of hopelessness for achievement and racism persists in American society as we approach the twenty-first century. These negative social and economic forces have their deleterious impact on young black males, and this, in part, accounts for their creation of and participation in violent gangs.

ED'S STORY: THE CASE HISTORY OF AN OG CRIP

The fiery violent crucible of the 1965 Watts riots in Los Angeles and the despair in the hood that followed in part influenced the formation of two now notorious black gangs, the Crips and the Bloods. These notorious names and their gang forms have spread to hoods all over America. The Crips and Bloods brand of gang is as well-known around the country to both gangsters and law enforcement as Coca Cola.

Ed (not his real name) was a typical Crip who rose in the ranks from a Wannabee to an OG. He grew up in the Watts and South Central areas of Los Angeles and from the age of nine ran with a number of gangs in his hood. He was on the scene when the first Crip gang was originated in 1968. Among the many notorious Crips that he knew over the years was Monster Kody, with whom he spent four years in Cellblock C in California's Soledad Prison. Ed did it all. At one time or another he participated in gangbanging, drive-bys, the Crip's drug business, and organized and directed an armed robbery crew that specialized in holding up jewelry stores. Along the way he admittedly participated in several gang murders.

Ed rose in the ranks of the L.A. Crips as a youth to become a respected OG in his gang. His insider's story of his thirty-year run with the Crips, in and out of prison, insightfully reveals an American black gang's structure, function, and activities in dramatic detail.

The first time I met Ed was in 1995. I had traveled to the Texas Department of Correction's Beaumont Prison to carry out a series of group and individual research interviews with young gangsters incarcerated in this medium-security jail. Ed, at that time, had become a responsible citizen. He had been drug and crime free for over five years as a consequence of his treatment and participation in Arizona's Amity Therapeutic Community Program and was working as a paraprofessional staff employee for Amity in the Beaumont Prison. Given the fact that he was now a law-abiding citizen who trusted me because we were colleagues in our work with incarcerated gang youths for Amity, he felt free to fully reveal his criminal past with considerable candor.

On one of my visits to the Beaumont Prison to direct a gang focus group, Ed was standing at the front gate of the prison ready to usher me into the special cellblock within the walls that was known as Amistad de Tejas. This was an Amity Therapeutic Community (TC) project in the cellblock for about 400 prisoners, most of whom were black and Chicano gangsters. The project was administered by a staff of around forty ex-criminals/addicts, including Ed, who had been rehabilitated in the Amity TC facility located at that time in Tucson, Arizona.

Accompanying Ed at the front gate was thirty-seven-year-old Sheila, the director of the TC prison project, herself a former addict/criminal who at the time was clean for over ten years and a valued employee of the Amity TC. As Ed and Sheila greeted me and were ushering me into the bowels of the prison to the Amity project cellblock, they received a continuing flow of friendly greetings from inmates who were behind barb-wired fences in various prison big yards, apparently on their recreation hour. I basked in the reflected glow of the inmates' acceptance and apparent affection for Ed, Sheila, and the enthusiastically accepted, lifesaving Amity program. (The therapeutic community approach will be discussed more fully in chapter 7.)

Over a two-day period, through the good auspices of Ed, Sheila, and the Amity staff, I was able to garner some significant research data for this book through interviews with individual gangsters and several special and extraordinary gang-focused groups. Because my respondents truly liked and trusted Ed and the Amity program, they were exceptionally open and forthcoming to me about their life as gangsters in and out of prison.

During my several gang-focused research groups, Ed was always at my side, and I was able to get some material about his life as a Crip. As indicated, he had "been down" with the South Central L.A. Crips gang since their inception in 1968, an active OG participant in the gang through various phases of its development and growth. From the age of twelve, he had been in and out of California prisons for a span of almost twenty-five years. He had now been gang, crime, and drug free for five years. This gave him a unique perspective on his former life as a Crip gangster. My bonding as a friend and colleague with Ed involved a significant element of trust, and my several intensive interviews with him provided me with an unusually honest, revealing, and valuable case history of a Crip gangster.

ED: I was born in L.A. in 1956 and grew up in Watts. I had six brothers and two sisters. My father left us when I was four. My mother had to raise all of us, and of course, she had a helluva time trying to keep the family going. I've since learned that we had what you all would call a dysfunctional family. Also Watts was what you might call a dysfunctional neighborhood — the message in Watts was that everything that was right was wrong and everything that was wrong was right. I was fucked up from the beginning.

We moved from Watts to another South Central L.A. neighborhood, but I brought my stealing and going to juvenile hall along with me to the new hood. All of my six brothers with the exception of my oldest brother, who was raised in the South, went to prison for various offenses. Three of them, including me, did some long hard time in the state prisons. I eventually went to Soledad a few times, and one of my brothers was in Folsom.

When I was around ten or eleven, I began to hang out with a small gang of kids called the Pigmies. They came from a family of around twenty kids, and we all used to go into stores and steal shit. At thirteen, after several trips to juvenile court and detention in the county's juvenile jail, I was sent to a juvenile camp for various thefts, burglaries, and stealing cars right off of people. The new word for that is carjacking, back then it was just car theft.

One of my older brothers was in a gang called the Ex-Cons. In South Central L.A. you were automatically in a gang if you lived in the hood. When I was around twelve I joined by just going along with the homies. There was no big initiation like they talk about these days. I think most of those jumping-in stories are bullshit. Alls you have to do to be down is start running with the homies and do what they do. Back then you just had to show you had heart — and you began to do what the older dudes did. This involved stealing, burglaries, violence, and of course, helping out in gangbanging when your turf was invaded or disrespected.

Around that time in 1967, when I was gangbanging and all that, we didn't pay any attention to black politics. I now know a lot more about political leaders like Ron Karenga, and of course, Martin Luther King. The only group we paid any attention to and respected were the Black Panther's chapter in South Central. But we were still doing our gang thing, and they didn't affect our crime and gangbanging.

Around that time our gang was called the Avenues. Most of us did weightlift-ing, and we had like twenty-inch arms. In those days if you had the muscles, you had the power. We weren't into any heavy violence with guns. It was mainly stealing, especially from people in other areas. Like we would fight a guy and take his nice leather coat. We would go to parties, drink, smoke weed, and shit like that. Then we would get into fistfights, sometimes knives, and just bust some heads.

At that time, the Avenues was a close-knit neighborhood gang around Hoover Avenue in around a one square mile area. We had about forty guys, and we all knew each other. I had around ten to twelve arrests and did a few tours at the probation camps for burglaries and robberies.

Along the way I became a Crip. The Crips began around 1968. The name came about in a funny way. At that time we were doing a lot of robberies. We were mugging a lot of people on the streets when the situation was right. A rich target for a mugging were some of these Japanese ladies who lived in the hood. We found out that the cops in the area from the 77th Division of the LAPD had these block meetings with the citizens, including the Japanese ladies. At these meetings citizens were told if someone was robbing you, the thing to do was to scream, make a lot of noise, and wave your arms so the police will come.

After one of these police block meetings, a group of old Japanese ladies were walking on Central Avenue. A group of dudes, including Raymond Washington, a well-known OG who was the leader of his gang, started to rob them and take their purses. The old ladies started yelling and making noise, the gang ran, and the police came. The women were all excited when they were talking to the police. And one Japanese lady, who could hardly speak English, kept repeatedly yelling "a crip, he was a crip." The police finally figured out that one of the attackers had a cast on his leg — and the woman was trying to say she had been attacked by a "cripple." So that's how the name Crip came about.

After that our dudes accepted the name Crips for our gang. Another group from Pirue Street who were our enemies began to stand up to us. They called themselves the Pirus and later on they changed their name to the Bloods. Other gangs sprung up around the area using the name Crips — like the West Side Crips.

We were the original gangsters from the streets and that was where the label OG Crips came about. Our original group of guys became known as OGs. The dudes who joined in the camps or CYA (California Youth Authority) were known as "jailhouse crips" and there were some Wannabees. Yes, we did use that expression back then for kids who were claiming things they weren't and had not yet put in their work. We would use expressions back then like OG, Jailhouse, or a Wannabee Crip.

I'll give you an example of a Wannabee. If some dude wanted to be down with the gang and they weren't in, we OGs would say, "You wannabe in the gang, well you're going to have to put in some work by taking this gun and shoot someone." For example, there was this young kid around fourteen, and he wanted to be with us all the time and go to parties and things. We liked him and we let him be with us. One time we had this problem, and we went on a drive-by. I said, "You wannabe with us, take this gun, and when we spot these motherfuckers, we'll see what you do." So when it was going down, he took the gun and shot this guy standing in front of his house. I don't know whether he killed him because we didn't stop to check it out but I saw the guy go down.

Some OGs would use Wannabees to do their dirty work. For example, in a burglary it can be dangerous to enter a house. You don't always know if there is some motherfucker sitting their with a gun who might blow you away. So you might say to a Wannabee who's with you on his first job, "you go in the window first, cause you're smaller." Or you might hand the kid a gun in a store robbery.

When we would do a drive-by you never knew for sure if you killed anybody. None of us really had any training with guns. Everything would be in the spur of the moment, and you were never sure exactly who you hit. You try to do as much damage as you can. And you might look in the paper next day to see if you killed anyone, but you can't be sure. I'm sure that over the years I killed three people, one in a drive-by, and two times in robberies. Other times, I never stopped to find out if a guy I shot was just wounded or dead. The advice I was always given by my homies was, "Fuck man don't worry about it, what's done is done."

In those days we would do some crazy shit like going to a funeral home and fucking up our dead enemies' caskets and even his body. We were pretty crazy. After we killed a guy, we would sometimes do some more shooting at the funeral parlor because we knew our enemy's homeboys were going to be there. Once me and a couple of my homeboys got arrested for shooting up a funeral. This was around the third time we had done this crazy shit, and the police were waiting for us. To this day, if you see a dead homie's funeral you can bet his homies will be there with guns, and the police will be watching for an attack by his enemies.

You know [as I'm telling] these things, I can't believe I did this shit like fucking up some dude's body at a funeral home, but it's good for me to get all of this shit out of me. You have to know that back then, my Mom was working two jobs. When I went to school — which I rarely did — when I got home there was no one there. My homies were the only people around for me. I had no one else. In a way they became my family. We did a lot of wrong, but my homies were the only people who accepted me. There were few places for me to go. In those days there were some clubs where you could lift weights. And if you weren't in the gang, you couldn't get in to the club. Being part of the gang made me somebody.

At that time I did a lot of things that, in my mind, I really didn't want to do. But belonging to the gang was my life. For example, me and two dudes from my set, Kenney and Eddie, would stand on the corner by our school and just rob kids coming or going to school. We would take their lunch money and go buy some beer or weed. I liked some of these kids we stole from, but if they didn't do what they were suppose to and give us their money fast, we would beat the shit out of them. I didn't like it, but I knew what side I wanted to be on. I would rather be on the side of giving the beating than on the side of the guy that was getting the beating. If you weren't part of the power in my hood, then you were the prey. I didn't always like what I did, but I felt I had to do it to be down with my gang. Looking back, it wasn't much of a family, but it was the only family I had — that I trusted. The only love and trust I got from anyone back then came from my homies.

If you were part of the gang, you could trust your homies. For example, no one would snitch on you. In those days your homies stood up for you. Nobody snitched, so no one could find anything out about what we did. There may have been a few snitches, but most of the time a gangster would rather go to the joint than give up a homie. Going to prison wasn't that big a price to pay for keeping quiet. Because many of your friends were in the institution. And a snitch always ran the risk of getting killed.

I was arrested around twenty-five times from around the age of twelve to seventeen. Most of the time I was cut loose from the juvenile court with a warning. A few times I would be in juvenile hall or sent to probation camp for six months. Finally when I was seventeen, I was sent away for four years to CYA for robbery, rape, kidnapping, and grand theft.

We had kidnapped this white lady — I remember her name was Jane. We took her down by Redondo Beach. We robbed her possessions, and then me and my partner raped her. She refused to get out of the car, so we knocked her out and stole the car. After we left, like a fool, I ran a red light. A police car stopped us and checked us out. I had no license, and it was a stolen car.

They wanted to try me as an adult at seventeen, but I was fortunate enough to get sent away to CYA in 1972 as a juvenile. If I was eighteen I would probably still be in prison for kidnapping and rape. Back then, you would be arrested maybe twenty to thirty times before you would get sent to CYA. Many of the dudes in CYA were in for robbery, murder, and really heavy crimes.

The Crips had been going on in the hood for around five to six years by the time I went away to CYA. By then, even though I was pretty young, I had done a lot of work and was a highly respected OG. There were around twenty Crips from my neighborhood during my four years in CYA. In CYA they reviewed me at the end of two years, but my conduct was so bad, they kept me another two years until I was twenty-one.

When I got out of CYA, I was only on the streets for around two months. Then I got busted for grand theft. This was for pickpocketing around the Forum in L.A. I was trying to steal with more finesse — but I got caught. This time I was sent to a real prison at Soledad in 1975.

In Soledad some of the older prisoners hated the Crips. Because on the streets in L.A. some of their relatives had been killed. In the prison there weren't too many of us Crips, but we had to stay strong and together for our protection. The prison gangs at that time included the Mexican's La Familia and the beginning of the Mexican Mafia, the Black Guerrilla Family, the Aryan Brotherhood, and there were white biker-type gangs. The main problem in prison was always racial, although there was some black-on-black, and Mexican-against-Mexican violence.

Back then these groups ran the prison. As Crips we had to watch our back all of the time because we didn't have too many homies there at that time. But then later on — when Crips and Bloods started going to prison in bigger numbers — we began to get a lot of power. Even in prison the Crips and Bloods hated each other, but because we were getting a lot of violence from the Mexicans and whites, we would join forces at times.

When I got my release date and was thirty days away from getting out of Soledad, some real shit went down. This black dude, one of our Crips, had snitched, and there was a big shakedown in some cells and they found different weapons. He was one of ours, and we had to take care of him. We had this meeting and I got the contract. Now I didn't want to do it because I was set to go home in thirty days. A good friend of mine took it over from me, and he killed this snitch with a shank (a knife).

When I got out, I noticed people began to look at me differently in my hood. I was now a big homie because I had been to prison. I got more respect, and people were afraid of me. I enjoyed the way people were treating me. I had no intention of getting a job or anything like that. I was an OG in the 89th Street East Coast Crips.

Around that time I got involved in a drive-by. One of my younger homeboys had been killed, and we knew the gang that did it. Someone stole a car, and we loaded all of our weapons in the car. We rolled into their neighborhood, and we knew where they would be kickin' it. We pulled up as close to them as we could get, and then we unloaded on them. I knew I had hit and killed this one motherfucker, and when I got back to the hood I was braggin' on it. We talked about it for a week. At that time we would think it was funny if a dude who got shot screamed or cried like a bitch when he got hit.

It seems crazy to me now, but back then with all the violence there was love for your homies. Like three of my homies that got killed, younger guys, I remember them with love. I had a strong rep and I tried to help them, but they got killed gangbangin'. These kids kind of idolized me, and when I was in the penitentiary, they would go to my house and drop $200 to $300 on my Mom to send to me to buy things in prison. They were my friends, and in a kind of memorial, I have their three names tattooed on my back.

During my being locked up in prison, for a few years I decided that money was more important than gangbanging, so in the early 1980s when I was in my late twenties I became involved in armed robberies. Making money from my crimes began to make more sense to me than crazy gangbangin'. My specialty was jewelry stores because those jobs were very profitable.

LY: Why did you switch over to robberies from gangbanging?

ED: Gangbanging was OK for the kids in my set who were coming up. They were putting in work to make their reputation. And when they came to me for advice about some problem with another set, I would tell them what to do. But at that time I wanted to make some real money. The crew that did robberies would still do gangbanging, but these were the guys with plenty of weapons, out to make some money. These were the guys who had nice cars, apartments, and all that.

Right now, let's say there are around thirty Crip sets in L.A. Every set has an OG who has organized a crew that does robberies. He will, as I did, use a younger homie in a robbery who showed heart, was cool, and had no fear in his crew. An important thing I always made sure of, if I brought a kid along in my crew for a robbery, was that the kid, if caught, would not snitch. The most important thing about a younger homie that I would take in my crew would be — will he shoot to save my life! I wouldn't want anyone with me who wouldn't pull that trigger if my life was in danger. I wasn't into killing anyone in a robbery for senseless shit — but if he was going to kill me, I'll get him first, and everyone in my crew has to be there to watch my back.

LY: Why robbing stores, why didn't you get more into the drug thing?

ED: My thing was robbery. Some crews in gangs were mainly involved with drugs. I tried to get into selling drugs. But I'm no dope dealer. I tried, but I can't sell no dope. I would use it or give it away. When I tried to sell dope, if someone came to me with a bullshit story and had no money — I would just give him the shit. In order to sell dope, you got to be a coldhearted, chickenshit person.

I did have a personal bout with drugs. One time when I got out of prison and I was trying to sell rock cocaine, I experimented with the shit and got hooked on crack. That was the worst time in my life. I did a lot of stupid shit for crack. I would sometimes be beggin' my homies for crack or money to buy it. I carried a pistol and I would sometimes rob a homie for the shit. If anybody trusted me, I would burn 'em and that wasn't like me. I even was put out of the gang at that time. If anyone tells you that gangsters are using drugs, that's bullshit. They smoke weed and drink, but they don't fuck with that hard-core shit. I lost a lot of respect from my homies behind that shit.

Some dudes made a fortune selling drugs. One guy I knew was Freeway Rick. He was with the dudes from the Hoover Crips. Rick was a wild man! He would put ninety keys of dope in a car and drive somewhere like a madman. He was one of the first guys I saw who used guns with silencers. With all his money and drugs — he had to have firepower.

I don't know about Freeway in particular, but a lot of guys would kidnap a rich dealer and hold him for ransom. The last I heard was that Freeway was getting drugs from the police and then he turned informant on them. I don't know what really went down, but I believe he's doing time now.

LY: So, in a way, what you're telling me is that today's gangs have many purposes.

ED: That's right. The gangs now are like a big melting pot. In my earlier days the groups were smaller, tighter, and more like a family.

I was sent back to Soledad a few times. I was there between 1981 and 1983. I was also in Chino (prison) for what they call diagnosis for a time. When I was there I got into some trouble. Me and my homies attacked a guard, and I was sent to the hole for about four months. But I liked it there. You got away from the prison bullshit, and you could kick back, read, and think. From Chino, they sent me back to Soledad in 1984.

My last long stretch was from 1984 to 1989 in Soledad. You asked me about Monster Kody. I met him around 1986 in C Wing in Soledad. He immediately, when he got in, started organizing the Crips in the prison. You had to respect Monster. He was intelligent and sharp. We respected each other and got along, even though we were from different Crip sets. I knew he was going to move out of the black-on-black violence because he was being educated by some older dudes in the joint who were political and against that shit. Like he taught me some Swahilli. He was into his African roots, and this had calmed his violence down.

But he wasn't totally out of the Crips and he organized us. One time, he did beat up some guy who was suppose to stand "post." Standing post is like standing guard. Like when we black guys were showering, someone had to stand post to guard us from the Mexicans and whites. When you're showering you are naked, vulnerable, and have no protection. This guy fucked up, and went off his post to watch some TV program. Monster later on punished him by beating the shit out of him. Normally, he would have been killed.

I got out of Soledad in 1989, and some of my homies had made a lot of money selling dope. They staked me for awhile, then like a fool I got hooked again on crack. After a while they just cut me loose, and I had to earn some money on my own, and I began to rob jewelry stores on the West Coast.

Ed became involved in a set of criminal and judicial circumstances when he was committing jewelry store robberies around the Southwest, which landed him in jail in Tucson, Arizona, in 1990, accused of robbery and conspiracy to commit first-degree murder. For various reasons the murder charge was dropped, and a set of circumstances arose that motivated Ed to enter the Amity Therapeutic Community. Since his entrance into Amity in 1990, he has remained free from drugs and crime. (I will resume Ed's chronicles related to the therapeutic dynamics that resocialized Ed in Amity in chapter 7 on the TC approach to treating criminals/addicts and gangsters.)

GANGSTERS AND GANGS IN PRISON

In general, as Ed and others have pointed out, the structure of gangs is more cohesive in prison than on the outside. This is largely due to the close physical proximity of gangsters in prison and also to a more intense need for security and protection from other prison gangs. The factor of a more cohesive gang in prison was validated by about 80 percent of the respondents to my questionnaire on this subject. One gangster I interviewed shortly after he was released from California's Folsom Prison responded simply and succinctly to my query about the difference between gangs in and out of prison: "In prison there's no place to go or hide."

My friend and colleague sociologist John Irwin was incarcerated for five years as a prisoner in Soledad Prison for armed robbery. He later returned to Soledad as a graduate student to research his doctoral dissertation at the University of California at Berkeley. His research was the basis for an excellent book he later wrote, *Prisons in Turmoil.*[4]

In an interview with him, he described some of the fundamental problems of prison gangs that exist in Soledad and most other prisons around the country. Irwin asserts that violent racial and ethnic prison gangs in the pursuit of loot, sex, respect, or revenge will attack anyone who is not in their group. This, Irwin told me,

> has completely unraveled any remnants of the old codes of honor and tip networks that formerly helped to maintain order in prison. In a limited, closed space, such as a prison, threats of attacks like those posed by racial and ethnic groups cannot be ignored. Prisoners must be ready to protect themselves or get out of the way. Prisoners who have chosen to continue to circulate in public in prison, with few exceptions, have formed or joined a clique or gang for their own protection. Consequently, violence-oriented gangs dominate most, if not all, large men's prisons in the United States.

Irwin emphasizes that gang-type structures are developed along racial lines in prisons and that the level of violence and potential violence has escalated. He writes,

> Racial conflicts among blacks, whites, and Hispanics in American prisons have produced a situation in which groups of prisoners regularly rob and attack other prisoners and retaliate when members of their clique or gang have been threatened or attacked. This has intensified the fear and widened the gap between prisoners, particularly between prisoners of different

races. The problem of racial conflict has substantially increased the level of prison violence and made many prisons almost impossible to manage.[5]

In my direct research with prisoners in prison gangs, I encountered the secrecy and violence factor of prison gangs noted by Irwin. My research into prison gangs involved several individual and gang-focused group sessions. At one of my group research sessions at the R. J. Donavan California Corrections Prison in San Diego, I decided it would be useful to videotape one of my gang-group interactions.

There were about fifteen men in the group who had volunteered to talk to me about gang structure and behavior in and out of prison. There were two Caucasians in the group and the rest were equally divided between Chicano and black convicts who had an extensive background and experience with gangs. I assured them up front that I only wanted to discuss some of the general aspects of gangs and that I was not interested in specific names or criminal behaviors that might get someone in trouble.

Before the discussion began, two Chicanos raised their hands to tell me that they would not discuss anything until the video camera was turned off. I decided I wanted to keep it on, and five Chicanos excused themselves from the session on the basis of their fear of Mexican Mafia retaliation. I later determined that their fear had a basis in reality.

Their resistance related to the violent aftermath of one of the most authentic movies made on Mexican prison gangs. The award-winning film made by Edward James Olmos entitled *American Me* is virtually a documentary on Chicano gangs in and out of prison. Two individuals who were very familiar with Mexican gangs, and especially the Mexican Mafia, served as technical consultants on the production of the film. A brutal side effect of the production of the film was that the Mexican Mafia felt that the film was disrespectful of their gang. In retaliation, from prison they contracted two assassination-type homicides on the two technical advisers on the film.

The Chicano prisoners in my gang-focus research group were all well aware of these brutal homicides, and under the unspoken admonition that discretion is the better part of valor, these two respectfully chose not to participate in my research. A sizable number of Chicano and black gangsters in the prison did cooperate with my research and provided me with some valuable and insightful data.

In my varied forms of research into prison gangs, I have observed that Chicano gangs in recent years are more coherent and cohesive in prison than black gangs. Two major and powerful prison gangs in the Southwest are the Mexican Mafia in California and the Texas Syndicate in Texas. These gangs deal in drugs and maintain their strong position through assassinations. Both gangs, but especially the Mexican Mafia, or M, have gang sets in each prison with connections throughout the California and Texas prison systems.

Two other gangs that are always in conflict, sometimes exploding into prison wars, are the black gangs, one known as the Black Guerrilla Family, or BGF, and various white gangs, varyingly known as the Aryan Brotherhood or the White Aryan Race. Of course, Crips and Bloods also pervade the California prison system.

The East L.A. barrio is the spawning ground of the M, and reflects a typical area that creates M gangsters. Many youngsters growing up in this area have limited choices since their fathers, uncles, grandfathers, and other role models are gangsters. In recent years the problem of racial violence has been accentuated by the evolution of more clearly defined prison gangs. Almost all of these groups have some connection to the neighborhood gangs the inmates formerly belonged to in their communities of orientation.

My research with several veteranos of Mexican prison gangs indicates that the prison gangs began when Chicanos in large numbers were sent to prison in the late 1960s for drug trafficking. These new Chicano prisoners were often greeted by groups of veterano Los Angeles Mexican Mafia with disdain and ridicule. The older inmates sneered at the new young convicts and regularly preyed on them for money and sex. The victims responded in kind and formed a new Chicano prison gang known as La Familia. Pitched battles for power became common in prison between these two gangs. This conflict resulted in a number of assassinations. These La Familia killings "cooled out" the Ms, gained the Ms' respect, and later on La Familia merged with the Ms and accepted their name.

In earlier years the M gang operated openly under an informal system of peaceful coexistence with state prison officials. The leaders were sometimes permitted to roam the halls at will, to enter the normally secure solitary areas for private meetings, and even to use the prison's staff conference room. Prison officials admit to having cooperated in the early days. One veteran California Department of Corrections worker commented, "We were trying to use them as a way to control the violence inside. It didn't work."

There were many murders of rivals and gangsters who didn't follow the rigid rules of secrecy and conformity of gang leaders. A rough estimate is that around 200 assassinations were carried out in the California system between 1970 and 1996, and many more gang murders emanating from the prison conflicts were committed in the barrios of California. Mexican American youths participated in the M in their barrio and inside prison. A gangster's street reputation followed him from his neighborhood into prison and vice versa.

Chicano gang youths tend to assume a high visibility in the prison world. They wheel and deal. They dress in what is know in prison as a "bonnarue" style with sharp well-laundered prison garb. They meticulously care about appearance and use their prison connections to get better clothes. Mexican OGs or veteranos have a number of young gangsters who do their bidding and carry out their orders without question. Many Chicano gangsters in prison entertain little or no hope for life on the outside. Their youth has been spent learning to optimize the quality of the environment inside the camps, youth facilities, and prisons that are too often their homes for most of their life.

For veterano gangster prisoners with some prestige in the world of organized drug crime, prison is a time for lying low, for avoiding attention from the authorities, and for spending energy on getting out. It also importantly involves some effort at maintaining the street business of drugs outside the walls. This commerce in drugs came to a head in 1995 as the result of an FBI investigation and a large number of indictments. I had an opportunity to have a valuable research meeting with several agents involved in the FBI Gang Task Force and learned a great deal behind the scene about the FBI's findings and about gang's dynamics.

The arrests and indictments reveal that the M got a cut of the commerce of drugs in and out of the prison. They insured their vicious enterprise by ordering homicidal hits on anyone who got in their way. Through these violent assassinations, the pernicious tentacles of the M clearly extended beyond prison walls into the barrios of the larger society.

The federal indictments revealed a great deal about the M. The FBI, as previously mentioned, indicted twenty-two members and associates of the Mexican Mafia prison gang, who for several years relied on murder and intimidation in an attempt to organize drug trafficking among hundreds of Latino street gangs in Southern California. The twenty-two people, ranging from the organization's reputed godfather to street-level enforcers, were charged under RICO — the federal Racketeer Influenced Corrupt Organizations Act — with crimes including murder, extortion, and kidnapping. One of those arrested was accused of helping plot the death of the two consultants who worked on *American Me*.

The indictment marked the first time the RICO Act was used against a gang in Southern California. The eighty-one-page indictment painted a chilling picture of this Los Angeles underworld, signaling an unprecedented degree of organization and ruthlessness in the long and bloody history of Chicano gangs in and out of prison.

The indictment indicated that one of the principal goals of the Mexican Mafia was to control narcotics distribution by street gangs. Two of the kingpins indicted were at the time incarcerated at the California Pelican Bay Prison. The authorities were attempting to get a conviction under the RICO Act in part because it would allow them to have key M gangsters transferred to a federal prison. The goal was to remove them from the gang's power base in the California penal system.

The indictment revealed that the M was "the gang of gangs," with a membership of 400 in prison and control over hundreds of youths in street gangs on the outside. The gang was reputed to control narcotics distribution, gambling, and prostitution at many state prisons, and their power reached from the prison into the community.

In one instance, the indictment charged that the M kidnapped a local drug dealer who failed to pay $85,000 in "taxes" as part of their extortion arrangement with him. They eventually let him go after he agreed to pay four kilos of cocaine to settle the score. To deal drugs in a two-block area near Downtown Los Angeles, the indictment charged, drug dealers were required to pay the Mexican Mafia $15,000.

In general, the FBI alleged that the moneymaking potential and violent power of organizing the estimated 60,000 Latino gang members from about 450 gangs in Los Angeles County alone was enormous. A sign of the M's power emerged in the summer and fall of 1993, when M members held a series of meetings with gang members from Riverside to Los Angeles. Relying on fear, intimidation, and rhetoric steeped in cultural unity, the M ordered the street gangs to halt drive-by shootings and settle their differences face-to-face or else face the deadly wrath of the syndicate's ability to hit from behind bars. Their move was not altruistic, it was to control the senseless gangbanging in order to maintain their lucrative drug business. The move, which initially resulted in a drop in Latino gang killings, was welcomed by many residents of L.A.'s violent barrios. The violence, however, resumed, as evidenced by the 120 gang-related murders committed by Mexican gangs in L.A. in 1993.

A Common Bond: The Macho-Syndrome and the Machismo Characteristic of Gangsters

The most violence-provoking epithet you can hurl at a black or Chicano gangster is one that identifies him in some way as having feminine character-istics. If you have the temerity to seriously call him a "pussy," a "faggot," or a "punk," you may be committing suicide. The common meaning of all of these terms is that the G is less than a man. If you insult a G this way, be prepared to physically defend yourself because an attack is coming — either immediately or at some future point. Although there is a lot of homophobic joking around about homosexuality and "fags," a G can't allow a serious intentional attack on his masculinity to go by unpunished, especially if it takes place in front of his homies.

Being a supermacho man not only involves proving it with physical violence, it is characterized by the way a gangster walks and talks. You can often tell that someone is a macho G by his unique swaggering walk down the street or his walk and physical posture out in the prison's big yard.

Most gangsters spend a good part of their life in custodial institutions. In this context prison homosexuality has always created identity problems for gangsters. Long before today's era of racial-ethnic prison gangs, many prison-ers, particularly those with youth prison experiences, regularly or occasion-ally engaged in homosexual acts as the dominant sexual partner with prison "queens," "kids," or "punks," though not without some cost to their own masculine self-definitions and reputation. There is a cynical accusation repeated frequently in the informal banter among prisoners that those in-mates who engage in homosexual life too long finally learn to prefer it and, in fact, become gay.

On the issue of homosexuality and violence in prison, John Irwin states,

> Violence has always been a popular solution for inmates in prison con-flicts. Short of a prison riot, violence is a constant element in contempo-rary prison life. This super-macho form of violence involves an exaggerated form of masculinity. This pattern of super-macho toughness is the most important value and attitude in the violent men's prisons. It means, first, being able to take care of oneself in the prison world, where people will attack others with little or no provocation. In addition to threats of robbery, assaults, and murder, the threat of being raped and physically forced into the role of the insertee (punk or kid) has increased in the violent prison world. It was a jocular credo that after one year behind walls, it was permissible to kiss a kid or a queen. After five years, it was okay to jerk

them off to "get 'em hot." After ten years, "making tortillas" or "flip-flopping" was acceptable and after twenty years anything was fine.[6]

These expressions refer to the homosexual "turning out" of some prisoners.

In my research involving encounters with tough criminals of all ages, in and out of prison, I have always felt their extreme macho posturing had a humorous tinge to it, however, I have always been careful not to challenge it — for fear of a violent reaction. I have never had any interest in being hurt in the process of my work.

Many men, young and old, are macho and this kind of posturing is not necessarily pathological. It becomes pathological when it becomes an extreme perspective on life that pervades an individual's thoughts, physical posture, and his verbal expressions. It is a significant aspect of the gangster's view of the world and his culture.

I define the term "macho-syndrome" as a pathology that involves an attitude and posturing of being a superman for the purposes of survival in a real or imagined hostile world. Almost all gangsters have this affliction, which affects most of their social interaction and relationships. It is a tough-guy criminal mask to the world that states for self-protective reasons a posture and an attitude reflected in the one-liner I have heard many times from gangsters: "Don't fuck with me or you will regret it."

The macho-syndrome stems in part from a traditional and somewhat perverted perspective on gender roles that has changed only slightly in the past decade. American men are supposed to be supertough and invulnerable; women are supposed to be supersensitive and vulnerable.

An aspect of the macho equation for males growing up in a gang environment is the notion that "the world is a hostile place and in order to survive I have to always be on guard and present a tough masculine posture to others." In this sense the macho-syndrome is a rational response to a hostile environment. It reflects a rational motivation not to be violated or victimized. On many occasions I have heard the following in one form or another: "I can never let anyone see me as a punk. They always know what I'll do if anyone messes with me." This rationale accounts for the continuing and often bizarre acting out of senseless violence by gangsters for the maintenance of their status in the gang and the hood. In this context being a superman, feared by others, is a shield against being in the opposite role of being a feminine punk who is violated and victimized. In popular jargon, "a good offense, is the best defense."

The macho-syndrome (hereafter referred to as M-S) is partly caused by the gangster's early life experiences. My many intensive in-depth case studies of youths who become gangsters reveals that they suffer a disproportionately high number of the indignities of physical, emotional, and sexual abuse when compared to youths who are socialized in a more normal or positive family environment. They are more often than not physically abused by one or both parents and older siblings. In a defensive reaction-formation to this early treatment, they believe, and with some justification, that their continued existence requires a tough-guy macho attitude.

In one typical case of this abuse phenomenon, I ran a group therapy session in prison involving a young man I will call Roy. Roy blamed his two older brothers for his criminal behavior and incarceration. In a poignant role-playing session, I had him confront his two older brothers, played by two inmates in the group. At one dramatic and insightful point in his session, Roy said,

> You motherfuckers put me in this place. All my life you fucked with me. Kickin' my ass when I was a little kid five years old. You fuckers, joking around, forced me to smoke dope when I was eight — and that kicked off my drug habit. And the main way you fucked me up is that I don't trust anyone. I am always suspicious of people, and I really don't know how to have any friends. Even in my gang I was always a loner.

Roy in his general behavior in prison walked and talked the self-protective, distrustful M-S.

An element that contributes to M-S for some gangsters is the already discussed fact that they were sexually molested at an early age. In the intimate sanctuary of various therapy groups, personal interviews, and therapeutic-community group sessions that focused on this issue, I have heard a large number of gangsters reluctantly disclose their sexual victimization experiences. Many of these youths revealed how their fathers, mothers, and sometimes older brothers and sisters sexually abused them. In one memorable case, a young Chicano told about how his father, who was a minister, sexually abused him. He related that on numerous occasions, his father masturbated himself and the boy from the age of eight until he was ten. He went on to state in a therapeutic-community group, "Now that I am in therapy, I have talked more openly to my sisters and brothers and found that he had also sexually abused them."

Most youths who become gangsters spend some time locked up in juvenile jails of various kinds. For several years I worked in a juvenile detention facility. In this juvenile jail, despite the efforts of staff to prevent the phenomenon, a variety of acts of sexual abuse, including rape, by older inmates on younger ones was a common occurrence. A common bad joke in a lockup is the warning, "When you are showering never bend down to pick up the soap." I recall one incident where two youths in a juvenile institution were standing in a chow line. All of a sudden one of them turned around and with his metal tray began to severely beat the kid standing in back of him. He later explained his violent behavior with the paranoid comment, "I could tell that the motherfuckin faggot was eying me, and I wanted to let him and everyone else know I am not a punk faggot." His macho violence was his defensive way of asserting his masculinity.

In this same vein, I recall having an in-depth individual therapy session with a sixteen-year-old gangster who was notorious for manipulating and forcing younger kids to "give him a blow job," in some cases, he would sodomize them. In discussing his proclivities for these violent homosexual acts, he, of course, vehemently denied the possibility that he was a homosexual. In our discussions, at a certain point, with an embarrassed demeanor, he revealed the secret that he had been raped by his older brother and later on by some older inmates in an institution where he had been previously incarcerated. I asked him, "You know how horrible you felt when you were victimized, how could you do the same thing to another kid?" Through this youth's response and the response of other youths with whom I have discussed this syndrome, I have concluded that being in the role of the controlling perpetrator of the homosexual act removes the rapist as far as he possibly can get from being the punk-victim. In a convoluted and pathological way, being a super-macho gangster rapist validates the perpetrator's masculinity and places him in a less vulnerable nonvictim position.

In the gangster macho-syndrome, especially in prison, a gang rape involves multiple rapists attacking one victim. In some cases this form of gang rape is often enacted with the curious rationale of ferociously punishing a person who has snitched or violated some important gang rule or code of honor. Perversely, the sodomizing gang rape performed by multiple gangsters validates in their mind their masculinity and turns the victim who is being punished into a feminine punk. This punitive sodomizing sexual act is vividly enacted in the film *American Me*. In one dramatic scene, a Mexican prison gang punishes a gangster who has violated the gang's code of honor by five gang leaders each in turn sodomizing the helpless victim.

MACHISMO AND CHICANO GANGS

The described macho-syndrome is a significant factor in Chicano gangs under the label of "machismo." My review of various literature on the subject reveals that machismo, the Chicano form of M-S, may have its roots in the early twentieth-century history of Mexico. In the Mexican Revolution, peasants led by Pancho Villa and Emilio Zapata in the early years of the twentieth century created a bond involving a fight for honor, land, and liberty. Most peasants in these armies were poor and illiterate and untrained as soldiers. They made up for their deficiencies by what they considered to be fearless acts of super-masculinity. In this context, a basic pillar of machismo became a willingness to kill or be killed for their brothers in arms, their land, and their freedom. Honor and pride as a man, or machismo, in this context — in terms of Mexican culture — was worth the sacrifice of one's life.

There was, of course, a logical reality to the revolution led by Villa and Zapata, which is somewhat absurd in its adaptation to the Chicano gangs of today. Poor peasants in the earlier era were fighting for land and rights of freedom that were their due, and the victory sought after was a valuable achievement. This originally honorable code of machismo from that time has been perverted as it has become an important value in the Chicano gangs of the barrios of many cities throughout the Southwest.

A Chicano friend of mine nicknamed Munchie, an ex-veterano who was a drug-dealing gangster/criminal for over thirty years but has now been clean for over fifteen years, has become a legendary figure in the resocialization of Chicanos in prison. (I worked alongside Munchie in an Amity Therapeutic Community prison project in a special cellblock for 200 prisoners in the California Corrections R. J. Donavan Prison.) Munchie presented me with some interesting observations on the concept of machismo, cogently describing the absurdity of machismo in contemporary violent gangs to me as follows:

> In today's Chicano gangs our kids are killing themselves in astronomical figures for the simple reason of demonstrating their machismo. This characteristic is so imbedded in Chicano gangsters that they don't blink an eye in killing somebody or getting killed. In the process, they stupidly cause the destruction of two lives — one dead, the other doing twenty years to life in prison. This simultaneously affects two families with irreparable damage, not to mention the killing of a blood brother.

In directing Chicano prisoner groups, Munchie often presented this viewpoint on the absurdity of machismo in the gang. I have heard him in several group sessions give his reasons for Chicanos to acquire a more sensible understanding of the real meaning of machismo in Mexican culture. In one session he gave the following message to a group of Chicano gangsters, who viewed him as a positive role model and did appear to absorb his commentary:

> The guy who puts so little value of appreciation on his life and is not concerned about those who are victimized (children, spouses, relatives on both sides) is not in my estimation a man of high values or worthy of respect. It takes much more machismo to maintain a job, be responsible to our dependents, meet our debts, and be respected for living up to our commitments. This kind of machismo would also involve a man becoming a good role model as a father to his children.

Working off of Munchie's logical viewpoint, I directed a psychodrama session with Raoul, a Chicano veterano gangster in the Amity program who was concerned about his son, who was following his machismo gang lifestyle. Raoul was now around forty years old and had spent half of his life in prison for a variety of offenses. He was now in the process of attempting to turn his life around in the Amity program. He was convinced that his son was following his pathway into a life of crime and prison, and he wanted to have a psychodrama on how he might be able to handle this unfortunate situation. In the psychodrama, I had another younger inmate play the role of his son.

The moment-of-truth in the two-hour session was Raoul's diatribe to his son about machismo, drugs, and gangs. In part he told him,

> Listen man, there's no glory or honor in killing a blood brother just because we had a fight over some drugs that he was selling in my territory. I know, I've done that. And now that I've come to my senses, it's hard to live with that memory. I can still see his face when I blew him away. And over what? Some stupid white powder bullshit that we were fighting over. Because I was in the gang, I had to kill him or look like a pussy and lose the respect of my homies. Look at me now. Look at the price I'm paying with my life in this joint just to show those guys that no on can fuck with Raoul and get away with it. I see everything differently now. Don't be a machismo asshole like I was. It's not worth killing someone and losing your freedom for life.

In another situation on the theme of machismo, an ex-gangster I will call Ricardo revealed to me a murder he had committed to maintain his machismo honor. He was around twenty-eight years old, had been through a therapeutic community rehabilitation program, was functioning as a paraprofessional drug counselor, and at the time was clean around five years. When he was driving me to the airport after I had directed a group session in the prison where we both worked, I asked him to give me his viewpoint on machismo. He responded by telling me the following story:

> When I was about thirteen, I was in a gang and I was trying to get my reputation. One day, this older twenty-year-old guy, a loco vato in the gang, got me alone in back of this building. We smoked some good weed that he had, and then when we were both loaded he forced me at knifepoint to suck his dick. At that time I was a weak kid without any power. I never told anybody this story because it was too humiliating to me.
>
> I just took my time and waited for my opportunity to get my revenge. He was still around, and around five years later, we were in this group just hangin out on the corner and talking about this and that. I told him that I had some good shit, a kind of inhalant, and why don't we go and get loaded. The two of us went to a private place and got high on this shit. When I could see that he was kind of mumbling and out of it, I took this rope I had hidden in my jacket, put it around his neck and strangled the motherfucker until he was dead. For me, with my thinking at that time, there was no way I was going to let him get away with what he had done to me. I was honor bound to kill him for the way he had disrespected me when I was a kid. I never told anyone until now, how and why I killed him.

In summary, the basic concept of machismo as originally rooted in Mexican culture, involving honor, respect, and reputation as a man, is a laudable concept. The attitude is perverted in contemporary Chicano gangs into a rationale for many violent acts that have no relationship to logical and respectful behavior. The macho-syndrome is rampant in both black and Chicano gangs. In some ways it is derived from the larger society. Much of the contemporary mass media depict pathological killing as heroic, glorious, and honored behavior. Not just gangsters, but millions of average citizens, young and old, pay millions of dollars to see blockbuster movies that glorify the inhuman, sociopathic macho-syndrome behavior and homicide. A partial fallout of the atrocious macho-violence too often affirmed, honored, and patronized by the larger society is that it validates a parallel form of sociopathic violence by gangsters in the context of their gangs.

5.

Why Gangs Kill: The Sociopath Factor

○ ○ ○ ○ ○ ○ ○ ○ ○ ○

ODY SCOTT HAD AN interesting viewpoint on gang murders:

> Who fired the first shot? Who knows? But, too, who cares, when one of theirs is lying in a pool of blood with his brains blown out. This question becomes weightless in the aftermath of a shooting where someone has died. Thus the goal becomes the elimination of the shooter or as many of his comrades as possible. This inevitably leads to war — a full scale mobilization of as many troops as needed to achieve the desired effect: funerals.[1]

Monster Kody's commentary on the appropriateness of gang murder is a prima facie example of advocating what I would term senseless sociopathic violence. There is a distinction to be made between a sociopathic personality and sociopathic behavior. A characteristic of sociopathic gang behavior includes the dehumanization of other people, especially enemy gangs, and the necessity "to murder them before they murder us"; the ruthless behavior of robbery, carjacking, and burglary; the use and distribution of deadly drugs; and murder through drive-bys, which around half the time kills innocent victims. Most violent-gang behavior is sociopathic; however, many but certainly not all gangsters can be characterized as having sociopathic personalities.

A comprehensive analysis of the concept of sociopathology and the sociopathic personality, in my view, is vital to understanding gangsters and the overall gang problem. Sociopathology is a complex social psychological pathology largely because sociopaths most of the time appear to speak and behave in ways that are socially acceptable. They don't communicate like seriously pathological people do, in a jumbled word salad, and they don't usually hallucinate or hear voices. Their pathology becomes most apparent in their acompassionate treatment of other people.

In my efforts to understand the sociopath in my work in prisons and psychiatric hospitals over the past forty-five years, I have interviewed and attempted to treat several thousand sociopathic individuals. A number of these individuals have committed violent acts, including murder. Based on my extensive experience, it is useful to note that sociopathic killers, including gangsters, most of the time behave like an average person. This is often true, even when they are convicted and discussing their crime. In brief, a sociopath to the untrained eye can present the appearance of being an intelligent, charming, considerate person except when they are acting out their pathology in some kind of sociopathic behavior. The sociopath's overt appearance belies his underlying amoral character disorder.

A good example of this sociopathic pattern is the serial killer Ted Bundy, who viciously murdered over thirty women. Even the judge who sentenced Bundy to death was sufficiently charmed and conned by Bundy to comment at his sentencing, "It's too bad you went down the wrong path, partner, you would have made a good lawyer."

Jeffrey Dahmer, the flesh-devouring madman — who kept the severed heads of several of his fifteen dismembered victims in his refrigerator so, as he stated, "they wouldn't leave" — in court appeared to be a gentle person who was accepted by the people in the apartment where he lived as a "nice guy" and a quiet neighbor. The Hillside Strangler's live-in girlfriend, before he was caught, perceived Kenneth Bianchi, who with his cousin Anthony Buono tortured and killed around fifteen women, "as a wonderful husband and father to my daughter."

In one brief encounter I had with Charlie Manson at the Haight-Ashbury Free Medical Clinic in the late 1960s, before his family went on their murder spree, I found him to be a nice fellow. At the time he was very concerned with getting his girls the medical treatment they needed at the clinic for their varied social diseases. Although he was spouting deranged platitudes about the crazy state of American society, he seemed to be another benign, loving hippie of that era. Another example is Susan Smith, who murdered her two children by driving them into a river to drown, fooled the world when she acted out the role of a normal, kind, and sympathetic mother. Her crying and lying about the kidnapping of her children masked the sociopathic personality that facilitated her bizarre, violent act.

Part of society's intrigue with the trial of O. J. Simpson was based on the general belief that a man with the good-guy public personna of O. J. couldn't possibly slaughter two innocent people. This was the jury and some of the general public's reaction to the question of his guilt, despite the overwhelming scientific facts and other information that implied he was a brutal wife beater and appeared to show he was most likely a murderer.

In this context of benign overt appearance by sociopaths, most violent gangsters, young and old, usually do not appear to be violent offenders. For example, Monster Kody, who committed numerous violent acts including murder, appears in his book and on television interviews as a literate, intelligent person concerned about the negative aspects of the society that motivates gangsters to kill. Most all of the killers I have described can be defined as sociopaths. And most individuals who fit this characterization appear to be normal human beings most of the time, except when the sociopathic side of their personality is full blown.

In contrast with my view of violent gangsters as sociopaths, some gang theorists and researchers persist in perceiving contemporary gangs as "families" and normal adolescent groupings. These viewpoints present a distorted perception of gangs as normal rather than pathological collectivities. Contemporary gangsters do not fit the models of camaraderie, brotherhood, and solidarity that characterized earlier gangs. The sociopath factor explains how and why gangsters can kill without remorse or regret.

DEFINING THE SOCIOPATH

For many years the catchall label "psychopath" was applied by psychiatrists to all individuals whose behavior deviated markedly from normal, yet could not be clearly categorized as severely neurotic or psychotic. In the past decade the term "sociopath" has been used interchangeably with "psychopath" to describe individuals who, because of a severe character defect involving a lack of compassion, act out self-destructive and other harmful behavior. In the following analysis I will use the term "sociopath" rather than "psychopath" to describe this personality disorder that encompasses the psychiatric theory of the psychopath.

The sociopathic offender is characterized by what has varyingly been called a "moral imbecility" or "character disorder." This type of offender may know right from wrong, but lacks any coherent, appropriate discretionary ability in the realm of compassionate, moral behavior. A number of psychiatrists, psychologists, and sociologists have contributed to the understanding of this complex personality disorder, and it is useful at the outset, before relating the concept to violent gangs, to review some varied perspectives on the sociopath.

One of the first and most cogent viewpoints on the sociopath was presented by Hervey Cleckley in his appropriately entitled book, *The Mask of Sanity*. He defined the sociopath as: "chronically antisocial individuals who are always in trouble, profiting neither from experience nor punishment, and maintaining no real loyalties to any person, group, or code. They are frequently callous and hedonistic, showing marked emotional immaturity, with lack of responsibility, lack of judgement, and an ability to rationalize their behavior so that it appears warranted, reasonable, and justified."[2]

Paul Tappan, a sociologist, in an interview I had with him, described the sociopath as "an individual with a condition of psychological abnormality in which there is neither the overt appearance of psychosis or neurosis, but there is a chronic abnormal response to the environment." According to Harrison Gough, a psychologist, the sociopath is "the kind of person who seems insensitive to social demands, who refuses to or cannot cooperate, who is untrustworthy, impulsive, and improvident, who shows poor judgement and shallow emotionality, and who seems unable to appreciate the reactions of others to his behavior."[3]

Albert Rabin succinctly describes the basic trait of a defective social conscience in the sociopathic personality: "There are two major related aspects to this notion of defective conscience. . . . The first aspect is represented in the inability to apply the moral standards of society to his behavior; he cheats, lies, steals, does not keep promises, and so on. He has not absorbed the 'thou shalts' and the 'thou shalt nots' of his society and cultural milieu. The second aspect is that of absence of guilt."[4]

Guilt is an important part of any well-developed conscience. When a normal person violates a moral code, he feels guilty; he feels unhappy and blames himself for the transgression. Guilt is an unknown experience for the sociopath, who has no controlling superego. The sociopath has no automatic self-punishment that goes along with the commission of immoral and unethical acts. They behave irresponsibly, untruthfully, insincerely, and antisocially, without a shred of shame, remorse, or guilt. Sociopaths may sometimes express regret and remorse for the actions and crimes they have perpetrated; however, these are usually merely words, spoken for their effect or to extricate them from a punishing situation. Their regret is not sincerely felt.

In brief, the sociopath's overt personality and behavior traits would include most, if not all, of the following factors:

1. a limited social conscience;
2. egocentrism dominating most interactions, including the "instrumental manipulation" of others for self-advantage;
3. an inability to forego immediate pleasure for future goals; and
4. a habit of pathological lying to achieve personal advantage.

Most of the violent gangsters I have researched appear to manifest these personality characteristics in their behavior.

FACTORS THAT CREATE THE SOCIOPATHIC GANGSTER

It is of value to analyze the causal factors that produces the sociopathic gangster. The following analysis reveals some of the family and parental socialization factors that help to create the gangster's sociopathic personality.

FAMILY IMPACTS

An adequate social self develops from a consistent pattern of interaction with rational adult parents in a normative family socialization process. Effective adult role models, especially two parents, help a youth learn social feelings of love, compassion, and sympathy. This concept of adequate self-emergence through constructive social interaction with others, especially parents, is grounded in the theoretical and research findings of a number of social psychologists.

For example, sociologist G. H. Mead, on the issue of the proper personality development that results from effective parental socialization of a child, asserts,

> The self arises in conduct when the individual becomes a social object in experience to himself. This takes place when the individual assumes the attitude or uses the gestures which another individual (usually his parents)

would use. Through socialization, the child gradually becomes a social being. The self thus has its origin in communication and in taking the role of the other.[5]

Social psychologist Harry Stack Sullivan perceived the self as being made up of what he calls "reflected appraisals." According to Sullivan,

> The child lacks equipment and experience necessary for a careful and unclouded evaluation of himself. The only guides he has are those of the significant adults or others who take care of him and treat him with compassion. The child thus experiences and appraises himself in accordance with the reactions of parents and others close to him. By facial expressions, gestures, words, and deeds, they convey to him the attitudes they hold toward him, their regard for him or lack of it.[6]

In brief, a set of positive sympathetic responses by socializing agents, usually the child's parents, are necessary for adequate self-growth. This component is generally absent in the development of youths who become sociopathic gangsters.

The basic ingredient, missing in most sociopathic gangster's socialization, is a loving parent or adult. Based on extensive research, Joan and William McCord assert,

> Because the rejected child does not love his parents and they do not love him, no identification takes place. Nor does the rejected child feel the loss of love — a love which he never had — when he violates moral restriction. Without love from an adult socializing agent, the psychopath remains asocial.[7]

Psychologist's Edwin Megargee and Roy Golden carried out extensive research cross-comparing psychopathic delinquent youths, including gangsters, with a control group of nondelinquent youths. Based on their research they concluded that sociopathic delinquents had a significantly poorer relation with their parents than nondelinquents; and the sociopathic delinquents had significantly more negative attitudes toward their mothers and their fathers than those of nondelinquents.[8]

Dr. Marshall Cherkas, an eminent psychiatrist, in his thirty years of experience as a court psychiatrist interviewed several hundred delinquent sociopaths, including a number of gangsters. His conclusions about the origin of the sociopathic delinquent's personality summarizes the observations of other theorists on the subject. I concur with the following statement he presented to me in an interview on the causal context of the sociopath's early family life experience:

> Children are extremely dependent upon nurturing parents for life's sustenance as well as satisfaction and avoidance of pain. In the earliest phase of life, in their first year, infants maintain a highly narcissistic position in the world. Their sense of security, comfort, reality, and orientation is focused on their own primitive needs with little awareness and reality testing of the external world. As the normal infant develops, its security and comfort is reasonably assured. There occurs a natural attachment, awareness, and interest in "the Other." As the child matures, the dependency upon "the Other," its parents, diminishes, but the strength of the self is enhanced, and the child develops an awareness that its narcissistic needs are met through a cooperative, adaptive, and mutually supportive relationship to its parents and others. In other words, the child recognizes that even though its selfish (narcissistic) needs are extremely important, they can best be served by appropriately relating to other people, especially its parents.
>
> Infants whose needs are not adequately met because of the parents' own exaggerated narcissistic needs develop feelings of mistrust, insecurity, and wariness about the capacities of their provider. In order to protect itself, the child may perform many tasks to gain attention, support, and interest from the parent. The child also begins to feel that it cannot trust others, and that its needs can only be met through self-interest. The child who cannot count on its own parents begins to become egocentric and therefore sociopathic in its behavior.

Based on my experience, I have determined that the basic reason for the sociopathic gangster's lack of trust noted by Cherkes and others is primarily a result of the physical, emotional, and sexual abuse that he has received from his parents in the context of his socialization process. The emotional abuse is often in the form of the absence of any socialization of the needs of the child or of outright abandonment.

The parental factor in the socialization of a gangster has several roots and implications. Children who are physically, sexually, or emotionally abused or abandoned by their parents develop low self-esteem and are more prone to commit acts of violence. They also denigrate themselves, feel worthless, and are less likely to care about what happens to them. These negative social-psychological forces contribute to the acting out of self-destructive behavior, including drug abuse and violent gangster behavior.

THE SUBSTANCE-ABUSING PARENT

Most youths who become sociopathic gangsters have parents who are alcoholics or drug addicts. In extreme cases, at birth they are physiologically affected by being born to a mother who is an addicted crack-cocaine, heroin, or alcohol user. These children are sometimes born addicted and have severe physiological and psychological deficits.

As most research and my own observations over the years have revealed, substance abuse is an egocentric problem. The drug addict or alcoholic is consumed with the machinations of his or her habit. In a significant sense, whether or not the parents have a sociopathic personality, their behavior in the throes of their addiction is self-centered and consequently sociopathic in their relationship to their child. This form of parenting is not conducive to effectively socializing a child into a caring, compassionate, loving person. Children who are socialized in the chaotic world of a substance-abusing family tend to have a limited trust of others, become egocentric, and acompassionate. These sociopathic personality factors facilitate their participation in the violent gang. In brief, based on this varied research and its theoretical implications, it can be concluded that the proper and functional adult role models necessary for adequate socialization are usually absent from the social environment of youths who become gangsters.

Most gangsters come from dysfunctional families with brutal or absentee fathers. The negative adult role model that a youth growing up without a father may emulate is often the "ghetto hustler" — a fixture in the black hood. Malcolm X in his autobiography described this type of negative role model as follows:

> The most dangerous black man in America is the ghetto hustler. . . . The ghetto hustler is internally restrained by nothing. He has no religion, no concept of morality, no civic responsibility, no fear — nothing. This type of individual's hustle may be drugs, and he is often a father who has abandoned his son.[9]

A significant factor in this cauldron of substance-abusing, negative parental impacts is related to ineffectual discipline. Essentially there are four basic forms of discipline in the socialization process of a child: strict, sporadic, lax, and none. Research reveals that the most damaging form is sporadic discipline. In this form the child seldom knows when he or she is right or wrong. Substance-abusing parents tend to administer this type of discipline. They are out of any parental loop most of the time; however, they randomly will appear with some form of discipline that is often not connected to their child's "bad behavior." Children subjected to this type of discipline tend to develop a dim view of justice in their life and the justice that exists in the larger society. The results of this pattern of sporadic discipline feeds into the sociopathic viewpoint of distrust of others and a gangster lifestyle.

The children of substance abusers are also influenced by their parents' lifestyle to accept drug use as a way of resolving their emotional pain. Following in the path of their parents' substance abuse becomes for the gangster a way of ameliorating their painful feelings of low self-esteem and their sense of hopelessness in life.

In my work with delinquents, especially in psychiatric facilities, I have observed the impact created by drug-abusing parents on hundreds of youths who develop sociopathic personalities and become gangsters.

One typical example is a thirteen-year-old WB whose gang name was L.K., short for "Little Killer." L.K. was emotionally and physically abused from the age of four, several times a week, by his drug addict father. The physical beatings and verbal abuse administered by his father often had little relationship to L.K.'s good or bad behavior. He would be beaten or verbally abused for a variety of "offenses" chosen at random by his irrational father. His father assaulted whenever he had a need to act out his drug-induced personal frustrations with the world around him; a convenient target was his son and his wife. According to L.K.,

> He would beat the shit out of me for no reason — just because he was loaded and mad at the world. I've always felt like a punching bag, or maybe more like a piece of shit. If my own father thinks I'm a punk and a loser, maybe that's what I am.

The irrational behavior of L.K.'s father led to several consequences. The indiscriminate physical and verbal abuse had the effect of producing low self-esteem in the youth. He tended to feel humiliated and worthless. As a result of these feelings, he thought he was a loser. The only place where he found he had power, respect, and a reasonable sense of self was with his homies in the Venice gang that I have previously identified as the Insane Baby Crips. The gang gave L.K. some level of the positive approval he so desperately needed and sought.

L.K.'s typical dysfunctional family helped to create a sociopathic gangster in several ways. First, the youth had no one in his family he felt he could trust. Second, there were no significant people in L.K.'s basic socialization who were positive role models, demonstrating how a person shows love and compassion to another person. A child can't learn to be compassionate if he never sees any examples of caring in his crucial early years. Third, because he was abused by his father, L.K. developed a low self-concept. In a reaction to these feelings of inadequacy, he developed a macho-syndrome that he acted out in the gang as a "little killer." Fourth, the gang gave this emotionally needy youth some sense of self-respect and power in his chaotic world. All of these socialization factors converged to produce a violent sociopathic gangster.

SOCIOPATHIC PERSPECTIVES ON THE GANGSTER

THE APPEARANCE OF NORMALITY

Despite their horrendous and often violent behavior, sociopathic gangsters in a one-on-one conversation are often able to manifest a charming, or "good guy," personality. They can maintain this overt posture except when they believe their ego is being disrespected or attacked. I can recall many instances in my direct work with gangsters in therapy groups where we were having a logical conversation, and they suddenly burst into a fit of rage, when they felt they were "dissed," or disrespected, by other members of the group. Because of their underlying sociopathic personality, they are capable of shifting from a good guy posture to a homicidal terrorist position in a matter of seconds.

CORE AND MARGINAL SOCIOPATHIC GANGSTERS

Not all gangsters are sociopaths; however, most of the gang's behavior is sociopathic. Drive-bys, gangbanging, and random assaults on innocent victims are behaviors that demonstrate a total disregard for the life of the gangster and his victims.

The degree of the gang youth's sociopathic personality is a determinant of the level of participation and involvement of the individual in the violent gang. The less sociopathically disturbed youth is more likely to become a "marginal gangster," whereas the more sociopathic youth tends to become a core gangster. Core gangsters are heavily, almost completely, committed to sociopathic gang activity. They belong essentially because it is an easily accessible social structure in which they can function with some level of acceptance and adequacy. The malleable nature of the violent gang makes it a useful vehicle of illusionary achievement for the defectively socialized youth. Sociopathic core gangsters, with a low level of social ability, function in the social system of the gang more effectively than they can in the larger society.

Marginal gangsters are less likely to have sociopathic personalities than core gangsters. Marginals participate in gang activity largely because of an enormous psychological need to belong to some form of community, or "familia," and to have a sense of power. Most core gang members demonstrate by their commitment to violence and their acompassionate behavior that they are sociopaths.

The core sociopathic gangster is a highly impulsive and explosive youth for whom the moment is a segment of time detached from all other. His actions are unplanned and often guided by his whims of the moment. The sociopath gangster is aggressive. He has learned few socialized ways of coping with frustration. Because he feels little if any guilt, he can commit the most appalling acts and view them later without remorse. The sociopathic gangster has a warped and limited capacity to love and be compassionate. His emotional relationships, when they exist, are shallow, fleeting, and designed to satisfy his own egocentric desires.

Because of the absence of loving parental or other role models in his environment, the core sociopathic gangster has no reference groups where compassion, love, and affection are manifested. Because of this deficiency in his life experience, he tends to be self-involved, exploitative, and disposed toward violent outbursts. He is characteristically unable to experience the pain or the violence he inflicts on another since he lacks the ability to identify or empathize with others.

ATTITUDES ABOUT SEXUALITY

Gangsters tend to perceive females as objects to be used and abused in satisfying their sexual needs. This is, as has already been indicated, found in gangsta rap. In the most violent and atrocious form of sexual activity, they participate in "gangbangs," which involves multiple males raping one female. The gangster attitude toward women has an overt disdain for girls often combined with covert homosexual overtones. Each pattern almost rules out the possibility of a warm, empathic human relationship. One gangster's response to a question in my questionnaire on the role of females in the gang was succinctly stated in one word, "PUSSY."

This sociopathic mode of relating to females by violent gangsters entails disdain and exploitation. In this pattern, females are viewed as objects to be manipulated or used for ornamental rep making and ego gratification. The female becomes a target for hostility and physical brutality, which when reported back to the gang confers prestige on the violator. "Why waste your time with bitches?" "You can't trust them." "I belted her a few times because she wasn't behaving." These are common expressions that reflect the gangster's general viewpoint toward females.

Young gangsters often parallel the behavior of adult Mafia mobsters toward their women. They implicitly define two types of women. One type is called a "ho" (whore), or a bitch, and the other type is a saintly wife or girlfriend. Some gangsters do fall in love and fantasize their girlfriend as a perfect female ideal. The allusion by another gang member that his girlfriend is a ho or prone to promiscuous relations will invariably produce an explosive violent response.

Some gangsters attempt to maintain an illusion of virginity and perfection about their girlfriend that is often in conflict with the facts. Here again, he relates not in significant human interaction, but on what approaches a fantasy level of relating. For most gangsters a close, warm relationship with a female entailing mutual responsibility and empathy is rare.

Another factor worthy of note is that gangsters tend to be homophobic. Their insecurity about their own masculinity is a factor in their macho-syndrome. Some gangsters present themselves as supermen in an effort to compensate for some of their underlying feelings of insecurity in their role as a heterosexual male.

Along these lines there is evidence of homosexual experimentation among gangsters outside, but mostly inside custodial institutions. This is not usually overtly carried out by gang members among themselves; however, a common pattern for them is to become the passive recipient of homosexual relations with a seductive overt homosexual. The homophobic ritual that often recurs was expressed by one gang member as follows: "After this faggot blew us (laughs), we beat the hell out of him." He had no awareness of his own homosexual involvement in the act.

This pattern is more pronounced in prison. Here, certain individuals are turned out as punks and are used as sexual whores by many gangsters. In some cases, as previously indicated, punishment for an errant gangster against his gang involves his being sodomized. This "discipline" is carried out to humiliate the offender and demonstrate he is really a punk. Gangsters become furious when it is pointed out to them, as I have in group discussions, that when they play any role in a homosexual act, they are practicing homosexuality — and whether they are "pitchers" or "catchers" is irrelevant.

There is another element in the ineffectual way in which sociopathic gangsters relate to women that was interestingly revealed in the previously discussed film *American Me*. The main character is tough and often vicious in his role as an M gang leader. However, he is appropriately shown as relatively weak and inadequate when it came to his relationship with the woman from his barrio he "loved." His failure to perform adequately sexually or in assuming any responsibility to "his woman" is effectively dramatized. In the film it is clearly pointed out by his woman and by his behavior that years in prison and gang life do not create the appropriate male personality for relating in a positive way to a woman. This fictionalized version of a failed gangster-girlfriend relationship is reinforced by my research observations and the group therapy sessions I have directed over the years with sociopathic gangsters.

SUICIDAL TENDENCIES

A line in the rapper Ice T's song "Colors" is "My color's death." Because of their dysfunctional backgrounds, a characteristic of the sociopathic gangster is that they have a limited concern about whether they live or die. In a real sense they manifest suicidal tendencies in their everyday behavior by their involvement in dangerous and deadly situations.

On a number of occasions in the process of directing therapy groups with gangsters, I have raised the issue of gang behavior as tantamount to suicidal behavior. The usual response I would receive was an angry denial: "Hey man, you're crazy, I ain't suicidal." I would then have the group review as many incidents as they could where they had exposed themselves in fights, drive-bys, and other gang activities in enemy territory where they made themselves vulnerable to being maimed or killed. In many groups, after extensive discussion, they would acknowledge that their gang behavior might be potentially suicidal.

To reinforce their more rational conclusion, I would jokingly reinforce the gang as a vehicle of suicidal tendencies by stating that I was an abject coward and at the same time a self-loving egomaniac who would never, if humanly possible, place myself in a situation where I might be violently harmed or killed. They would get the point.

I recall a fifteen-year-old gangster with whom I worked who accounted for his being wild in the streets in this way:

> My father always beat me up since I was a little kid. When I hit fourteen, we would still wrestle and fight. Sometimes I would beat him up — but mostly he won. Our fights would totally piss me off, and when I hit the streets I was full of rage and looking for trouble. I had fights every day, and when our gang went gangbanging I was always up in the front line. I never cared what happened to me or anyone else. Everybody dies!

In another case, a psychodrama I directed in a psychiatric hospital with a gangster named Henry, he revealed some of the underlying suicidal dynamics of some sociopathic gangsters. I learned in the session that when he was sixteen he had attempted suicide by stabbing himself in the chest with a hunting knife. In exploring this self-inflicted wound with him, it became apparent that the incident revolved around the many conflicts and fights he had had with his father, whom he hated because he had sexually violated him and his sister.

During one of these many fights with his father, Henry picked up a kitchen knife. In a soliloquy I had him do à la Hamlet, he verbalized that it came down to a toss-up between killing his father or himself. Henry believed that either act, killing his father or himself, would end his emotional pain. In the end, he stabbed himself and was rushed to the psychiatric hospital, where he became a participant in my therapy group.

Another case in point relating to the suicidal tendencies of gangsters was brought to my attention by Tonya, a female gangster. She came from a dysfunctional family of gangsters and had been sexually abused by various "fathers," "uncles," and brothers for most of her childhood. She became a crack-cocaine addict who hung out with gangs for kicks and drugs. She was usually sexually available to any member of the gang who had the right amount of cocaine; she was, in the lexicon of the gang, a "coke whore."

Tonya's relationship to the gang was typical. Most gangs have female counterparts like Tonya. The females will participate in the gang in many ways including fighting, drug commerce, and often, like Tonya, they will sexually service their male homies. They are essentially used and abused by male gangsters, even though they have a fierce but misguided loyalty to "their" gang.

Tonya was an unusual case in that her mother at one point had a job that had health insurance. Most gangsters' parents do not have this benefit and do not appear in psychiatric hospitals for treatment. After an arrest for drugs, the judge gave her a choice of jail or psychological treatment. Tonya was hospitalized, and I worked with her in several sessions in an adolescent therapy group in a psychiatric hospital.

Because of her serious past of sexual and physical abuse, Tonya, of course, manifested low self-esteem. One fallout was a practice of self-mutilation. She slashed herself with razor blades and almost died on several occasions. She very obviously had a low self-concept and considerable rage emanating from her early life experiences of being victimized.

In one encounter group therapy session she was in, I delivered a diatribe at the end about the deadly, destructive effects of drug abuse and gang behavior and remarked, "Drug addiction is a form of slow suicide." As I delivered my impassioned sermon on the death-dealing results of drugs and gangs, I noticed Tonya's eyes light up and a smile came over her face. I later asked her about her curious response to my sermon, and she commented, "Your lecture on drugs and gangs really came through to me. Now I know why I do drugs. I feel like a worthless piece of shit, and if I had enough courage I would kill myself. I often feel, especially when I smoke crack, maybe I'll die painlessly and suddenly from an overdose. I want to die, and my choice is to kill myself slowly with drugs." I apparently had no positive impact on Tonya. The insight she gained from my lecture was that she was suicidal, and her choice was to carry it out with drugs.

DEFECTIVE SOCIAL ABILITY

In a discussion I had with a detached gang worker who was attempting to redirect Crip gangsters into a more responsible and rational way of life by creating jobs, I asked how effective he was. His response revealed much about the gangster's inability to accept employment as a basic social responsibility:

> Through several community leaders and corporate executives, I have been able to acquire over fifty jobs during the past year. The pattern is clear. Some of the more marginal gangsters will take a job and follow through with their new responsibility. However, the more core gangsters who I get jobs for are back on the corner a week or two later up to their old tricks. The gang gives them more prestige and a feeling of power than any job I can get them. Also most of these guys are too pathological to have the fortitude to hold down a job.

Gang violence is better than a minimum-wage job as a readily available means for sociopathic youths to achieve some form of the success-ego-gratification so desired in American society. The selection of violence by the sociopathic youth in his adjustment process is not difficult to understand. Violent behavior, especially behind the barrel of a gun, requires limited training, personal ability, intelligence, or even physical strength.

In addition to the importance of violence as a prestige symbol in the gang, the larger society covertly approves of, or is at least intrigued by, that which is depicted in literature, radio, television, the movies, and other mass media. Although on the surface most members of society condemn violence, on a covert level there is a tendency to aggrandize and give recognition to perpetrators of violence. The sociopathic personality who commits intense, sudden acts of violence is the "hero" of many plays and stories portrayed in contemporary mass media, especially in film. The socially incompetent sociopathic gangster senses this condition, and this accounts in part for his selection of the violent-gangster role, a role too often approved, romanticized, and glorified in the American mass media.

Sociopathic youths gravitate to the gangster role because the violent gang provides for them a vehicle through which they can acquire and achieve gratifications consistent with their defective social ability for achievement through the usual societal channels. The sociopathic youth, who is a failure in the larger society, selects or helps to construct in the violent-gang role patterns in which he gives the appearance of being a "successful" person.

Gang youths hear a form of false propaganda through the mass media that sells the ideology that almost all social statuses are available to all citizens of America. This is obviously not the case. It is clear that the facts of class, religion, ethnicity, race, and other background factors sharply limit certain segments of the population in achieving social goals. The possibility and means for acquiring many of these highly valued social statuses and objectives are slight for most youths, particularly for those who come from a lower-class background or a minority group. Although they are not fully blocked from the means for achievement that are available to other segments, the degree of availability and the starting point are not fully equal.

Given these varied social dislocations, the sociopathic youth, who is, after all, socially disabled, has a more difficult time achieving any status or respect in the success-oriented and competitive larger society. He can more easily become a success in the gang. Through the gang and the commerce of drugs, he has a chance to be successful in both the gang and elsewhere: because of the enormous financial rewards of drug dealing, he can acquire some of the symbols of success so highly valued in the larger society.

LIMITED EMPATHY, SOCIAL CONSCIENCE, AND EGOCENTRISM

In acting out their violent behavior, the core sociopathic gangsters give no indication of having a social conscience involving a real concern for others. A limited empathy for others is a basic factor of their personality, even though they may at times manifest a concern for others when it serves their manipulative purposes. Their incompetency in the area of demonstrating real compassion or empathy is a result of the fact that they have seldom seen or learned from any loving role models in their socialization process.

Most people do not commit violent acts on others because they would empathize with their victim and feel their pain. Core sociopathic gangsters are capable of senseless killing because they have a limited concern, or in some cases, no concern, about the feelings of their victims. As one gang boy who had shot and killed another youth described his feeling about the incident, "Man are you crazy? Of course, I felt bad. I knew I was going to get caught and locked up."

Most sociopathic gangsters have a marked inability to be empathetic, to take the role of other persons and understanding their feelings, except for the goal of manipulating others for their own egocentric ends. Their primary concern is for their own material and emotional comfort. This is a bottom line in their behavior, even though they pretend to have a real concern for their homies. As previously indicated, I have observed many instances where their concern for their brother gang members immediately disappears when their self-interest is at stake, notably in police stations or in court, where one homie will enthusiastically implicate and snitch on his "bro," his brother gangster, if he can get cut loose or work out a deal for himself with the police or the justice system.

In a clinical sense almost all sociopathic gangsters are egocentric. They have limited social feelings, identity, and compassion for others. Their sociopathic personalities reflect some if not all of the following characteristics: (1) a defective social conscience marked by limited feelings of guilt for destructive acts against others, (2) limited feelings of compassion or empathy for others, (3) the acting out of behavior dominated by egocentrism and self-seeking goals, (4) the manipulation of others in a way possible for immediate self-gratification (for example, sexual exploitational modes of behavior) without any moral concern or responsibility.

LIMITED REGRET, GUILT, OR ANXIETY

Most sociopathic gangsters have little or no regret for their destructive behavior, even though they will, when it is in their self-interest, express regret. I recall an incident that demonstrates this component of the socio-pathic gangster's personality. As part of my job in a juvenile jail that also housed the juvenile court, I accompanied a sociopathic gangster into the courtroom part of the building. He had been in the courtroom on numerous occasions for the commission of a variety of violent acts, and his latest probation and evidence reports finally and clearly recommended that he should be sent to the state reformatory. The judge asked him if he had anything to say before he pronounced the expected sentence.

The youth went into an unbelievable dramatic explanation of regret for his past behavior and how he would "never do it again." As the saying goes, there wasn't a dry eye in the house, and even a veteran police officer who was present shifted over to accept the youth's posture of sincere regret in his impassioned appeal for leniency. The judge cut him loose. As we walked out of the court back to the detention facility to get his clothes and process his release, I noted a marked change in his demeanor. With a big smile on his face, he looked up at me and said, "Hey man, I did pretty good, didn't I?" It was clear that everything he had said in court was from his viewpoint an insincere but convincing act devoted to getting released.

Sociopathic gangsters appear to have limited guilt or anxiety about their negative behavior toward others. Anxiety often results from the phenomenon of internally reviewing the right or wrongful nature of behavior. Since the sociopath has a limited regard for the right or wrong of a self-serving act, for him it is an irrelevant emotion.

RATIONALIZING VIOLENT BEHAVIOR, SELF-DECEPTION, AND PATHOLOGICAL LYING

Sociopathic gangsters have a remarkable propensity for rationalizing and excusing their horrendous behavior. They are capable of the most outrageous rationalizations. A notable rationalization that I heard from a gangster in prison with a life sentence for killing his cousin, for whom he claimed to care, was, "I had to kill the motherfucker. We were at war, and he had moved to another turf and joined our enemy set."

In this same context, Kody Scott in his autobiography dispassionately describes a series of violent atrocities that he is "obligated to commit" as a gang member because his enemies happen to live six blocks outside of his Crip gang's territory. The need to commit violent atrocities by gangsters in "war" is not related to any rational considerations. The war is created in their paranoid minds, in order for them to act out their sociopathology. Most gangster behavior is a thinly veiled rationalization for enacting their unfeeling, distrustful sociopathic tendencies.

The perceived motivation of gang members to "fight for their turf" and commit Rambo-like acts of violence in a coherent defense of their comrades in arms masks the real reasons for their behavior. Their underlying sociopathic personality dictates their atrocious behavior, and their overtly stated gang motivations are rationalizations for their senseless violence.

An interesting characteristic of sociopathic gangsters is that they do not see themselves as others do. They tend to see their behavior rationale, even when it is senseless pathological behavior. A notable example is manifest in Scott's autobiography. For the first third of his book, he describes in lurid detail his clearly pathological violent and sometimes murderous behavior. In one typical episode, among many other ruthless acts of senseless violence, he describes how he leaned into the window of an enemy's car, put a gun to his enemy's head, and pulled the trigger. Later, he muses that he probably killed this person, and it didn't matter to him whether his victim lived or died. He goes on like this ad nauseam, describing a series of violent and senseless atrocities that he had committed.

Later in the book he comments about being pursued and arrested by the police for his many crimes. In the process of reviewing his arrest, he converts himself from being a perpetrator of violence into being the victim of a pathological snitch and the police. According to Monster, "The enemy gang member who snitched me off to the police was a mentally ill cat named Teddy." From a rational viewpoint, all of Monster's violence was senseless and pathological. Yet he saw no madness in his own behavior. Teddy, the snitch, was "mentally ill"; Monster Kody, however, was a courageous warrior!

Rationalizations and self-deception are part of the sociopathic syndrome that enable the gangster to escape the consequences of their vicious behavior. In this context, sociopathic gangsters are usually pathological liars and will lie with a blazing recklessness that contradicts the obvious reality they are discussing. Most sociopaths are unconcerned with the truth and are capable of blocking out and denying reality. Others are aware that they are lying; however, the truth for them is irrelevant. The irrelevancy of the truth is especially manifest in getting out of the tight legal situations that are characteristic of the gangster's lifestyle.

When a gangster is under the gun, he will say anything that might work to save himself from being imprisoned or in some cases killed. I have noted that imprisoned sociopathic felons after a period of extensive lying about their criminal behavior begin to repress the memory of their horrendous crimes and truly begin to believe that they are innocent. (In my opinion, the celebrity who was acquitted of the crime of the century, involving the butchering of two people, is a good example of this self-vindicating phenomenon.)

LOW SELF-ESTEEM

The sociopathic gangsters, despite their self-presentation as tough macho-men are, often driven by their deeper feelings of low self-esteem. This feeling of being a nobody is partially derived from the abuse and abandonment of their family. Because of this and other factors in their early life, they are constantly in a quest of proving their masculinity to compensate for their underlying low self-concept.

The senseless violence committed by gangsters is perpetrated for ego status and also encompasses a search for kicks or thrills. The kicks involve a type of emotional euphoria. Gangsters use violence for the emotional charge, which serves to validate their existential state and makes them feel good, at the expense of anyone who gets in their way. Many sociopathic gangsters have told me about the emotional high they get from their violent behavior.

Youths who become gangsters, as indicated, are usually socialized in family situations that involves child abuse or neglect and abandonment or both. This treatment impacts their self-concept and gangster behavior. In summary, the following sequence of events depicts the early socialization process in the background of the typical sociopathic gangster: (1) As a child he is emotionally, sexually, or physically abused or neglected by his primary socializing agents, his parents. (2) Because he is treated in negative ways and with limited respect, the child feels humiliated, demeaned, and unworthy. As a consequence of this pattern of socialization, he develops a low self-concept and feels self and other rage and hatred. He tends to accept on some deeper emotional level a message he is repeatedly given, which he interprets as, "If these powerful people in my life, my parents, think that I am stupid, inadequate, and unworthy of love and respect, I must be an inferior person." (3) Mixed in with this creation of feelings of low self-esteem is a rage against the parents who abused or neglected him, and this rage is often displaced to others in a society that also treats them with a level of disrespect.

The violent gang is a viable collectivity for youths with these complex social backgrounds to enact their rage. The malleable structure of the violent gang enables sociopathic youths to commit atrocious violent acts, and then rationalize their senseless behavior in the context of their gang's asocial norms. The sociopathic factor is a significant concept for explaining violent-gang behavior.

PART THREE
TREATMENT APPROACHES

o   o   o   o   o   o   o   o   o   o   o

6.

Some Effective Interventions

○ ○ ○ ○ ○ ○ ○ ○ ○ ○

W HATEVER ULTIMATELY DETERMINES THE emergence of a specific violent gang at a particular time and place, there is no doubt that the existence of violent gangs as a continuing social phenomena in American urban areas is ultimately related to deeper, more general dysfunctions in the overall social system. If this consideration is relevant for an overall assessment of the problem, it must be equally relevant to the issue of a thoroughly effective attack on the pathological roots in the social system that produce the violent gang.

A society that fails to find remedies for its own institutionalized social inequities, including racism, discrimination, poor educational facilities, and dysfunctional family life, including teenage pregnancies, is likely to continue to suffer with the existence of gang violence, drug addiction, crime, and delinquency. On the broad societal front, therefore, governmental and private programs aimed at reducing social and economic inequalities, equalizing opportunities, facilitating the integration of new populations, and improving educational facilities would have the effect of ameliorating some of the causal factors of the gang problem.

The continuance and proliferation in the 1990s of senseless violent gangs in conjunction with the increased drug use are indicators of the deep despair and alienation experienced by many minority and ghetto youths because of these root causes. The existence of the violent gang is strong evidence that many significant social dislocations continue to exist in American society, and these social conditions need to be improved. These apparent and complex societal causal factors are not amenable to quick solutions; however, there are short-term methods and interventions that can be effectively utilized short of dramatically changing the overall American social system.

Programs can be developed that can provide viable pathways into law-abiding society for youths who are vulnerable to participation in violent gangs. There are a variety of these types of social programs that have been tried in some measure and have resulted in a degree of success. This section on treatment will delineate a variety of interventions and approaches that have been effective and show promise for preventing and controlling gang violence.

These include the enrichment of educational programs in the schools especially directed at young gang-prone youths; family therapy; special job-training programs; special recreational and athletic facilities and programs in community centers; more vigorous outreach probation officers, with small caseloads, trained to understand gangs and resocialize at-risk youths; and the employment of former gangsters, who were "once on the scene" and have changed their behavior, to reach these youths and redirect them into a more positive lifestyle through the development of special "therapeutic community" programs for gangsters in and out of prison. (This latter type of project shows great promise for ameliorating the gang problem and will be presented in detail in chapter 7.)

Social programs devoted to controlling gangs require an effective police presence in the community. The incarceration of some core gangsters, is, of course, a necessary part of any overall program to control gangs; however, when the get tough attitude by society is the only or dominant response, it often exacerbates the problem. Too often ghetto youths who look and dress like gangsters but are law-abiding citizens are captured in emergency police dragnet efforts. Indiscriminate police sweeps often pour gasoline on the fire. The single-minded approach of more vigorous law enforcement, in the absence of social programs is about as effective as the failed federal "war on drugs."

Most gang youths will respond to a variety of logical and humanistic programs when they are reasonably available to them. The insertion of these social programs in a community in conjunction with a rigorous and logical police effort can connect many alienated gang youths into law-abiding society and significantly reduce the horrendous consequences of senseless violent-gang behavior.

DETACHED GANG WORKER PROJECTS

One methodology expressly designed for the violent gang that has been effectively employed is the "detached gang worker" approach. In this approach a professional, often a probation officer or a social worker, is assigned to the gang problem in a hood or barrio. The essential goal of the worker is to reach out to the youths in an area and redirect them from destructive gang behavior patterns into constructive activities in their community.

A significant detached-worker program, which has served as a model for gang control in large urban areas nationally since its inception in 1946, is the approach designed and utilized by the New York City Youth Board. The Youth Board established seven goals for work with street gangs: (1) reduction of antisocial behavior, particularly street fighting; (2) friendly relationships with other street gangs; (3) increased democratic participation within the gangs; (4) broadened social horizons; (5) responsibility for self-direction; (6) improved personal and social adjustment of the individual; (7) improved community relations.[1]

SOME GENERAL ISSUES INVOLVED IN DETACHED GANG WORK

Reaching the gang through detached youth workers, utilizing the above-stated principles and goals, is often effective. However, the process entails pitfalls not specified in policy or in the manuals. Foremost among these potential problems is the possibility of inaccurately diagnosing gang structure. Distinctly different treatment methods are required for treating more benign gangs of youths and more aggressive violent gangs. The gang workers in their initial period of intervention must accurately diagnose the structure of the gang with which they are working.

Different levels of involvement among the core and the more marginal gangsters dictate different treatment prescriptions. The wannabee, more marginal younger gangster can generally be reached through the more conventional methods of recreation, providing a job, and some counseling, whereas core Gs and OGs require a different approach that often includes working with them in a custodial institution.

The diagnostic assumption that working through the violent gang leader will redirect the gang can pose another problem. Often working through the leader of a violent gang solidifies its structure. Official sanction of some sociopathic gang leaders by a worker may give them more status and solidify the gang.

Merely gaining access to violent gang participants is frequently mistaken for acceptance and rapport. Contrary to popular belief, getting in touch with the gang is not difficult for a detached worker. However, the meaning given to the relationship by gangsters varies and is of major significance. If the gang worker appears as a "mark" to most members, a do-gooder who doesn't know the score, they will simply use him for money, cigarettes, or whatever favors they can obtain.

In this regard, some detached gang workers, rather than resocializing gang members, are taken in by the gang. They may rationalize their personal motives toward "adventuresome" gang behavior as necessary to maintain their relationship. In fact, this behavior is not necessary. Becoming themselves a gang member by overidentifying with the gang neutralizes their impact as an adequate adult role model. The negative nature of the gang worker's mistaken assumptions is revealed by the following statement of a detached gang worker who, in my view, was taken in by the gang he was sent to change:

> One afternoon the boys were hanging around and a crap game started. I decided it would be strategic for me to participate so that I might get closer to them and improve my rapport. During the course of the game one of the fellows turned to me and said, "Say, man, you're supposed to be out here to change us and it seems like we're making you like us instead."

When an overzealous detached gang worker is duped by the gang or misinterprets the meaning of a situation, he is reinforcing rather than modifying their behavior. In his capacity as gang worker, he is, in effect, a carrier of the values and norms of the larger society. Initially, gangsters resist the intrusion and possible changes into their subculture. The gang will attempt to get what it can without changing and then seduce the detached worker into becoming part of the gang. The gang worker should be aware of the negative implication of compromising the relevant norms of the larger society in order to gain false acceptance and superficial approval. When he does this, he is fairly quickly eliminated as a force for changing the gang since they begin to view him as a mark or sucker susceptible to manipulation. This defeats the objectives the worker is attempting to achieve.

Given these caveats and potential pitfalls, reaching the gang in its own milieu through a detached gang worker, whether he or she is a university-trained professional or an ex-gangster paraprofessional, is a valuable approach to the violent-gang problem. However, several issues require revision and redefinition if this approach is to modify rather than solidify or reinforce violent-gang structure and behavior. The following guidelines are suggested for an effective detached gang worker approach:

1. It is necessary for the detached gang worker to be trained to properly diagnose the structure of the gang he or she is working with.
2. Accurately diagnosing the violent gang will reveal different degrees of participation and involvement on the part of each gangster. Marginal members may be approached through more conventional treatment; core violent-gang participants and leaders require a different and more intense form of treatment in many cases, including incarceration.
3. A violent gang can become more integrated by working through some leaders, and this error reinforces the gang's cohesion.
4. The detached gang worker is an official representative of the more inclusive society and must avoid sanctioning or participating in deviance to gain what will turn out to be a false acceptance and rapport. He should serve as an adequate law-abiding adult role model. In this way he may become a bridge or vehicle for bringing the larger society's positive values and norms to the gang.

Utilizing these principles and methods, the worker should consciously dismember the gang, starting from the outside marginal gangsters and working toward the more core participants, as if he were peeling an artichoke. The marginal Wannabees, once they hook into more constructive enterprises, will find less energy and time for violent-gang activity. These constructive activities should be viewed less for their intrinsic value and more for their usefulness as a gimmick, a means for extricating marginal Wannabees from participation in the violent gang and involving them in activity within the inclusive society. And the more core gangsters who require closer supervision and treatment need to be incarcerated for a time in a therapeutic community-oriented program.

LEO CORTEZ: A POSITIVE EXAMPLE OF A DETACHED
GANG WORKER IN ACTION

When the issues and caveats I have delineated are effectively incorporated into the detached gang worker approach, the intervention of detached gang workers in a community can make a positive difference. An excellent case example is revealed in the following report from the *Los Angeles Times* on the work of one effective detached gang worker, Leo Cortez. His response to a gang shooting in L.A. indicates how a detached worker can intervene in a positive way in a serious situation within a gang and a community.

The night before, a youth with a sawed-off shotgun had shot a middle-aged mother who was picnicking with several small children in an East Los Angeles park. And now, although the woman's sons and their friends were probably plotting a bloody gang revenge at this very minute, Leo Cortez found himself sitting inside a small county office while assorted law officers and social workers drank coffee, ate doughnuts and wondered what to do about the youth gang problem in East Los Angeles. At times such as these, Leo Cortez, 37, a county youth worker and one-time gang member, wonders why he isn't out on the streets working with those he understands so well. So well, in fact, that many residents of that small 8.36-square-mile enclave known as unincorporated East Los Angeles, population about 140,000, are convinced that Leo Cortez has probably averted more gang wars and saved more lives than all the sheriff's deputies combined. . . .

[In this case,] Cortez drove directly to County-USC General Hospital where he made his way through the maze of corridors to her room, a crowded ward on the ninth floor. Momentarily, he stood at the bedside, silently surveying the damage. Her bruised body was riddled with at least fifty shotgun pellets, two of them only a fraction away from her right eye. . . . Because she was an East Los Angeles mother, she understood gangs. Her two sons belonged to one of the roughest gangs in the area. And, she whispered, with weary acceptance, "they only try to kill each other. . . ." The woman's clouded eyes momentarily cleared, filled with sudden, sharp alarm. "Leo, don't let them go for revenge. Make them stay home."

At a later gang meeting Cortez heard the typical calls for revenge. "Man, tonight we'll go down there and kill a couple of those vatos (bad dudes)," declared one skinny youth of fourteen. The only problem was that, though they all suspected the assailant had come from one particular rival gang, nobody was sure. "I tell you something," shouted another boy of eighteen whose nick name was "Little Boy" and whose eyes were glazed over by something much stronger than liquor. "When we go, we'll be cool.

We won't go around shooting women and kids. We'll kill the vato who did it."

At the meeting patiently, in Spanish, Cortez urged them all to leave the park (where they met). Getting arrested wouldn't help anything. Better yet, why not visit the hospital? With surprising passivity, like small, uncertain children, most quickly agreed. Even Little Boy, who was reeling so badly he could hardly walk. And so Cortez gave him a lift home, not knowing, when he let the boy out, that in two days Little Boy would be dead himself — shot to death by youths from another barrio. . . .

Leo Cortez seems to know not only the names of almost every youth in East Los Angeles but also the names of their friends and their enemies. He also knows which kids are hard-core murderers, which ones can be influenced to kill, which ones never could, and, finally, which youths are "locos" — crazy enough to be altogether unpredictable.

According to Cortez, "What most people don't understand is that the kids out here, the gang members, don't consider themselves criminals. . . . Here, even when they kill, national standards just don't apply. Because, here, a gang member regards himself as a soldier, you understand? Even if he's only patrolling a few square blocks. No matter how small his turf is, he still regards himself as a patriot . . . protecting his homeland. Because that's all he's got, all he's ever had. . . . Too many kids nowadays aren't following any of the old rules. In the old days, gang members made certain that when they went on a retaliatory raid, they hit their enemy. But now, they often are sloppy, or heedless, simply speeding by an enemy house at night and spraying it with bullets, regardless of who's inside. I think that's why there's more violence here now. . . . They've got no future, nothing but their barrio and their 'homeboys.' So, they can only prove their manhood by standing up and getting killed, or killing." [2]

THE LOS ANGELES COUNTY PROBATION DEPARTMENT'S DETACHED GANG WORKER PROGRAM

The Los Angeles County Probation Department, under the leadership of Chief Probation Officer Barry Nidorf, has instituted a most effective detached gang worker program that utilizes both probation officers working with gangsters in the community and in custodial camp institutions. The department's gang workers are knowledgeable about gang structure, and they effectively combine their efforts with a blend of aggressive supervision, caring social work, and access to a number of custodial facilities. Marginal gang youths referred to the department from the courts are worked with in the community where they receive appropriate counseling and job training.

Hard-core gangsters, after adjudication, are placed in custody in a probation camp. The camps have a variety of programs that focus on changing gang affiliation, individual and group counseling, and preparation for the youth's reentry into his community. Some of the camps have a military-type boot camp approach. The department's varied programs have been successful in redirecting many gang youths from continuing their delinquent activities and being sent to big-time California prisons; they return to their community with some social skills, needed for leaving the gang and becoming responsible law-abiding citizens.

THE ADULT YOUTH ASSOCIATION APPROACH

Many community-based programs for reaching out to delinquents and gangsters were created in Chicago, Boston, and New York in the early 1930s during the economic depression of that period. So-called settlement houses and community recreation centers were developed to deal with the poverty and boredom that young people confronted in their lives. This methodology continues to be a viable approach for dealing with and involving alienated gangsters and redirecting them into more constructive activities. Most approaches of this type involve detached gang workers reaching out to youths in their community. As indicated, detached gang workers can operate in the context of a variety of community-based organizations, certainly including community recreation centers, and such official agencies as probation or parole departments.

A structure that I found useful in my own work with gangs in New York was built on the concept and experiences of earlier community-based organizations. It was called the Adult Youth Association and became known as AYA. The AYA program encompassed a variety of intervention methods. The AYA was based on one of the essential causes for a youth's participation in gangs: the absence of a positive adult role model in the hood or barrio.

The situation of youths without any positive male role models can be effectively attacked through an AYA type of project by producing natural relationships around recreation, project planning, and other activities that bring adults and youths together in constructive interaction. The use of citizen volunteers from a community who are willing to give of their time and energy is essential to an AYA operation. The usual approach of getting volunteers to help a social agency was reversed in AYA. Our social agency and its professional staff attempted to help and support the adults in the community to run their own programs that involved relating naturally with neighborhood youths.

The AYA type of project can be especially successful in peeling off from the gang the more easily reached wannabee youths and involving them in a meaningful relationship with an adult, thus helping to resolve the neighborhood adult-youth schism. The detached gang worker can serve as the bridge and coordinator. The activities utilized are not the primary factor in the AYA program; the involvement of indigenous adults working in interaction with youths from the neighborhood is at the core of the AYA approach.

The AYA approach can be self-perpetuating. Many Wannabees who successfully participated in the AYA program as youths tend to turn around at a later age and become adult surrogate-father role models to other neighborhood youths. The emphasis in the AYA approach is to build it into the natural structure of the community so that, whether the professional agency that initiates the program continues or not, something positive is at work in a somewhat changed neighborhood. It operates in terms of the biblical admonition here loosely paraphrased: if you give someone a fish, he is not hungry that day; however, if you teach him how to fish, he becomes self-sufficient.

RECREATION AS AN AYA APPROACH

Recreation is a good gimmick for involving neighborhood adults and marginal gang youths into interactions with each other in constructive activities. In the process of planning a recreational activity, a natural interaction takes place that is difficult to duplicate. Emphasis should be placed on some degree of organized league activity rather than on random play. The organizational procedures required for finding a gym or field for the league, developing rules, age limits, team size quotas, scheduling, and so on involves adults and youths in a natural and productive interaction. The main sports that are attractive to youths include baseball, basketball, and football.

In developing an athletic league, care must be taken not to make the gang structure more cohesive. In using the league idea, efforts should be made to have the teams form around athletic ability rather than around gang affiliation. A good league will reshuffle the neighborhood's gang structure and thus minimize violent-gang activity. Marginal gang members become involved in a social athletic club rather than their destructive gang.

Building the recreational activity into the social fabric of the neighborhood is basic. Emphasis should be placed on maximizing the involvement of local adult volunteers; utilizing neighborhood facilities — gymnasiums, meeting rooms, halls, and so on; and gaining local citizen monetary and moral support. The effort should be made so that whether or not the basic organizing social agent, the professional detached worker, continues on the project, there is sufficient community involvement to keep the adult-youth activity in motion on its own strength. And graduates of the program as youths should be encouraged to come back as responsible adults for the continuation of the program. This will enable the program to be self-perpetuating.

Prefabricated or overly prestructured recreation programs, prepared in advance by adults or professionals, into which youths are moved in an assembly-line fashion are of limited help toward involving the youth and resocializing him adequately. However, developing recreation activities in which the youths take a major role in defining what they want, what they get, and how they get it, combined with the assistance of interested and indigenous, inspired adult volunteers, produces activities that become part of their natural milieu.

THE COMMUNITY GANG COMMITTEE

In the New York AYA project that I instituted and directed, the AYA spearheaded, among other projects, a cooperative effort of social agencies and gang workers that became known as the West Side Gang Committee. Members of the committee included a number of ex-gangsters who were now responsible citizens, local police, interested citizens, and people from various social agencies in the community.

The gang committee met periodically, not only in crisis situations, and concentrated on exchanging information and knowledge about gang organization in the area. In addition to compiling data on gang patterns, the more than thirty members of the committee discussed effective programming for gang control and dealing with such special problems as drug dealing and drug addiction. Following is a summary of aims and activities developed and utilized by our gang committee:

1. *Gang Information.* Information (both rumored and factual) about the size, organization, and so on of gangs and delinquent groups was ex-

changed among the members of the committee. This interaction was carried on through such means as questionnaires, discussion at meetings, and phone calls.

2. *Gang-Work Techniques and Methods.* The committee attempted to discuss and continually develop more effective techniques and methods for detecting, preventing, dealing with, and eliminating gangs and related individual problems. These methods would include group discussion with gangsters, methods for working out social agency-police-youth relationships and dealing with gang/narcotics problems.

3. *Community Education Groups.* The committee disseminated information and educated the public on gang problems and issues that were of relevance.

4. *Ancillary Projects.* The committee, through college students from a local university, carried out limited-range surveys, research projects, and group therapy projects.

Group Psychotherapy and Psychodrama Treatment Methods for Gangsters

As part of the described programs and agencies devised for reaching gangsters, especially younger Wannabees, the treatment methodologies of group psychotherapy and psychodrama are very effective approaches. These quintessential treatment methods can be incorporated into programs in community centers, schools, probation, parole, and in custodial institutions.

GROUP PSYCHOTHERAPY

The use of group psychotherapy with sociopathic gangsters, especially younger Wannabees, is most useful for the purpose of modifying their behavior and helping them to lead more constructive lives. Group psychotherapy has some special advantages over individual therapy:

1. The therapist can be aided by cooperative youths within the group whom he can enlist to provide a bridge of communications between them and the more difficult, less communicative youths in the group.

2. Gang youths in a group are very insightful about detecting and dissecting

each other's problems. Essentially, multiple therapists are involved in the group if the group therapist effectively coordinates the situation.

3. The therapist encounters his clients in a more natural milieu in group therapy than in a one-to-one relationship. Most gangsters find it uncomfortable to talk to a gang worker alone without some of their homies present.

4. Group interaction brings to the surface more underlying problems than an individual situation produces. The all-in-the-same-boat condition of gangsters can help focus and resolve many of the problems they confront in their family and community and can lead to a positive change in their behavior.

PSYCHODRAMA

Since group psychotherapy is a more well-known methodology, I will go into more detail on psychodrama as a viable method for treating gangsters. (For a more comprehensive discussion of psychodrama, see my book *Psychodrama.*[3])

Psychodrama was invented in 1910 by psychiatrist J. L. Moreno. In the 1930s Dr. Moreno and a number of associates directed psychodramas in juvenile reformatories and in a number of prisons, including New York's Sing Sing Prison. Since then the method has been effectively used in a variety of institutional and community clinics for delinquents. I have employed the method over the past forty-five years with considerable success in reformatories, with gangsters on probation and parole, in psychiatric hospital programs for delinquents, and with convicts in several prisons.

The psychodramatic method can be briefly described. Psychodrama is a natural and automatic process. We all at some time have an inner drama going on in our mind. In this confidential setting, a person is the star of his or her psychodrama session and plays all of the roles. A person may encounter parents, an employer, a spouse, or a rejecting lover in the monodrama; these others are referred to in psychodrama as "auxiliary egos." In a session, an auxiliary ego will play the role of a significant other related to the subject's problem. Throughout this book I have presented a number of psychodramatic role-playing sessions to indicate some issues related to the gang. Following are two psychodrama sessions — one in the community and the other in a probation camp — that serve to illustrate how psychodrama can be utilized to treat the gang problem.

An Impromptu Psychodrama on Violence

Gang life often moves so fast that it is not possible to wait until gangsters are apprehended and placed in an institution to leisurely work with them in psychodrama. To prevent an act of violence, it is sometimes necessary to respond quickly to an emergency situation. In the following intervention to prevent a gang murder, I used psychodrama in the context of my role as a detached gang worker.

The psychodrama began with a sociopathic gangster known as "Ape," whom I knew from my work with the Egyptian Kings gang. I encountered Ape, accompanied by two of his gangster friends, as I was walking down the street near my office in New York. Without any hesitation or preliminary greetings, and a sullen angry demeanor, he surprised me by pulling out a deadly looking switchblade knife and announced that he was on his way to kill a youth who lived in a nearby neighborhood on the Upper West Side of Manhattan.

A number of factors were in place that enabled me as a detached gang worker at that time to intervene in this potential homicide. I was prepared for this emergency possibility since on a continuing basis I knew the relationships of various gangs and gang networks in the area. I knew the gangs that were feuding and the leadership patterns of each group. More than that, I had previously directed psychodrama sessions with Ape and other gangsters from his gang in my office.

Also, at the moment I encountered Ape, I asked myself, Why did he stop me before he went to stab the other youth? I suspected the chances were good that he really did not want to commit this violence and wanted me to help him find a convenient way out of committing a potential murder. In brief, some groundwork was in place for this psychodramatic intervention.

After some preliminary discussion about the situation on the street, I invited the trio to my office to discuss the matter further, and they reluctantly accompanied me. After we settled into my office, Ape elaborated on his previous brief remarks to me on the street. He said, "Man, I'm packing I got my blade (switchblade knife) right here. I'm going up to 130th Street to cut the shit out of Crazy Eddie" (a notorious enemy gangster) who had apparently shown disrespect for Ape by saying bad things about him.

After a warm-up discussion on options to murdering Eddie, Ape agreed to a role-playing session to explore his rage, the motivation for his anger, and from my viewpoint, to drive home to him the dire consequences of such a homicide. The session began with the use of another gang boy as an auxiliary ego in the role of the intended victim. A paper ruler replaced the knife (for obvious reasons), and the "killing" was acted out in my office under controlled psychodramatic conditions. Before Ape plunged the "knife" into "Eddie," I had him soliloquize his anger and the reason why he wanted to kill Eddie.

Ape (the subject) in his speech cursed, fumed, threatened, and shouted at Eddie. After he had explored much of his rage, I returned him to role playing with his psychodramatic Eddie, who hurled threats and insults in return. Ape worked himself into a frenzy and then stabbed the auxiliary ego (the gang boy playing the part) with the paper knife. The psychodramatic victim fell dead on the floor.

Ape was then confronted with the consequences of his act in all of its dimensions, including the effect on his life and his own family. He began to regret what he had done and was particularly remorseful when (psychodramatically) an auxiliary ego playing the role of a court judge sentenced him to death in the electric chair.

When he had calmed down from acting out the murder and seeing the possible consequence of his own execution, we psychodramatically explored his possible motivation for killing Eddie. As I expected, Ape was going through a rough period of conflict with his father, and in a role play of this father-son problem, it appeared in the overall two-hour psychodrama that his father was the real target of the rage he had wanted to act out against Eddie.

The psychodrama accomplished several things for this potential killer:

1. In the session he gained a certain amount of insight into the fact that at that time he had a lot of conflict with and hostility toward his father and that his potential attack on Crazy Eddie was a form of the displaced anger he felt for his father.
2. He no longer was motivated to kill Eddie since he had already in a sense accomplished this psychodramatically.
3. He was confronted with the consequences of his homicidal act. Most gangsters, like many people, operate in the spur of the moment and are unable to think ahead in a situation to the outcome. When a gangster has an opportunity to act out his homicidal tendencies in a psychodrama, he invariably gains some insights into his real motivations.

My intervention served as a deterrent to the actual commission of a murder. Of course, this boy required and received further therapy, which sought to deal with his more basic personality problems. Moreover, considerably more work was attempted on the gang networks so as to minimize their potential for violence. However, the emergency psychodrama, in what Moreno calls "in situ," the immediate situation, did deter Ape from committing a homicide, at least on that particular day.

Psychodrama in a Probation Camp

A student of mine, John Hill, whom I had trained to direct psychodrama in his work in a probation camp, used psychodrama to deal with a typical gang problem that often manifests itself in a custodial setting. Following is a previously unpublished report of the event that John and I coauthored, in which we discuss the rationale for using psychodrama and present a typical session for controlling violence in a custodial setting.

One of the major problems faced by correctional counselors in the care and treatment of gang youths in a custodial setting is the behavior of the aggressive, assaultive inmate. His violent attitude and behavior tends to disrupt the possibility of the treatment process in the institution. He presents unique difficulties in terms of control and adaptability, especially in the group-living situation, and since his behavior directly affects the behavior of his peers, his negative acting out exerts undue pressures on the group as a whole.

With these thoughts in mind, the possibility of utilizing psychodrama as a treatment tool in dealing with an aggressive ward named David became readily apparent based on four major assumptions: (1) Any aggressive and assaultive impulses could be channeled in a controlled, monitored setting, allowing full expression without the danger of physical injury. (2) The motives behind these impulses could be explored in a manner readily visible to the wards involved. (3) An immediate catharsis could be achieved, reducing the probability of uncontrolled aggression and pressure in the group-living situation. (4) Any precipitating problems could be alleviated, examined, and explored as they occurred by a restaging of the problem in a psychodrama.

The psychodrama of David presents an example of the process in action. David is a sixteen-year-old Mexican-American youth committed to the custody of the probation camp by the courts for murder. He is a large, heavyset boy, intensely gang oriented. His case file reveals a record of seventeen arrests ranging from assaults and robberies to the offense that had him committed to camp.

David entered "A" dormitory reluctantly. His initial reaction to camp was negative in the extreme. Within three hours of entering the program, he had managed to alienate virtually everyone in the dormitory, staff, and peers alike. His answer to every reasonable request was a resounding obscenity. The consensus of opinion by staff was that David should be removed to a security, or lockup, facility as soon as possible.

This would probably have been initiated in short order had he not become involved in an incident with the reigning Chicano in the dorm, Leon, a member of a rival gang. Staff intervened before blows were struck, and David and six other wards were taken to the office for counseling.

It was felt that the psychodramatic approach might prove effective in this case, and the transition from encounter group to psychodrama was made by setting the stage for a reenactment of the confrontation between David and Leon. Initially an auxiliary ego staff member played the part of Leon.

David was seated in a chair facing the staff member, a probation officer, who assumed the role of Leon.

DAVID: You bastards (*indicating the group as a whole*) are always messin' with me.

"LEON": Man, you come walking in here like vato loco trying to prove how tough you are, what do you expect? (*David does a double take and demands to know who the staff member playing Leon is.*) Is he to be a staff person or is he supposed to be Leon?

The ground rules were repeated, indicating that what we were trying to accomplish was to relive the incident so that we could see what the problem was. David was reluctantly cooperative.

DAVID: How come that punk (*indicating the real Leon*) don't do it himself?

Leon became visibly agitated and started to get out of his chair to confront his adversary. He was waved back. Staff explained that because of the charged atmosphere and raw feelings a substitute for Leon was being used. David was instructed to regard the staff person playing Leon as the real Leon for purposes of the psychodrama. The initial confrontation was reviewed with the wards, explaining that David had challenged Leon and that Leon had reacted by questioning David's right to enter the dormitory as a new boy and throw his weight around. The staff member, reassuming the role of Leon, picked it up from there.

"LEON": How come you think you're such a bad ass? You can't come walking in here talking all that crap and shoving people around. You better get your act together.

DAVID: Fuck you man! You don't tell Mad Dog [his gang name] what to do or not do!

"LEON": Mad dog? Mad dog? They usually put mad dogs to sleep. What does that mean Mad Dog? *(Leon laughs from the sidelines as David balls up his fists and glares at the group.)*

DAVID: I'm going to waste you, puto! *(This is directed toward the real Leon.)*

The psychodrama interchange continued for some minutes and was evidently a source of some satisfaction to David who began to relax as he realized that he could express himself verbally without fear of physical retaliation from Leon or the staff member playing Leon. Another ward, James, a black gangster who had been delighted with the exchange, was moved into position next to David to support him and act as his double. (A double sits behind the subject of the session and gives him support in expressing himself.)

"LEON": *(Continuing with the session)* I don't know how a punk like you stayed alive on the outs. If I'd seen you out there, I would have brought back your cojones [testicles] in a paper bag.

DAVID: *(His face reddening at this reflection on his manhood, David struggles with himself for a moment before answering.)* At least I got cojones. You ain't nothing unless you got your home boys around.

At this point James, who had obviously been anxious to participate, interjected himself as David's double, helping David to present himself more effectively.

JAMES: *(As David)* Yeah, you think you runnin' this dorm, tellin' everybody what to do all the time. You think you cool, but you ain't shit!

David was somewhat taken aback at the unexpected support he had found from James and warmed to his role. He began to reflect on his statements, picking up cues from James.

DAVID: Yeah, how come when I come in here you all of a sudden start giving orders? You ain't no better than me even if you been here longer.

Leon now entered the session as himself. The interchange between the two boys was now taking place in fairly normal tones as Leon, having vented his personal angry emotions, began dealing with David on the level of a person of authority trying to reason with a recalcitrant underling. David was resisting this process by pointedly ignoring Leon's arguments and discussing his own feelings of right and justice. While he played the role of the wronged party with obvious relish, it was apparent that he had little or no insight at this point into his role in the problem.

The staff suggested that the wards physically exchange places (a role reversal) and that Leon play the role of David while David assume the part of Leon. Both boys initially balked at the idea of role reversal, but caught up in the fun of the process and at the urging of others in the group, they reluctantly exchanged seats. Leon was the first to begin the dialogue. He assumed an exaggerated stance of braggadocio, fists clenched and lips drawn back. He stared defiantly at David.

LEON: *(As David)* You puto you ain't gonna tell me what to do!

David was obviously struggling at this point, not sure of how he should react. Then, apparently remembering Leon's tirade against him, launched into a vituperative monologue that continued for some minutes despite Leon's attempts to interrupt. The other members of the group seemed to be really enjoying the performance of the two tough gangsters in their power struggle.

When David in the role of Leon finally ran out of invectives, the staff asked him what he was feeling at that moment. He then returned to being himself.

DAVID: I don't know man, but I really got pissed off when he called me a puto and started staring at me like that. It made me feel like going off on him.

STAFF: Do you want to go off on him now?

DAVID: Yeah, yeah I do!

STAFF: *(Handing David a towel)* Okay, hit the desk with this. Hit the desk like it was Leon.

David took the towel and tentatively hit the desk; once, twice, three times. Then he knotted the end and brought it crashing down a half a dozen times.

STAFF: Who are you hitting, David?

DAVID: Him, Leon.

STAFF: *(Turning to the group in the room)* What's happening here?

GROUP MEMBER: It seems to me that he's getting pissed off at Leon for doing the same thing he always does himself as a gang leader.

MIKE: I think he's pissed off at himself.

STAFF: *(To David)* What do you think about that?

DAVID: I don't know what you're talking about.

LEON: Look, man, I was doing the same thing you were doing from the first minute you walked in here. So maybe you can see how you was coming off.

David struggled with the concept for a moment then again crashed the towel violently against the desk.

DAVID: *(Angrily)* You guys don't know shit!

David did not say this too convincingly, however. The rest of the group had had a glimpse of the truth and immediately began to belabor the point.

STEVE: Hey, man, maybe you got angry because you know the way it really is. You aren't the big shot here. Maybe you better face it.

JERRY: *(Changing allegiance)* Yeah, don't seem like you can take what you was giving out.

CARLOS: That's the trouble with you man, you don't know what's coming down even when everyone else can see it! . . .

Suddenly David lashed out with the towel actually striking Leon across the face, and then he screamed at the group.

DAVID: Damn it! Why don't you putos get off my back?

Leon reacted by pulling the towel out of David's hands and was about to hit him with the knotted end when the staff member intervened and pushed both boys back into their chairs. The other boys had leaped up, happily anticipating a fight.

STAFF: Okay, okay, now just sit down and calm down.

Leon was rubbing his face, looking daggers at David, who was sitting slumped in his chair breathing heavily. The other members of the group settled back as the staff member asked them to explain what had just happened.

JAMES: I think David knows what's happening and is afraid to face it. He can't admit he's wrong, so he has to take it out on somebody.

MIKE: Yeah, he acts just like my little brother when he doesn't get his way or what he wants. He has a tantrum.

JERRY: Yeah, he acting like a kid.

The others all echoed Jerry's sentiments as David sat in his chair fighting back tears. Leon, sensing that David had just passed through an emotional crisis, relaxed and began to talk. He became quite reflective and adult.

LEON: I don't know, sometimes it's hard to be real. I mean to really see yourself as other people do. *(He reflects for a moment.)* When I was on the outs [on the street] when I was a kid, I got into fights all the time. I guess I was a real vato loco. Everybody thought I was crazy, even my parents. I was in the hospital maybe five or six times. When I was fifteen, I got shot and everybody thought I was going to die. When I got back on the streets I was a big man. I was tough. Then I started thinking how weird it was that it took almost getting killed and having a hole in my side to make me a person of respect.
  Anyway, now I had my rep as a G and didn't have to go around personally going off on people. Sure, I done some gangbanging, but most of the time since then I kept laid back out of sight. I got things I want to do. I got a veija [woman] and a kid. I guess I know what David feels like. I guess he still got to make his rep. He's just not going about it the right way. Going off on vatos in camp ain't gonna make it. That way somebody is going to do him [kill him]. We all got to get along here and do our time the best way we can. We got to stick together. When I was sitting here doing his trip [in David's role], I was getting next to how he was feeling. I guess because I been there myself. Always needing to prove myself as a man.

Leon appeared to have lost all his animosity, and during the course of his talking David listened intently. David seemed surprised that Leon expressed feelings of empathy for him, especially in view of the towel incident. He was having difficulty in controlling his tears.

STAFF: *(To David)* Okay, how are you feeling now?

DAVID: I don't know man. I don't know how I'm feeling. I feel all washed out. I feel like I don't give a damn about anything. I'm tired.

LEON: You got to get with it. You were talking that everyone was down on you without giving you a chance. Well, it seems to me that you were down on everybody without giving us a chance.

DAVID: I don't know. With the putos on the street you got to get them before they get you, you know that, otherwise they walk all over you. I know you got home boys here, but no one is going to walk over me.

LEON: Okay, no one is going to walk over you here as long as you take care of business. There's too many dudes out there that want to see us firing on each other. You're just going to make it harder on yourself and the rest of us unless you're cool and you make some changes. I know how hard it is to go through some changes, but it's worth it. I have to if I'm going to do right by my wife and kid when I get out of here.

DAVID: *(Shaking his head to indicate doubt, reflects for a moment, then tentatively holds out his hand. He finds it hard to meet Leon's eye.)* Okay, okay, man, I see where you're coming from. I'm sorry I hit you with the towel. I guess I was pretty pissed off.

Leon took David's hand and shook it firmly, making the comment that he could clearly see why they called him Mad Dog. At this point David had some recognition of his responsibility to the group as a veterano in the camp and had taken the first step in accepting the camp program for his treatment.

For David the psychodrama was both a catharsis and an initiation into the group-living setting of the camp. A most important facet of the psychodrama was that, for the first time, it enabled David to see himself as others saw him — the beginnings of insight and hopefully a positive change from his past violent behavior. While the psychodrama was not a panacea for David's problems, it did provide an initial step into being integrated into the camp program instead of being transferred because of his violent behavior to a maximum security prison. The transfer would have placed him in an institution where a kid like him would be pulled even further into a violent hardcore gangster in the prison system.

THE VALUE OF GROUP PSYCHOTHERAPY AND PSYCHODRAMA
FOR TREATING GANGSTERS

Group psychotherapy and psychodrama provide the opportunity for actual direct role training. Here a youth can see himself and others by presenting his problems for group discussion and analysis. More than that, they are in a position to correct (or edit) their illegal actions in the presented situations. The gangster can try out or practice legally conforming roles in the presence of criminal "experts," his peers, who quickly detect whether he is conning the group or playing it straight.

Psychodrama enables a violent gangster to vent his anger in a controlled setting and get some insights into the causal context (usually his family situation) of his violent behavior. In the group he can act out his assaultive impulses without harming anyone and rid himself of some of these negative emotions. He can learn to verbalize his violent impulses rather than assault first and pay the inevitable negative consequences.

Because gangsters have difficulty controlling their immediate violent compulsions, they tend to live in the moment and often lack the ability to relate the past to the present, the present to the future. The thought of future punishment or past experience doesn't usually enter their conscious deliberations to serve as a deterrent to illegal action. Training in understanding time dimensions is therefore often useful in violence prevention through the group process.

Psychodrama as a group process provides such time flexibility. The offender can act out the past, immediate, or expected problem situations that are disturbing him. The process, therefore, is useful in working with a typical gangster's problem, his impulsive violent behavior.

In psychodrama the use of the "future projection technique," by which a person propels himself into a future situation, provides an opportunity for the offender to plan how to live within the law. This technique has been used with gangsters about to be released into the open community. In a session they are psychodramatically projected into relevant future social situations in which they will find themselves. These role-test and training situations include confronting potential problems in their community, on a job, with their family, with supervising probation officers, and others. It can provide them with some degree of flexible and appropriate behavior for dealing with difficult future situations.

As a case in point, I have often directed role-playing session with offenders for the purpose of applying for a job. In one session a gangster, who was soon to be released from prison, went through the motions of getting a job with a potential employer in a role-playing situation. His demeanor reflected an apparent disinterest in really getting a job. This fact was quickly and forcefully brought to his attention by other members of the group who were watching and evaluating his lackluster performance. This feedback produced some insights for the subject of the session and led to a valuable and emotional discussion on the basic need for employment to be able to go straight and stay out of prison.

The psychodramatic role-training process can also be utilized to build up the gangster's resistance to efforts on the part of his homies to seduce him back into gang activity when he is back on the street. Psychodrama, therefore, provides an opportunity for the impulsive gangster to review some of his past and future behavior with its many implications for preventing and controlling his delinquent tendencies.

For sociopathic gangsters, words are cheap and lying is easy. Based on my experience of directing hundreds of psychodramas with these youths, I have determined that it is very difficult to lie in action during group psychotherapy or psychodrama. Because group pressures make distortion so difficult, the offender is forced to assess his behavior and its rationale closely. This, combined with opportunities to try out law-abiding behavior patterns in role playing before such severe judges as his peers, helps a gangster to reexamine and reject his illegal behavior patterns and learn socially conforming practices.

Part of the difficulty of various group treatment processes is that gangsters are quick and enjoy pointing out the defects of their cohorts, and are hard-pressed to accept constructive criticism when they are on the hot seat. This, of course, is not only true for gangsters; the principle applies to the general population. An empathic group can help the violent offender understand the roots of his compulsive violence. In their psychodrama or group therapy sessions, they learn that the causal context of their rage usually emanates from the sexual, emotional, or physical abuse they were subjected to as children in their dysfunctional socialization process.

A valuable characteristic of psychodrama, group therapy, and other treatment approaches is that they provide an opportunity for violent gangsters to discuss or act out their illegal motivations in a controlled setting. After acting out and discussing their destructive impulses in a session, they may no longer have the motivation to carry them out in reality. This therapeutic process can take place in the community, in viable custodial institution programs, and most effectively in the context of a therapeutic community.

7.

The Therapeutic Community
Approach to Gangs

○ ○ ○ ○ ○ ○ ○ ○ ○ ○

T HE THERAPEUTIC COMMUNITY APPROACH was originated in
1958 in Santa Monica, California, by an ex-alcoholic, Charles
Dederich, who overcame his alcohol addiction through Alcoholics Anony-
mous. He based his approach on the AA principle that people who have
experienced a problem and have triumphed over their problem can be
effective in treating and leading others out of their difficulty. One significant
departure from AA that Dederich initiated, among many others, was that the
recovering alcoholics/addicts lived together in a residential setting for at least
a year.

Another major premise of the therapeutic community (hereafter referred
to as a TC) is that the TC was managed by people who had recovered from
the problem they were attempting to treat. The TC's recovered graduates,
along with professional therapists, became the main "therapists" in their
community. The concept was that this new type of ex-alcoholic/addict
therapist was uniquely qualified to treat others because he or she had personally experienced the problem, had gone through a process of changing
his or her behavior in a positive direction, and was staying "clean," or free
from their former problem. When they complete the program, a number of
graduates who have demonstrated talent in treating others are hired by the
TC as therapists. The majority return to their family and community; how-

ever, they are encouraged to maintain some contact with the TC that helped to save their lives.

I first heard about the TC approach in 1960 from Donald Cressey, a sociologist who had researched and written about Synanon. Since then, based on my considerable research into Synanon and other TCs in the United States and Europe, I have concluded that the TC process equips former addicts with long criminal backgrounds and prison experience to become effective therapists for younger delinquents, including gangsters. The ex-criminal therapist has had the street experience of his client, cannot easily be outmaneuvered by him, and can establish rapport. There is a communication that most professional therapists find difficult to establish with rebellious and defiant gangsters.

In a TC setting, this type of meaningful and honest communication takes place on a daily basis in a variety of groups and the results have proven to be phenomenal. The TC method since its inception has proven effective for thousands of former alcoholics and criminals/addicts who have gone through the program. (The method and its effectiveness has been delineated in two books I have written.)[1]

The concept and methodology of the original Synanon therapeutic community has been replicated in thousands of spin-off organizations in the United States and around the world. In 1996 there were several hundred TCs in the United States and hundreds of others throughout Europe and Asia. These replications of the original Synanon method have been developed and modified to fit the cultural characteristics of different communities in the United States and societies around the world. (An organization known as Therapeutic Communities of America has a membership of several hundred TCs in the United States and there is a worldwide association, the World Federation of Therapeutic Communities.)

As indicated, TC programs for criminals/addicts are housed in the open community. However, a number of community-based TCs have implemented their programs in prisons, employing ex-criminals/addicts who have been successful in the program as therapists. The success rate has been exceptional for criminals/addicts, including many gangsters, who have participated in TC programs both in prison and the community. In general, research data on individuals released from TCs as compared to other treatment approaches reveals that the usual 65 percent repeater arrest rate has been reversed. Around 65 percent of individuals released from a TC program are successful in the open community and are not rearrested for at least three years.[2]

The Therapeutic Community Approach
for Gangsters

In many respects the TC approach has already been implemented in the treatment of the gang problem since hundreds of gangsters have found their way into these various TC programs and have benefited from the process. The manner in which a TC can be utilized for specifically resocializing gangsters was revealed to me in the early days of Synanon. As I spent time, around five years, and interviewed a number of Synanon residents for my first book on TCs, *Synanon: The Tunnel Back,* I became aware of the fact that a number of Synanon residents had violent-gang behavior in their background. It struck me early on that for alienated youths who became gangsters, being part of a gang was a search for some kind of status, respect, and belonging to a community. In a gang these needs were met in a self- and other-destructive way. In a therapeutic community the same needs are met in a humanistic positive way. The following chronicle of Frankie, a former New York gangster, illuminates how the TC process can effectively treat gangsters.

FRANKIE

Frankie came from a dysfunctional family. Because of this background, his family became a notorious gang on the Upper West Side of New York known as the Villains. According to Frankie, the gang was his family until, as he put it, "King heroin took over my life."

When Frankie was twenty, a New York judge, tired of seeing him go through the city's revolving-door prison system at Rikers Island and knowledgeable about Synanon in California, gave him a choice: a long prison sentence at Sing Sing or a last chance in a TC. Frankie chose Synanon.

When he arrived at Synanon, Frankie's first reaction to the TC was confusion: "The first thing they hit me with flipped me. This tough-looking cat says to me, 'There are two things you absolutely can't do here, shoot drugs or fight.' Frankie said, scratching his head, "I was all mixed up, these were the main two things I knew how to do."Despite his initial confusion, he found the environment interesting and exciting and quite different from the prisons where he had done time.

There were, according to Frankie, "lots of hip people" in Synanon. Among them was Jimmy, who at forty-eight had been a criminal/addict and a con man for more than thirty years; he was clean at the time for over five years in the TC. Jimmy, who ran the kitchen at that time, was assigned as Frankie's sponsor. Frankie got his first job, scouring pots and pans and mopping the floors. According to Frankie, Jimmy could not be conned or manipulated out of position like the guards and therapists that Frankie had encountered on Riker's Island and at various federal hospitals for drug addicts. Jimmy, of course, "knew the score." To him, Frankie, with all his exploits, was a "young punk" who could give him no trouble. Jimmy told me, "I've met kids like this all my life, in and out of the joint."

According to Frankie, "At first, I hated this bastard Jimmy. He controlled me and always talked me out of leaving and going back to my old gang. I used to sometimes sit and plan ways to kill him." When Frankie wanted to fight Jimmy over a disagreement about work, Jimmy laughed and told him that if he wanted to fight, he would be thrown out of the place and get sent back to New York and a long prison term.

The usual prison situation was reversed, and this further confused Frankie. In prison, if Frankie got into trouble, confinement became increasingly severe, with the "hole" (solitary confinement) an end point. In the Bellevue Hospital psychiatric ward, where Frankie had also spent time, it was a straitjacket. In Synanon, they told him they would throw him out.

What made Frankie behave in order to stay in the TC? It was not only the potential threat of prison. In another setting his usual violent behavior would have propelled him out the door. What was important for Frankie was that there were others who understood him, had made the same "scenes," and intuitively knew his problems and how to handle him. Although, at first, he would only grudgingly admit it, he respected people he could not con. He belonged and was now part of a family and a community he could accept.

Given Frankie's delinquent background, he understood the necessity to acquire a reputation in any organization he belonged to, including gangs. Frankie found he could make a rep in the TC, without getting punished or locked up, as he would from his violent-gang activities. In prison the highest he could achieve in terms of the values of other prisoners was to become "king" of the inmate world, acquire a stash of cigarettes, obtain some unsatisfactory homosexual favors, and land in the hole. In the TC he felt he could acquire any role he was "big enough or man enough to achieve" and "growing up" carried the highest approval of his TC homies. He could actually move up the status-ladder and become a director in this organization, as other criminals/addicts had done. (The president of Synanon, at that time, was an ex-heroin addict. For the first time in his life, Frankie was achieving status, a rep, for being clean and nondelinquent.

Of course, when he first arrived Frankie attempted to gain a rep by conniving and making deals, in accord with his old habits. When he did, he was laughed at, ridiculed, and given severe "haircuts" (a Marine-like verbal dressing down) by other old-time con men in group sessions. They were, he learned, ferociously loyal to the organization, which had literally saved their lives and given them a new status in life. He, too, began to develop an esprit de corps in the TC. As he once put it, "I never would give three cheers for Riker's Island. But I'm part of this place. It's my home."

Frankie found that rep was acquired in this social system (unlike the ones he had known) by "putting in work of truth, honesty, and industry." The values of his other life required reversal if he were to gain a rep in the TC. These values were not goals per se on which someone moralized in a meaningless vacuum, but were means to the end of acquiring prestige within the tough social system of the TC, with which he increasingly identified as his "positive gang."

In the encounter groups he was required to attend three nights a week, Frankie participated in a new kind of group psychotherapy, unlike the kind he had fooled around with in prison programs. In prison he had to maintain his tough-guy, macho demeanor for self-protection. Consequently, he never talked about his underlying feelings or his difficult family background. In the TC, the truth was viciously demanded. Any rationalizations about past or current deviant behavior were brutally demolished by the group. There was an intensive search for each member's real self-identity. He found that in this process, which he began to trust, he learned something of what went on beneath the surface of his thoughts. Frankie admitted that for the first time in his life, he had found other people who really understood him. He had experienced individual and group therapy in prison and various other institutions, but in those situations he could con the therapist and, most important, "I said what I thought they wanted to hear so I could get out sooner."

Frankie, who at first had followed his usual pattern of self-centered manipulation of others, now began to care about what happened to others, who were real friends to him. He began to identify with the organization and learned on a gut level that if any other member failed, in some measure he, too, failed. Frankie began to comprehend what others thought in a social situation. The concept of empathy, or identifying with the thoughts and feelings of others, in this new community became a significant reality. The concept of no man is an island, often discussed at noon philosophical seminars, began to have meaning for Frankie.

In the status system, Frankie's rise in the hierarchy was neither quick nor easy. He first moved from the dishpan to serving food at the kitchen counter. After several months he began to work outside on a pickup truck that acquired food and other donations.

Here he had his first slip into his old ways, no doubt, in part, to test the waters. With two other individuals who worked with him on the truck, a group decision was made one day that smoking a joint might be fun. They acquired some marijuana from a dealer known to one of the group.

When they arrived back from work, their slightly loaded appearance immediately became apparent to the group. According to Frankie, "They spotted us right away." They were hauled into the main office and viciously (verbally) attacked and ordered to "copout" (tell) or "get lost." A general meeting was called, and they were forced to reveal their deviant behavior before the entire group, in a so-called fireplace scene. That night Frankie was demoted back to washing dishes.

Frankie learned the hard way that the norms of the TC were the reverse of the criminal code he had known in his gangster life. In another slip into negative behavior, Frankie, with two other members, went for a walk into town. One of them suggested buying a bottle of wine. (Of course, no drinking was permitted in the TC.) Frankie and the other member rejected the proposal. However, no one revealed the incident until two days later when it came up in group. The group jumped hardest on Frankie and the other individual who had vetoed the idea, rather than on the one who had suggested buying the wine.

Frankie and the other "witnesses" were expected to report such slips immediately since the group's life depended on keeping one another straight. For the first time in his life, Frankie was censured for not being a snitch. The maxim "thou shalt not squeal," basic to the existence of the underworld criminal culture, was reversed and fiercely upheld. In the TC, you were expected to tell on another in order to keep them straight.

Another area, the no-physical-violence rule, was at first difficult for a criminal/addict like Frankie to grasp and to believe in since his usual response to a difficult situation was to leap, fists first, past verbal means of communication into assault. As a result of the group's and other new patterns of interaction, Frankie's increasing ability to communicate began to minimize his assaultive impulses. Although at first he was kept from committing violence by the fear of ostracism, he later had no need to use violence since he had developed some ability to verbalize his anger effectively. He learned to express himself, in what was for him a new form of communication, on a nonviolent, verbal level. On occasion Frankie would regress and have the motivation for assault, but the system had taken hold. In one session I heard him say, "I was so fucking mad yesterday, I wished I was back at Riker's. I really wanted to hit this guy in the mouth for attacking me in a group session."

Frankie had a sketchy work record prior to entering the TC. On the street, most of his time was taken up with gang fighting, pimping, armed robbery, or pushing heroin. Apart from some forced menial labor in prison, he was seldom engaged in anything resembling formal work. His theme had been, work is for squares. He learned how to work in the TC as a side effect of his desire to rise in the status system. He learned similarly a startling new fact, that "talking to someone in the right way made them do more things than threatening them."

As a consequence of living in this new social system, Frankie's social learning and ability continued to increase. His destructive pattern of relating to others withered away. It was no longer functional for him in this new way of life. The TC developed his empathic ability. It produced an attachment to different, more socially acceptable values and reconnected him to the larger society in which the TC functioned as a valid organization.

The TC process unearthed a diamond in the rough. Frankie always had an interest in art. As he later described it to me, "When I was a kid, I always liked to draw, but no one paid any attention to my sketches, and I was teased by the other kids. I did some secret artwork in prison but tore it up." One day in a group that involved a discussion of future occupations, Frankie was asked what he would really liked to do when he grew up. Frankie told me "I was scared to say it, but I said, 'I want to be an artist.' It was amazing that for the first time in my life, no one laughed. They even encouraged me to go to art school."

The TC truly worked for Frankie, and he went to art school. It converted a potential gang killer into an artist. I met Frankie in 1993 at a Synanon reunion. He remains drug and violence free, works as a lithographer, and has created many interesting works of art.

THE THERAPEUTIC DYNAMICS OF A TC

Frankie learned how to do his time in reformatories, prisons, jails, and addict hospitals. None of these traditional approaches worked for him. In most traditional institutions, there is a tacit assumption that if the inmates follow the rules of the institution and properly interact with the staff, they will change and become better citizens who can function more effectively in the larger society. This model does not have an effective success rate. In fact, most custodial institutions are training schools for turning out more skilled offenders.

Gangsters are programmed with a set of attitudes for handling encounters with society's custodial institutions. They learn a set of attitudes in juvenile custody and on the streets from older gangsters that are reinforced in prison. Prison officials are stereotyped by the inmate code as authority figures. For most inmates, custodial officials are hated and perceived as objects to be manipulated for quick release or illicit favors.

Frankie quickly learned in the TC that everyone was a "right guy," including the administrators, most of whom had been in his position at one time. When he tried to play his usual institutional games, he was ridiculed in group sessions. He could not hate the officials in the TC because they were people like himself.

If Frankie wanted to "break out," or go AWOL (a basic subject of conversation in most institutions), he was invited to get lost by the TC staff. At every turn he discovered new responses to old situations and, most important, other people who knew how he felt and understood him. Instead of receiving a callous reaction, he was told, "I remember how I felt when I first got here," and this was often followed by a detailed description of the precise feelings he was experiencing at the time.

TCs are often disconcerting for TC newcomers with an institutional past because it is a new and strange situation. Yet, at the same time, the sight of others like themselves who made it gives them confidence. They have role models, people they can emulate. In a TC they find a new society. They encounter understanding and affection from people who have had life experiences similar to their own. They find a community with which they can identify, people toward whom they can express their best human emotions rather than their worst. They find understanding friends who will assist them when they begin to deviate or fall short of what they have set out to do, to develop and mature. In the new society of the TC, they find a vehicle for expressing their best human qualities and their potential.

The concepts of caste and stratification are two sociological concepts that help delineate the differences between a TC and most traditional treatment institutions. An inmate or patient subculture develops within most custodial institutions, producing a we-they attitude between the professional administration and the inmates. The underground inmate society has norms, patterns of behavior, and goals different from and often in conflict with those of the overall institution. Inmates and the official staff are divided into two segregated strata. Inmates can be viewed as a caste of "untouchables," restricted to an inferior power position in the hierarchy in the institution; there is no possibility of their moving up.

It is conceded by most administrators that this inmate-administration conflict situation contradicts and impedes therapeutic progress for the inmate. This is especially true in a custodial institution or prison. The inmate subsystem helps the patients or inmates cope with the new set of problems that they find in most institutions. They feel rejected by the larger society and try to compensate for this rejection. One way they do this is to reject and rebel against the administrators of society's rejection — the institutional staff, who are the upper class of people in the institution.

A true TC does not have a we-they caste system. It provides an open-ended stratification situation. Upward mobility is possible in the organization, and status seeking in the system is encouraged. The most macho, violent gangster in a TC has the possibility of moving up the ladder to a paying staff position. Another factor in a TC that helps to raise self-esteem is that members are not identified as inmates, wards, prisoners, or patients — they are residents. The resident can identify with the constructive goals of the organization for which he works. He automatically becomes an employee in the TC organization, at first on a menial level, and, later on, is encouraged to take part in the TC's management and development.

In traditional institutions most inmates or patients tend to feel helpless, dependent, and hopeless about their destinies in the institution and the society. They have limited power in the institution since it is run by administrators who are usually indifferent to the inmates' or patients' opinions about its management. Moreover, as I have noted, the institution's administrators are seen as representatives of society's rejection of the inmates, and this sets up additional barriers to progressing in the institution. Inmates have a clear authority object for their frustrations and hatreds — the staff. In a TC there is no such split since the administration consists of coworkers and colleagues. There is no "they" to rebel against within the organization.

Involvement in a TC helps to foster empathy in a person whose basic problem is alienation from society. Identification with the TC involves feelings of caring and concern for the other members and for the destiny of the total organization. The development of these empathic qualities reverses the person's past, often sociopathic lack of social concern and has a real impact on positive personality change. Vital to this personality change are various group processes, such as the encounter group, the resident's sponsor, and his caring circle of friends.

Group sessions in the TC are more closely related to the real-life interpersonal and work problems that confront the members. Given the lack of caste division, lines of communication are open throughout the organization. This, plus a goldfish-bowl atmosphere, support a more extensive examination of a resident's deeper, underlying problems. TC group sessions make intense efforts to surface all possible data about a member since this is vital to the protection and growth of both the person and the TC organization. Since all TC members work for the organization, many real on-the-job problems are funneled into the TC's group psychotherapy. All of these factors give a TC's group process a reality not found in the closed-off social systems of most traditional institutions.

There have been attempts at self-government in prisons and mental hospitals. In these settings, however, the inmates recognize that final decisions on important policy matters remain with the administration. In a TC, perhaps for the first time in their lives, the members assume a significant role in controlling their future, and they have a degree of power in their new family and community. Leadership in a constructive situation is a new experience for them, and it appears to develop personal responsibility and a sense of independence in TC residents.

Because there is a generally held belief by the residents that the TC saved their lives, the camaraderie in the organization is quite powerful. Few inmates would give three cheers for a hospital or a prison, but residents in a TC enjoy praising the organization that saved their lives and are involved with the growth and development of their organization.

In summary, the following elements reflect the significant difference between the social structure and dynamics of TCs and traditional correctional institutions:

1. There is a difference between indoctrination in a TC and in other settings. The agreement for therapy and the prospect's expectations of

success are different. That the prospect is indoctrinated by people who have themselves been in the newcomer's shoes and have succeeded appears to be a significant element, providing the newcomer with a role model. Also, the indoctrinator sees where he or she was upon looking at the newcomer, and this is valuable for reinforcing personal growth.

2. TCs provide the possibility of upward mobility, whereas most institutions are caste systems. Becoming a TC member provides incentive to change one's negative attitudes to an anticriminal motivation. The TC resident can, with the proper attitude and behavior, achieve any role in the organization. In contrast, in the custodial institution, an inmate or patient is locked into a dependent position.

3. There is a qualitative difference between the TC and the form of group therapy carried on in prisons and hospitals. This is partly a function of the described differences in the overall social-system context. The TC resident, as a voluntary participant, has little to gain by faking progress, whereas in other institutions, the appearance of being rehabilitated may be rewarded by an earlier release from custody. The TC person is encouraged to reveal and deal with problems honestly by others who have traveled the TC-established route to recovery and independence.

4. The work assigned in a TC is real work, unlike the often contrived jobs in prisons and mental hospitals. All work serves the immediate needs of the organization. This includes the functions of the food preparers, office staff, maintenance and service crews, automotive crews, and coordinating staff. Everyone in a TC is employed in meaningful work, which gives them a greater sense of belonging to the TC, of being perhaps for the first time in their lives, self-supporting.

5. The TC subculture is integrated into the larger societal structure in a way that traditional institutions seldom are. The flow of members of the community through a TC and the participation of TC members in the larger society place it closer to real-life situations than the artificial communities of traditional institutions.

Frankie's transformation from gangster to artist through the TC approach left on me a deep impression of the TC's value in treating gangsters. This viewpoint was made clearer to me as the result of a specific event that occurred in the process of researching this gang book in a Beaumont, Texas, prison. The prison, overall, housed several thousand convicts. The prison population was comprised of all types of offenders doing time for various crimes, including homicide, rape, drugs, robbery, burglary, theft, assault, and gang murders.

I made a number of research visits to a special unit in the center of the prison that housed 400 inmates involved in a TC program for prisoners. The project was directed by thirty-five ex-criminals/addicts, including several former gangsters, who had been rehabilitated and trained in the Amity Therapeutic Community in Tucson, Arizona. The Beaumont TC prison project was modeled after a successful TC prison program that Amity ran for the California Department of Corrections at their Donavan Prison in San Diego.

As previously indicated, the two Amity people who assisted me with my gang research at the prison were Sheila, a former addict who had been clean for over ten years, the director of the prison program, and Ed, the former OG Crip whose case history appears in chapter 4. Ed at this time had been free of drugs and violence for over five years as a result of his treatment in the Amity TC and was now a paid therapist in the Amity prison program.

During my research tour at the prison, after I had been involved in several special gang focus groups and interviewed several gangsters individually, Sheila and Ed received permission for me to visit a special maximum security unit that housed the most difficult, recalcitrant, and violent gangsters in the institution. These gangsters were placed in this special unit because they were a disruptive violent force in the general prison population. Many of these individuals were responsible for murders in and out of prison.

The unit was supervised by three guards, who had a sort of catbird seat so that they could maintain high twenty-four-hour security within the cellblock. The cells were built for solitary confinement, with a small slit for observation and sliding the prisoner's food tray into their cagelike cells. In the center of these cells was a large cell (approximately twenty feet-by-twenty feet) with bars from the floor to the ceiling that was sometimes used for visitors.

I had seen the film *The Silence of The Lambs* and recalled the prison scenes where Jody Foster, as an FBI agent, had interviewed the frightening, cannibalistic criminal Hannibal Lecter, played by Anthony Hopkins. My inner thoughts when watching this scene in the movie, based on my visits to many prisons, was that Hollywood had really gone overboard here. I had never seen a cell like the one in the movie, nor any sociopathic killer who acted as sinister and outrageous as Hannibal Lecter. In the Beaumont prison I was surprised to see this horrendous movie scene replicated — with me in the Jodie Foster role!

Accompanied by Sheila and Ed I entered the big cell to sit down and talk with one of the inmates released from his solitary cell to talk to us. The inmate, Jesus, was about thirty years old. I later learned that he had murdered several people. The part of his criminal background that was especially shocking to me was the fact that he had killed his father. He murdered his father as the result of a gang conflict, in part because his father had moved out of Jesus's gang territory and joined a rival gang.

He was, in my view, an awesome sociopath. He was stripped to the waist, possibly for security purposes so that the guards could see that he was not secreting any weapons. His body was covered with grotesque tattoos of snakes. One prominent tattoo stood out from the rest, a large TS on his upper arm signifying that he was a member of the violent and notorious Texas Syndicate, the counterpart of California's infamous Mexican-Mafia prison gang.

Sheila and Ed had met Jesus before, and they introduced me as someone who was writing a book on gangs. He was not impressed, nor did he say anything in response to my questions that was noteworthy. In response to one question related to the fact that he was serving a life sentence, I asked him if he had any regrets and what advice he would give to a young kid who wanted to join a gang. With a kind of snarling sneer, he belligerently said, "Hey man, that's the kid's decision, ain't it! I'm doing okay right where I am." This response clearly told me he was not going to reveal any useful information.

Despite the fact that Jesus had clammed up, the situation was for me a momentous and revealing experience. Sitting at my left was Ed, whose background and behavior for many years was no different than Jesus's violent commitment to his gang . Yet here he was now, an open, amiable, reasonable, and positive person who was dedicated to treating a significant and difficult crime problem. Sitting across from me was Jesus, a virulent example of the horrendous gang problem we were trying to treat.

It was necessary to keep Jesus in prison for the purpose of preventing his violent proclivities. It was also clear, however, that his sociopathic-homicidal attitude was going to intensify and become more brutal by his life sentence in prison.

Although for several decades I had touted the positive value of the concept of the therapeutic community for controlling and treating criminals and the violent gang problem, and although I knew of many core gang members who had been positively changed by their TC experience, somehow it all came together for me that day when I was in that cellblock with

Ed and Jesus. The significant difference between these two individuals was that Ed had been resocialized in a TC program and that Jesus's treatment in a standard punitive prison was a brutalizing form of cold storage. It drove home to me the point that many hard-core former gangsters like Ed, if effectively treated in a TC, can become a vital therapeutic force in ameliorating the American gang problem.

ED'S TRANSFORMATION: FROM GANGSTER TO THERAPIST

Ed's extensive criminal, gangster, and prison experience has already been detailed. Ed is representative of several hundred gangsters I have interviewed over the years who benefited personally from the TC approach and have chosen to become paraprofessional gang workers in TCs in the community and in prison programs.

After working alongside Ed in a number of gang focus groups and being enormously impressed by his technique in eliciting insightful responses from many youths in the group, I asked him to attempt to delineate the therapeutic process that worked for him in Amity. Following is a report of our lengthy session on his resocialization process in the Amity TC.

ED: I will try to describe for you how I feel the Amity Program turned my life around and gave me another viewpoint on how to live my life in a better way. Let me go back in time a little to explain how I wound up in Amity in the first place.

When I got out of Soledad prison in 1989, I found that some of my Crip homeboys were making a lot of money selling drugs. So to help me out, they gave me a little money and some crack to sell to get me started. I was no good as a dealer, and I began to use the shit myself. Of course, I got all strung out and was useless to my homies in the drug business. Pretty soon I had burned all my OG homies, and they didn't want to help me anymore, or really have anything to do with me. I needed money for my habit.

I always was good at armed robbery, and jewelry stores was my specialty. I joined up with this crew from the Crips, and we started to hit jewelry stores around the Southwest — like Albuquerque, Phoenix, and Tucson. I brought one of my young homeboys, Bootsy, who was sixteen, along with us in our work. In this one robbery in Tucson, everything went wrong. Bootsy was killed by one of the crew. The guy who killed Bootsy felt it was necessary because during the robbery Bootsy panicked and ran out on us and this put us in danger.

After this robbery we all headed back to California, and one of the crew got stopped in Arizona in this van we used in the robberies. They got fingerprints off the van, and this one guy told on me and everyone else. They found four of us, and we were all busted and wound up in jail in Tucson. We were charged with first-degree murder for Bootsy's killing and armed robbery. I liked Bootsy, and I had nothing to do with his murder, but being with the guys in the robbery, all four of us were charged with murder.

They had no evidence to prove that I was involved with the murder, so they dropped that charge but held me in jail for some robberies. I pleaded guilty to robbery because my fingerprints were on some of the stolen property. I was sentenced to a two- to five-year sentence and was waiting in jail to be sent to the Arizona State Prison.

At that time I had already been in jail for a year. I was thirty-five years old, and for some reason, I began to think about my life. Before they dropped the first-degree-murder charge, they were talking about me getting the gas chamber. That scared the shit out of me!

I figured if I kept doing what I was doing, I would spend the rest of my life in prison or be dead. I had heard about the Amity Program, and I knew the judge on my case liked that program. That year I spent in jail in Arizona, I was checking out Amity. So I wrote the judge a long letter telling him that prison had never helped me change, I wanted to do something about my life, and I felt that I could get the help I needed in the Amity TC Program. The judge went for it, and I was sent to Amity.

My whole purpose at that time was to get off of drugs, find out why I used drugs, and stay out of prison. I mainly wanted to learn how to stay off drugs so I could go back to sell drugs without using and make some money. I also had a secret that I'll tell you now. I never wanted my little homie Bootsy killed, and I was planning to get the motherfucker who killed him when I got out of Amity. So when I entered Amity, I wasn't being completely honest about my intentions.

The judge in Tucson cut me loose with an agreement that I would enter Amity and stay there for at least eighteen months. When I first arrived at Amity I was scared, so I didn't do much talking in any of the groups. The level of honesty with the way these people talked in groups about their problems and feelings really fucked me up emotionally. When someone talked about dope or things that had happened to them or their loved ones, I would break down and start crying.

I remember this one woman, Alice, who had been a crackhead, talkin' about how her son had been killed in gang activity, and I began crying like a baby. Another guy, Ron, had a son who was killed in a gang. I didn't say much in groups, but a side of me that I really didn't know was there began to open up in these honest groups. And whenever I saw Alice anywhere on the property, I would break down and cry. I felt real guilty about her kids being killed in gang activity. It was crazy, but I felt guilty and responsible.

Whatever was going on with me, I felt it was something I needed to do. I knew something good was happening to me, but I hated it, too, because it was so foreign to me to act like that. I hadn't cried about anything in years. That experience of their honesty opened me up. Then I began to share in the groups about who I am and things that I did that I was ashamed of for the first time in my life. It made me feel better to get some of this shit out in the open.

The first thing I began to share was out of anger. I was talking a lot of bullshit at first and holding back. Finally I opened up about my plan to kill the motherfucker who murdered my little homeboy. So, at first, I was talking mainly about revenge on the guy that killed Bootsy. One of the things I began to see in the group where I was blaming this guy was that I began to see my own responsibility in my homie's death. I began to feel guilty because I brought him along on the robberies, and I felt responsible for his being killed. When I became honest enough on this thing with my homie to tell on myself to the people in Amity, I realized, motherfucker, you have changed!

Their opinion on my plans for revenge was, 'you are a crazy motherfucker to be thinking like that.' Their opinion was the opposite of what I felt was necessary revenge for the death of my homeboy.

LY: So your conflict was about the rules of the gang versus a more rational opinion by the people in Amity. They saw your necessity for revenge as holding on to the values of the gang in contrast with your really becoming involved with the rules and norms of society.

ED: That's right, they believed that what I wanted to do as a gangster was really crazy behavior, and I had to figure all of this out. It was really the first time anyone told me that my way of thinking wasn't right. Other people — my mother, at school, cops, judges, and all — had told me what was right, but these people at Amity were like me, and I listened to them.

After that experience, where I decided that killing that cat was crazy, I accepted a wider circle of friends in Amity. I still had trouble talking in groups, but I found one guy from New York, Jimmy T., who had been clean over ten years in Amity. I trusted him and felt I could talk to him about anything. And he helped me a lot to get my crazy gangster thinking of the need for revenge straightened out.

I felt bad that I had done a lot of violence in the past and killed some people. I was afraid of getting convicted on some old beefs, and things like that. So I learned to not identify times and places. So many things I had done in gangs began to come out, both to some trusted guys and I also began to become more honest in the groups. When I began to dump this old shit, I felt like a burden was lifted off of my shoulders.

My changes didn't come easy. (*Give me an example of a turning point in your life in Amity.*) In a retreat, that's like a forty-eight-hour series of groups that opens you up, they showed this movie, *The Boys in the Hood*. This retreat happened before I unloaded my insane secret of revenge and my plan to kill this cat who had murdered my homeboy. The movie was shown to kick off some group discussion. After the movie, people were asking questions and giving opinions on gangs. What they were saying about gangs upset the shit out of me. Rod, the group leader, saw I was agitated, and he asked me if I had something to say. I went stark raving crazy. I said, "Yeah, motherfucker, I got something to say. You all motherfuckers saw this movie and now you're going to be an expert on my hood, my people, and my gang." I cussed and I threatened people for their forming all these wrong opinions on where I come from. It drove me up the wall because they didn't know what the fuck they were talking about, and I resented all of their bullshit opinions. What made me so mad, at that time, was that they saw this one movie and thought that gangbanging was insane behavior.

When I think back to the showing of *Boys in the Hood* and my crazy explosion, I would analyze it this way: I felt that was me up there on the screen, and they were talking about me personally. And when they said that gang violence and murders was crazy, they were saying that I was crazy. I felt at that time that I was still affiliated with my homeboys. I now realize that at that time I was defending my gang insanity. In other words I now see that what they said about gangbanging and all that shit was right. It was kind of a turning point for me to give up some of my old crazy gang ideas, join the Amity community, and learn how to express myself in a more sensible way of life.

When I talked honestly about my past, people would be touched and would hug me and tell me they loved me. I thought they were crazy. In my past the only love I would get from my homeboys or anyone is if I did something violent for them, or they might like me out of fear. In Amity I found people who liked me for myself. And the more honest I became, the more I felt I deserved to be loved.

LY: Correct me if I'm wrong: the more honest and open you became the more you began to feel that you could relate to more people and help someone else.

ED: Exactly, I can't take anyone, like some of the younger dudes in Amity, anywhere that I wasn't willing to go myself. I learned in Amity that in order for anyone to be honest with me, I had to be honest with them. I began to feel I could help some of the younger gang kids in Amity get their act together for a better way of life."

Ed has been gang, drug, and crime free as a result of the positive social-psychological impact of the Amity TC program for over five years, and he has become an effective paraprofessional in TC prison groups and working with gangs. Based on my extensive research into TCs, I have concluded that former criminals like Ed are uniquely qualified to become effective peer therapists for three important reasons:

1. They have been through the throes and conflicts of their original problems. They know many of the rationalizations and self-deceptions that keep a person on the criminal merry-go-round: from the streets, to jail, to prison, and back. They comprehend on a deep, emotional level from their own experience what a criminal life is like. They have been there themselves.
2. They have gone through the complex resocialization process of personal change in a TC program. They know, on a firsthand basis, the painful emotional crises and traumas of confronting their own lives more directly. They have experienced the various phases of reorganizing their relationships with their families and friends. They have developed valuable coping mechanisms for dealing with the temptations of sliding back into their former existence and for breaking off relationships with former partners in crime. They have learned how to stay away from crime, drugs, and gangs and are succeeding as responsible citizens.
3. As a result of these two sets of experiences, a past life as a criminal and firsthand knowledge about the recovery process, former offenders have usually developed some special insights and skills. They are not easily outmaneuvered or conned. They quickly acquire the respect of their "clients" because they can see through the rationalizations and ploys that they once used themselves. The result is a communication that has more therapeutic power than that usually achieved by more traditional professional therapy. These paraprofessionals also know from their day-to-day experiences the self-discipline required to continue to lead a crime-free life.

In this context, paraprofessionals like Ed have clearly acquired the necessary experience for becoming a paraprofessional peer therapist: (1) He has had the street and prison "educational" background necessary for understanding the causal context of gang behavior on a personal level; (2) he has some surface and deep insight into the personal behavioral modification processes in a TC program that changed his behavior into a law-abiding member of society; and (3) for several years, he has stayed drug and crime free and functioned in a paraprofessional role, helping young delinquents change their behavior.

In 1996, Ed became a detached gang worker in a paid job in a Beaumont,

Texas, project. Ironically, one of the gangs Ed was assigned to worked with in Beaumont called themselves the Hoover Crips, despite the fact that they have no L.A. connection.

Based on my observations of the effectiveness of TCs for gangsters like Ed, Frankie, and many others, in chapter 10 I will detail a projected plan for treating gangsters utilizing the TC methodology.

PART FOUR

GANG THEORIES & TREATMENT

8.

Varied Theoretical Viewpoints

o o o o o o o o o o

A NUMBER OF SIGNIFICANT sociological and social-psychological theoretical and research efforts have contributed to the understanding of the structure and function of gangs, and many of them have been woven into the context of the book. It is useful to summarize these relevant theories for scholars and others interested in gang theories. Also, these theoretical perspectives serve as a prelude to the presentation of my own theory of the violent gang as a near-group in the following chapter.

ALBERT COHEN

In his book *Delinquent Boys*, Cohen views the gang as a subculture with a value system different from the dominant ones found in the inclusive American culture.[1] Working-class children, according to Cohen, use the delinquent subculture (the gang) as a mode of reaction and adjustment to a dominant middle-class society that indirectly discriminates against them because of their lower-class position.

The thesis developed by Cohen is that working-class youths, trained in a different value system, are not adequately socialized to fulfill the status requirements of middle-class society. Despite this differential socialization and subculture value condition, they are unfairly exposed to the middle-class aspirations and judgments they cannot fulfill. This conflict produces in the working-class youth what Cohen has termed "status frustration."

In a "reaction-formation" to this problem, these youths use the gang as a means of adjustment. In the gang such youths act out their status frustrations in "nonutilitarian, malicious, negativistic" forms of delinquency, which according to Cohen, represent their way of reacting against the described status dislocation of the social system.

Cohen provides illustrations of the working-class boys' difficulties in such middle-class-dominated settings as the school and community center. Here the working-class youth finds himself exposed to generally middle-class agents of the society (for example, teachers and social workers). Their efforts to impose such middle-class rules as orderliness, cleanliness, responsibility, and the virtues of ambition on him are met with sharp negativism.

Cohen specifically presents nine cases of middle-class values that are rejected by the working-class child. These are (1) ambition is a virtue; (2) an emphasis on the middle-class ethic of responsibility; (3) a high value on the cultivation of skills and tangible achievement; (4) postponement of immediate satisfactions and self-indulgence in the interest of achieving long-term goals; (5) rationality, in the sense of forethought, planning, and budgeting of time; (6) the rational cultivation of manners, courtesy, and personality; (7) the need to control physical aggression and violence; (8) the need for wholesome recreation; and (9) respect for property and its proper care.[2]

Cohen contends the lower-class child in a reaction-formation to these unfair impositions substitutes norms that reverse those of the larger society. He states, "the delinquent subculture takes its norms from the larger subculture, but turns them upside down. The delinquent's conduct is right by the standards of his subculture precisely because it is wrong by the norms of larger culture."[3]

The dominant theme of the delinquent subculture is the explicit and wholesale repudiation of middle-class standards and the adoption of their very antithesis. In this negative polarity of just for the hell of it vandalism and violence, working-class youths attempt to adjust their status frustration and hostility toward the larger society's unfair imposition of middle-class values on them. The gang is implicitly defined by Cohen as a cohesive collection of working-class youths pursuing their delinquent activities in consort with one another. The individual delinquent is, according to Cohen, more "the exception rather than the rule."

Cohen's position on the gang's relation to the community and the family parallels the conceptions of the earlier Chicago School. According to Cohen,

> Relations with gang members tend to be intensely solidary and imperious. Relations with other groups tend to be indifferent, hostile or rebellious. Gang members are unusually resistant to the efforts of home, school and other agencies to regulate, not only their delinquent activities, but any activities carried on within the group, and to efforts to compete with the gang for the time and other resources of its members.[4]

In summary, the delinquent subculture described by Cohen represents a collective effort on the part of the youths to resolve adjustment problems produced by dislocations in the larger society. In the gang the norms of the larger society are reversed so that nonutilitarian deviant behavior (especially violence) becomes a legitimized activity. The gang thus provides a legitimate "opportunity structure" for working-class boys to strike back at a larger society that produces their status-frustration problems.

HERBERT BLOCH AND ARTHUR NIEDERHOFFER

In their book *The Gang,* Bloch and Niederhoffer, somewhat differently than Cohen, analyze gang behavior as that of a universal and normal adolescent striving for adult status.[5] They assert that the gang pattern may be found, if looked for, in all cultures as a vehicle for achieving manhood. The pattern is more pronounced in cultures where youths are normally cut off from the possibility of manhood for a prolonged period.

They reach their hypothesis about gangs by the utilization of considerable cross-cultural material that attempts to reveal the differences and similarities of the adolescent condition in a variety of societies. Their basic position is presented in the following concise statement:

> The adolescent period in all cultures, visualized as a phase of striving for the attainment of adult status, produces experiences which are much the same for all youths, and certain common dynamisms for expressing reaction to such subjectively held experience. The intensity of the adolescent experience and the vehemence of external expression depend on a variety of factors, including the general societal attitudes towards adolescence, the duration of the adolescent period itself, and the degree to which the

society tends to facilitate entrance into adult hood by virtue of institution-alized patterns, ceremonials, rites and rituals, and socially supported emotional and intellectual preparation.[6]

Bloch and Niederhoffer assert that when societies do not make adequate preparation, formal or otherwise, for the induction of its adolescents into adult status, the youths will make their own culture for this transition, and they assert that the gang is this social form. They believe the gang structure in American society apparently satisfies deep-seated needs experienced by adolescents in all cultures.

In their analysis they attempt to assess anthropological data on adolescent cross-cultural behavior attached to such cultural patterns as "puberty rites," "self-decoration," and "circumcision." An emphasis is placed on relating the "rites" of other cultures to American adolescent "rites in the gang." Attention is focused on symbolic evidence of the "urge for manhood." The gang and its machinations are viewed by Bloch and Niederhoffer as a vehicle for accomplishing the assumed highly desired status objective of manhood.

Using data about adolescents from such diverse groups as the Mundugu-mor, the Manus, the Kaffir children of South Africa, the Comanche and Plains Indians, and a tightly knit delinquent New York gang, Bloch and Niederhoffer attempt to draw the inference that the "ganging process" provides symbolic evidence of the urge to manhood. At the end of their analyses they conclude the following: (1) Adolescent gangs may be profitably studied by using as a frame of reference the theory of power. (2) The gang's attempt to gain status and power through the domination and manipulation of persons and events is a collective representation of the individual gang member's guiding fiction, which is "to prove he is a man." (3) The presence of the gang — real, constructive, or symbolic — gives the individual member ego support and courage. He gains a psychological sense of power and manhood, which he does not possess at all when he is on his own.[7]

With regard to the "urge for manhood" and power, Bloch and Niederhoffer assert a point that is related to contemporary gangs. The problem, however, is today's gangs have distorted the concept of "manhood." The Wannabee's perspective on manhood as a gangster is earning money by any means necessary, using violence to settle disputes, perceiving women as objects and ornaments, and strutting this status in a violent manner. In brief, manhood in contemporary gangs involves the macho-syndrome, which in some distorted way is the gangster's approach to striving for manhood.

WALTER B. MILLER

Miller, in an article "Lower Class Culture as a Generating Milieu of Gang Delinquency," uses cultural concepts in a somewhat different fashion than Bloch and Niederhoffer.[8] He projects a lower-class adolescent theory of gangs. He maintains (in a fashion somewhat similar to Cohen's position) that the values of lower-class culture produce deviance because they are "naturally" in discord with middle-class values. The youth who heavily conforms to lower-class values is thus automatically delinquent.

Miller lists a set of characteristics of lower-class culture that tend to foster delinquent behavior. These include: (1) Trouble. Miller asserts that concern over trouble is a dominant feature of lower-class culture. He defines "trouble" as a situation or a kind of behavior that results in unwelcome or complicating involvement with official authorities or agencies of middle-class society. For men, trouble frequently involves fighting or sexual adventures. (2) Toughness. According to Miller the concept of "toughness" in lower-class culture represents a compound combination of qualities or states. Among its most important components are physical prowess, evidenced both by demonstrated possession of strength and endurance and athletic skill; masculinity, symbolized by a complex of acts and avoidance (tattooing, absence of sentimentality, nonconcern with art or literature, conceptualization of women as conquest objects, and so forth); and bravery in the face of physical threat. (Miller's view of toughness corresponds to my concept of the macho-syndrome.) (3) Smartness. This, according to Miller, involves the capacity to outsmart (outfox, outwit, dupe, "take," con) another or others and the concomitant capacity to avoid being outsmarted oneself. In its essence, smartness involves the capacity to achieve a valued entity — material goods, personal status — through a maximum use of mental agility and a minimum of physical effort. (4) Excitement. Miller states that for many lower-class individuals the rhythm of life fluctuates between periods of relatively routine or repetitive activity and sought situations of great emotional stimulation. Many of the most characteristic features of lower-class life are related to the search for excitement or "thrill." Involved here are the widespread use of gambling of all kinds. (My notion of existential validation tends to correspond to Miller's view of excitement.)[9]

Miller, like Bloch and Niederhoffer, suggests that gang activity is, in part, a striving to prove masculinity. In this context, females are exploited by gangsters in the "normal" process of relating. They are, as he specifies, "conquest objects" utilized to prove and boost the masculinity of the street-corner male.

Miller's emphasis is placed on the fact that lower-class youths who are confronted with the largest gap between aspirations and possibilities for achievements are most delinquency-prone. Such youths, according to Miller, are apt to utilize heavily the normal range of lower-class delinquent patterns of "toughness, shrewdness, cunning, and other devices in an effort to achieve prestige and status . . . toughness, physical prowess, skill, fearlessness, bravery, ability to con people, gaining money by wits, shrewdness, adroitness, smart repartee, seeking and finding thrills, risk, danger, freedom from external constraint, and freedom from superordinate authority." [10] From my perspective the WB's efforts to achieve status in the gang and become a G is reflected in Miller's viewpoint.

RICHARD CLOWARD AND LLOYD OHLIN

In their book *Delinquency and Opportunity*, Cloward and Ohlin present an in-depth analysis of the lack of fit between American success goals and the lack of means provided for the achievement of these goals by lower socioeconomic groups in American society. The central explanation presented by Cloward and Ohlin for the emergence of gangs is derived from the "goals, norms, and anomie" theories of Durkheim and Merton. Their basic view is "that pressures toward the formation of delinquent subcultures originate in marked discrepancies between culturally induced aspirations among lower-class youth and the possibilities of achieving them by legitimate means." [11]

The relation of their thesis to youths striving for cultural goals is heavily based on Emile Durkheim's original theory of anomie, later developed by Robert Merton. Durkheim in describing two categories of need, physical and social, makes the point that physical needs are satiable, whereas social gratification is "an insatiable and bottomless abyss." Given this condition, Cloward and Ohlin state that when men's goals become unlimited, the "norms no longer control men's actions and a state of 'normlessness,' or anomie, exists." Building on the theoretical base of anomie, they cogently assert the core of their theory in the following statement:

> The ideology of common success-goals and equal opportunity may become an empty myth for those who find themselves cut off from legitimate

pathways upward. We may predict, then, that the pressure to engage in deviant behavior will be greatest in the lower levels of the society. Our hypothesis can be summarized as follows: The disparity between what lower-class youth are led to want and what is actually available to them is the source of a major problem of adjustment. Adolescents who form delinquent subcultures, we suggest, have internalized an emphasis upon conventional goals. Faced with limitations on legitimate avenues of access to these goals, and unable to revise their aspirations downward, they experience intense frustrations; the exploration of nonconformist alternatives may be the result.[12]

Cloward and Ohlin attempt to account for gangs as an alternative road to social "success-goals." Alienated youths band together in the collectivity of the gang in an effort to resolve mutually shared problems.

Cloward and Ohlin posit that there are three types of delinquent gang norms and activities: violence, theft, and drug use. Each of these dominant themes, they contend, provides the focal concern of three basic gang types: conflict gangs, criminal gangs, and retreatist gang drug users.

This delineation refers essentially to a kind of ideal type. Cloward and Ohlin recognize that "the extent to which the norms of the delinquent subculture control behavior will vary from one member to another." Because of this, their descriptions are stated in terms of the "fully indoctrinated member rather than the average member."[13]

The criminal gang is devoted to theft, extortion, and other illegal means of securing an income; in the conflict gang, participation in acts of violence becomes an important means of securing status; in the retreatist gang, the most enigmatic group, the consumption of drugs is stressed and addiction is prevalent.[14]

Although there is considerable merit in Cloward and Ohlin's conceptualizations of gangs, especially in their analysis of anomie and opportunity structures, their delineation of three types of gangs is no longer accurate for the analysis of contemporary gangs.

One major flaw in the Cloward and Ohlin model with regard to today's gangs is related to their "retreatist subculture." Most contemporary gangsters use alcohol and smoke marijuana; however, the gangster who gets too involved with today's drugs, especially crack-cocaine or heroin, becomes a gang dropout. The gangster who becomes addicted gets on the drug-seeking treadmill and becomes unreliable as a gangster. His primary aim in life is to get high, and he gets the money necessary to get high by any means necessary. His concern with anyone else is simply as a mark, a victim to be conned or cheated, or possibly as a criminal accomplice in a "quick score" of money for acquiring drugs. The flux of the addict's life condition provides no stability for any group formation, even one with very limited cohesion. Drug addicts, as social isolates, may be in some physical proximity to each other, but their lack of ability to relate even minimally makes a social group unlikely. The retreatist subculture can thus not be rationally regarded as a category of gang on the contemporary gang scene.

My viewpoint is, as previously delineated, that contemporary violent-drug collectivities are multipurpose gangs. And in this genre, black and Chicano gangs encompass many deviant opportunity subgroups for gangster WBs, Gs, and OGs. In the modern gang you can, under the same gang banner, be a violent gangbanger, operate as a thieving delinquent, or use and participate in the commerce of drugs.

James F. Short, Jr., and Fred Strodbeck

Short and Strodbeck, together and individually, carried out a series of gang studies in Chicago over a number of years and wrote a series of articles, including "Youth Gangs and Society," that contribute enormously to our understanding of gang behavior.[15]

Among the conclusions of their varied studies is the assertion that aleatory (or chance) elements play a considerable part in gang behavior. According to Short and Strodbeck gang activities, whether for fun or profit, usually involve a degree of risk. Most of the time these activities are engaged in without serious consequences, but sometimes something happens and the outcome is calamitous. They discuss the implication of these aleatory risks in the following statement:

> Our use of the term aleatory does not restrict it to events which are independent of the actions of the persons involved. It was incidentally true that the events in question were not, for this stratum, punished by society. However, we now wish to go beyond this feature and direct the argument to instances of serious aggression in which the outcome is not desired either by the boys or the community, and for which serious consequence, like imprisonment, may result from the response by the larger society. We do not say that all cases of serious aggression result from action with such an aleatory element, but that, etiologically, those which do should be distinguished from cases in which serious injury is the clear intent of the actor.[16]

Short and Strodbeck adopted an approach consistent with the earlier poverty area research of Clifford Shaw and Henry McKay and the group delinquency perspective found in the theories of Cohen, Cloward and Ohlin, and Thrasher. They found that it was difficult to locate gangs that corresponded to those described in most theories. This led them to examine in greater depth the processes and values that lead to gang delinquency.

Short and Strodbeck specify five specific indices of gang activity: (1) conflict; (2) institutional social activities; (3) sexual behavior, hanging out, and selling alcohol; (4) homosexuality, fathering illegitimate children, and common-law marriages; and (5) involvement in minor, correlated crimes, conflict, and alcohol use. They observed that these behaviors were not greatly different from the more routine activities of adolescent males.[17]

In accord with my findings they determined that gangs had a shifting membership and structure, with allegiances vacillating over time. Leadership was seldom strong, and generally incapable of exacting discipline from members. Concomitantly, few strong group norms laid claims on the behavior of individual gang members. They found in Chicago gangs, as I did in L.A. gangs, that any threats to the status of the gang were particularly important and conflict often emerged from disputes about the reputation of the gang.

Barbara Tomson and Edna R. Felder

Tomson and Felder, in their book *Gangs: A Response to the Urban World*, analyze the impact of the neighborhood on gangs.[18] Their general assumption is that gang membership is a response to the difficulties of the depressed urban situation. Their research dealt with the gang member's response to the urban structure, the political structure, and the mass media. According to Tomson and Felder, "these are institutions in which they are unlikely to have formalized individual contacts . . . for youngsters who are not in touch with the larger society the gang provides a positive identity for their individual members."[19]

They summarize their viewpoint as follows:

> The urban setting in which gangs thrive reduces varied pressures: the need to deal successfully with strangers, the need to deal with a money-based economy, loneliness, and lack of privacy. The delinquent responds to these pressures by identifying with the gang, which offers him symbols of identity, activities, and helps him obtain money, companionship, and friends.

... The purpose of the political machinery is to provide services and resolve conflicts for members of the society. Delinquents assess the political situation correctly by concluding that they do not belong to society and are not wanted. They can, however, identify with and be understood by their gang.[20]

IRVING A. SPERGEL

In his first book on gangs, *Racketville, Slumtown, Haulberg,* Spergel explored three different styles of delinquency in three different lower-class areas of a large eastern city.[21] Spergel's study was based on firsthand field-study interviews and contains the verbatim responses of gang youths.

Spergel's fundamental assumptions parallel Cloward and Ohlin's theories of gangs. He asserts that delinquent subcultures are created and thrive under the impetus of socially unacceptable opportunities available to youths for achieving acceptable, culturally induced goals. He defined three major types of delinquent youth subcultures: one characterized by racket activities; another, by violent conflict; and a third, by theft. These patterns, according to Spergel, depended on the interaction of conventional and criminal opportunities. Spergel states that "drug addiction in these neighborhoods develops mainly as a variant and transitional pattern for older adolescents and young adults, many of whom have been participants in the major delinquent-youth subcultures."[22]

In a later book, *The Youth Gang Problem,* Spergel asserts that there are four basic strategies for dealing with youth gangs: (1) local community organizing and mobilization of citizens, community groups, and agencies; (2) social intervention, often outreach counseling and detached work; (3) provision of social and economic opportunities, especially jobs, training, and remedial education targeted to gang youths; (4) suppression, including both formal and informal mechanisms of control.[23]

In accordance with my viewpoint, Spergel states that the ideal plan of intervention and suppression, as well as prevention, depends on appropriate analysis of the community's gang problem and the resources available and needed to deal with it. In his approach, Spergel emphasizes the importance of police suppression and interrelating these strategies with priority strategies of community mobilization.

He specifies that violent gangs should be selected for special attention, based on shared organizational and community-group information. He asserts that gang youths should be targeted for special controls, social services, and provision of social opportunities in the following order of priority: first, leadership and core gang youths; second, high-risk gang-prone youths who give clear evidence of beginning participation in delinquent or criminal gang activities; and third, regular or peripheral members with special needs for social control and intervention through a variety of educational and socializing services.[24]

MALCOLM W. KLEIN

Klein, in his role as director of the University of Southern California Delinquency Control Institute, over several decades has carried out a large number of research projects into gang structure and behavior. His decades of research findings on gangs and the work of other notable gang researchers and theorist are incorporated in a book of edited articles, *The Modern Gang Reader.*[25]

Based on his studies of Chicanos and black gangs in Los Angeles, Klein defines gangs as

> any denotable adolescent group of youngsters who (a) are generally perceived as a distinct aggregation by others in their neighborhood, (b) recognize themselves as a denotable group (almost invariably with a group name) and (c) have been involved in a sufficient number of delinquent incidents to call forth a consistent negative response from neighborhood resident and/or enforcement agencies.[26]

Based on his varied research findings, Klein concluded that gang leadership is not a position, as many have theorized, but is rather a collection of functions. Leadership varies with the activity, such as fighting, athletics, and girls. He asserts that the gang's leaders are often difficult to pick out except by the reactions of other members, and that age is an influence in leadership.

Also, according to Klein's findings, gang boys portray a caricature of adolescence:

> They behave and react in excess, and they definitely overplay roles. Gang boys have little confidence in themselves and are insecure with respect to their own abilities and social relationships. These feelings of inadequacy often result in a dependence on the peer group and, consequently, on arrest-provoking behavior. Adolescents float together as they reject and are rejected by their community. Thus the gang is a cluster of youths held

together by their individual incapacities rather than common goals or interests. It serves a need satisfaction and leads to delinquency only secondarily.[27]

Martin Sanchez Jankowski

For his book *Islands in the Streets*, Jankowski conducted ethnographic studies of gangs over a ten-year period in New York, Boston, and Los Angeles.[28] In the process of his research, he was a participant-observer of thirty-seven randomly selected gangs representing eight different ethnic groups (including Chicano, Dominican, Puerto Rican, Central American, African American, and Irish). His work, based on "living the gang life," provides a distinctive viewpoint on gangs. He describes gang members as "defiant individualists" who possess several distinctive character traits, including competitiveness, wariness, self-reliance, social isolation, and strong survival instincts.

Jankowski perceives the gangs he studied as "formal-rational" organizations, having strong organizational structures, well-defined roles, rules that guide member activities, penalties for rule violations, an ideology, and well-defined means for generating both legal and illegal income. He observes that gangs function much like most groups and maintains that many gangs have positive relationships with people in their neighborhoods, often performing essential functions, such as looking out for the well-being of the community in which they live. In this regard, the functions include such things as protection against unscrupulous businesses as well as organized crime. He labels the links between gangs and their neighborhoods as a form of "local patriotism."[29]

In his research Jankowski has utilized, as I did, a number of gangsters to assist him in his research with their gang. He notes that they are involved with a territorial imperative that includes violence for the protection of their territory. He also perceives the gang as having a significant level of intense camaraderie that involves the recreational act of "kicking back." In this regard, he concludes that the use of almost all drugs with the exception of heroin is condoned by the gang.

He is one of the few gang researchers who has focused in on personality factors in his research. He observes that the juveniles who join gangs are those with what he terms defiant individualism. He perceives these youths as the most competitive individuals in a community, who organize and join gangs for the purpose of acquiring what he terms the scarce resources of lower socioeconomic communities. He notes that their competitive edge to win these resources accounts for gangbanging behavior. In overview, Jankowski concludes that gang behavior is often an appropriate response to the pathological conditions that exist in the inner cities of the United States.

WILLIAM B. SANDERS

Sanders' book *Gang Bangs and Drive-bys* is based on his research with gangs over a ten-year period in the San Diego area.[30] He utilized what he terms "by any means necessary research." His approach employed participant-observation and some statistical analysis. Apart from his research findings, his book effectively delineates an excellent research approach for studying and analyzing gangs. He analyzes a panorama of gang issues, including an analysis of the gang's motivation for violence, organizational characteristics, leadership factors, and territorial imperatives.

From his research base Sanders defines the gang as follows:

> A youth gang is any transpersonal group of youths that shows a willingness to use deadly violence to claim and defend territory, and attack rival gangs, extort or rob money, or engage in other criminal behavior as an activity associated with its group, and is recognized by itself and its immediate community as a distinct dangerous entity. The basic structure of gangs is one of age and gender differentiation and leadership is informal and multiple.[31]

JEROME H. SKOLNICK

Skolnick has contributed to the understanding of gang behavior in a number of articles. Notable among these is his analysis of drug gangs.[32] Based on his extensive interviews with prison inmates and police, Skolnick concludes that there are two types of gangs: "entrepreneurial gangs" and "cultural gangs." His basic premise is that as gangs become more enmeshed in the drug trade, they become less of a strictly cultural phenomenon and more of a business enterprise. This evolution, he concludes, poses a significant problem for law enforcement officials.[33]

Skolnick presents the viewpoint that the cultural gang is more likely to involve gangbanging and some social activities, and those gangsters involved in the drug trade would be more a part of what he refers to as the entrepreneurial gang. My research reveals that both the entrepreneurial drug activity and the cultural aspects of gang behavior exist within the same organization, which I refer to as the multipurpose gang.

JOHN M. HAGEDORN

Hagedorn, in his varied writings, has focused on the injection of the drug business into gangs and how this factor has affected the gang's structure and function in recent years. Based on his research into gangs in Milwaukee, he posits the concept that most adult gang members cannot be described as "committed long-term gang participants" in the drug economy. Most of the gangsters he has interviewed reveal that they have been sporadically involved in the drug trade and that they move in and out of the gang into conventional labor activities.[34]

Hagedorn develops a typology of adult gang members and identifies them in four categories. He places the four ideal types on a continuum of conventional behavior and values: (1) "Legits" are those few gangsters who have gone legitimate and matured out of the gang; (2) "Homeboys" are those gangsters, who comprise a majority of both African American and Latino adult gang members, who alternately work conventional jobs and take various roles in drug sales; (3) "Dope-fiends" are those gangsters who are addicted to cocaine and participate in the dope business as a way to maintain access to the their drugs; and (4) "New Jacks" are gangsters who regard the dope business as a career.[35] Hagedorn's last three categories include most of the types of gangsters I studied who are participants in the multipurpose gang.

GEORGE KNOX

Knox, as editor and founder of *The Journal of Gang Research,* has made a major contribution to the understanding of gangs. In the many important and diverse articles published in the journal, Knox and his colleagues in the "New Chicago School" of delinquency present a considerable amount of valuable data about gangs. Apart from his contributions to the journal, Knox has over the past decade written a number of significant articles and books on various aspects of the gang phenomenon. His book *An Introduction to Gangs* is an important contribution to the field.[36]

Notable among Knox's other publications is his book *Schools under Siege,* an extensive study of gangs in schools, written with David Laske and Edward Tromanhauser.[37] In their book the authors note that research over the past decade reveals a direct correlation between the presence of gangs in and around schools and increases in school violence. They assert that the relationship between gangs and schools hinges on several factors.

(A) Street gang members have easier access to weapons than do non-gang affiliated students and are more likely to use these weapons; (B) gangs can more easily afford to purchase weapons using the money earned from drugs; (C) historically territorial conflicts fuel gang violence because entrepreneurial street gangs involved in drug trafficking use terror to protect their sales market area; (D) the presence of street gangs in schools increases the percentage of students who carry guns. Both gang affiliated and non-affiliated students begin to carry weapons for protection; (E) the school environment brings rival gang members in close proximity to one another and blurs haphazard turf lines which leads to confrontations and challenges within schools, on school property and on the streets surrounding the schools.[38]

Schools under Siege is a relevant book for school administrators since it presents viable methods for dealing with gang violence in and around the school.

In another useful research project, Knox and a number of associates in 1995 completed a comprehensive study entitled "The Economics of Gang Life," which involved gathering information from over a thousand gang members. The premise of their research was "to understand the costs and benefits associated with gang life in America today." The research collected data in different types of social contexts, including adult and juvenile correctional facilities and community programs.[39]

Their data was collected in five states: California, Illinois, Iowa, Michigan, and Ohio. Knox and his associates determined in their study that there were differences between gangs on their level of organizational sophistication. According to their findings,

the higher level gangs were more organizationally sophisticated and appeared to have a number of formalized economic functions and capabilities. In this context they determined that most of the gangs they analyzed were fairly sophisticated, had some formalized rules, and their own argot or gang language. Their sample of gang members included both youths and adults, "but the top leaders were for the most part adults with long tenure in the gang."[40]

Although the gangs that Knox and the others researched in Chicago appear to be more organized than the gangs that I studied, they appear to have the component of being multipurpose gangs.

Summary and Conclusions

Several central themes emerge from the various notable theories and research reports that I have here reviewed. Most gang researchers share the following viewpoints:

1. gangs have a fierce involvement with their territory in their hood or barrio, and gangs will fight and gangbang to protect their turf;
2. gangsters have different levels of participation — partially based on age — and can be characterized as core or marginal participants;
3. different gangs have diverse patterns of leadership;
4. many gangs and gangsters participate intensely in the commerce and the use of various drugs; and
5. gangs are, in part, generated by their cultural milieu in a response to a society that blocks their opportunity to achieve the success-goals of the larger society.

My review of the literature reveals that gang researchers have amassed a wealth of significant data on gangs; however, as we sociologists are wont to say at the end of almost every book and article, more research is needed. At the 1995 Academy of Criminal Justice Sciences meetings in Boston, sociologists Scott Decker and Ronald Huff, based on their extensive research into the field, presented a valuable seminar and paper that attempted to summarize early and recent field studies of gangs. Notable in their presentation was data from Ronald Huff's book, *Gangs in America.*[41]

In their presentation they concluded with a number of significant and relevant suggestions for future research on gangs, which were contained in an article by Scott Decker. Decker delineates a number of issues and questions that deserve further field studies:

(1) Does gang membership precede the onset of serious criminality? (2) What affect, if any, does gang membership have on other members in the family, and conversely, what affect does the family have on gang members? (3) What is the process by which gang members leave their gang? (4) How do gangs grow in size? (5) How do gangs spread from one city to another? (6) Are there links between gangs and organized crime groups? (7) What is the genesis of inter-gang and intra-gang violence? (8) How are roles within the gang established, and how are individuals selected for those roles? (9) What role do economic factors and motivation play in the actions of gangs and gang members? (10) What is the relationship between gang members and social institutions? (11) What are the protective factors that insulate some individuals from gang membership? and (12) How does the gang change over time?[42]

The perspectives on gangs presented in this review of the literature reveal two notable areas of conflicting viewpoints on gang theory and research that require additional research and analysis. One involves the personality characteristics of youths who participate in gangs, Do gangsters manifest emotional pathologies that differ significantly from nongangster youths? A second controversial issue is the structure of gangs, Are gangs the cohesive groups perceived by some theorists or the inchoate structures that I have found in my research? My viewpoints on these two issues have been deline-ated throughout the book; however, in the following chapter, I will present some additional clarification on these two significant issues in the context of my theory of the gang as a near-group.

9.

The Violent Gang as a Near-Group

○ ○ ○ ○ ○ ○ ○ ○ ○ ○

THE DEVELOPMENT OF AN adequate theory on the violent gang requires an extensive foundation of relevant research data. The importance of such research for adequate theory building and the pitfalls of not carrying out such empirical investigation are cogently expressed by the sociologist Robert Merton: "Empirical research initiates, reformulates, refocuses, and clarifies the theories and conceptions of sociology. It is evident that any theorist who is remote from all research, of which he learns only by hearsay, runs the risk of being insulated from the very experiences most likely to turn his attention in fruitful directions."[1]

RESEARCH ISSUES IN THE DEVELOPMENT OF GANG THEORY

It is apparent from my overall analysis of the literature on gangs that there are diverse sociological and psychological viewpoints on the organization and behavior of gangs. The diversity is partly explained by the chameleon nature of gangs, by different time periods engendering different changes in gang structure and behavior, and perhaps more importantly, by the perspective of the researcher.

186

Before presenting my theory on gangs, I believe it is useful to examine some of the travails and issues involved in the process of researching gangs as they relate to defining a relevant social-psychological theory on gang structure and function.

Different researchers have studied the gang from different perspectives. Camera positions in the production of a film serve as a relevant metaphor. Some gang researchers operate in the ivory tower, from an academic distance, having no direct communication with the gangster subjects of their research. They base their theories on reports from the gang battlefront and have a long-distance viewpoint. In film parlance they are viewing the gang from a camera long shot. Other researchers perceive the gang in a close-up. Their perception is based on a study of one or two gang entities up close and personal. Somewhere in between is a two-shot. My research camera has attempted to encompass all of these perspectives, including what might be termed a long tracking shot over a time span of close to fifty years.

Differing perspectives on gangs may also be explained by the old parable of the six blind men and the elephant. After each man had inspected a part of an elephant by feeling it in a particular place, each one was asked to describe the appearance of an elephant. Of course, the man who felt the trunk described the snakelike characteristic, the man who touched the leg described it accordingly, and so on, and so on.

RESEARCH PROBLEMS AND PITFALLS

The generally suspicious violent gangster is not easily approached in his habitat on the streets of his barrio or hood. Also, most gangs tend to change over a period of time with such factors as family movement, arrests, incarcerations, police pressure, and drug involvement. These factors tend to change the personnel and structure of a gang, and this also impacts the researcher's findings. Consequently, certain types of formal sociological research are not functional for researching gangs.

The development of an effective methodological design for systematically studying gangs remains a challenging and formidable research problem. Long-distance views about gangs emanating from questionnaires that are not administered directly to gangsters, outdated research findings, or research related to delinquency in general rather than to the gang in particular are prone to lead to theoretical misconceptions.

Another issue that relates to some of the contemporary viewpoints on gangs is that too many current theoretical conceptions of gangs rely too heavily on the theories and empirical data contributed by the early Chicago School. It is apparent that there have been significant social changes in American society over the past fifty years, and these changes have altered the sociocultural causal context and the structure of gangs. The earlier methodologies of using personal documents, case materials, and direct interviews, characteristic of the Chicago School research approach, remain vibrantly valid; however, drawing conclusions about contemporary gang structures with outdated gang data can lead to erroneous theories.

The development of accurate gang theories, in the light of the foregoing research pitfalls, requires an innovative type of research that gathers a variety of documentary data about gangs through diverse methods in different settings. William Sanders, in his book *Gangbangs and Drive-bys*, refers to this type of data gathering as research by any means necessary.[2] Sanders' use of various research methods for the collection of data serves as a viable approach to studying gangs.

An appropriate model for current gang research might very well be the anthropological field-study approach, usually reserved for more "exotic" foreign cultures. In this type of research, the researcher literally moves into a barrio or hood and experiences the various social forces operating in the community. From this vantage point he or she is in the ideal position to gather the wide range of data that would prove most useful toward developing gang theory. Such data would include information about various types of gangs, leadership patterns, the meaning of membership, activity analysis, violence patterns, gang language, and gang-youth personality types. William F. Whyte lived in "Cornerville" near Boston, and Martin Sanchez Jankowski adapted this approach for his book, *Islands in the Street*.[3] I utilized this in my early gang research in New York and to some extent for this book, since I live in close proximity to the gang area of Venice, California.

In the development of my theory of gangs, I have carried out gang research with all of the approaches alluded to and two additional methods that have seldom been employed. My fundamental data on gangs is derived from traditional field research in the community, interviews with individual gangsters, and the use of an extensive written questionnaire that acquired over sixty useful responses.

In addition to these research methods, my research with gangsters in prison, in gang focus groups, in group therapy and psychodrama proved to be valuable approaches for enhancing my understanding of the phenomenon of violent gangs. In my research with gangsters in prison, I found that my gangster respondents' boredom with prison life contributed enormously to my research data. My captive audience, having nothing better to do and having plenty of time on their hands, figuratively and literally, sat for hours in individual interviews, in gang focus groups, and in therapy groups. They were much more amenable to discussing their gang organization and behavior, past and present, when they were in prison than they were on the streets.

An important facet of their willingness to cooperate with my research interests when they were in prison was related to the fact that they were already convicted and sentenced. They had a limited resistance to discussing their past violent-gang behavior in detail because their revelations would not result in any additional punishment. Of course, the murders some of my gang subjects had committed and admitted to had no statute of limitation and were discussed with a certain level of obfuscation and discretion, with an assurance on my part that I would not reveal this information.

Another relatively unique aspect of my prison gang research that led to openness and candor was the fact that most of the gangsters I studied were in a therapeutic-community treatment program that stressed the open and public discussion of their past and present personal life. My role as a group therapist and psychodramatist in the program enabled me to collect data on the participants in my groups from a more logical vantage point than simply interviewing them about their motivations and personal life. A considerable amount of relevant personal data emerged in the context of the group therapy sessions I directed. At times, after an emotional therapy session, I would follow up with a one-on-one discussion on a particularly relevant subject with an individual who had become emotionally wide-open and was highly motivated to explore a significant personal issue in his life.

In the context of my groups, as previously discussed, former rivals from different gangs were more amiable with each other. I would encourage them in the nonviolent and nonthreatening environment of a prison TC to share their past experiences with each other in an effort to better understand their violent emotions. The positive social environment of the TC enabled former deadly enemies to see each other as human beings.

In the general prison population gangsters were separated by their racial and ethnic backgrounds by choice, and this was facilitated by the prison administration. A significant impact of the TC involved the integration of around 200 Chicano, black, and a few white convicts in their cells in one cellblock. This integration enabled me in my gang focus groups to place a Crip and a Blood or a Chicano and a black in a face-to-face position and have them discuss the senseless nature of their hatred of each other as enemy gangsters.

After a heated confrontation, I would say, "Here is a guy who has many of the same problems of family and feelings about society that you have. In a way, despite the racial and enemy gang bullshit that divides you, you have essentially the same kinds of problems as human beings. Why do you hate and kill each other?" In the discussions that usually ensued, some gangsters would see the foolishness of their hatred for each other, the senseless nature of gangbanging, and reveal a great deal of personal information that was most useful in understanding their motivation for participating in gangs. These insightful dialogues produced invaluable data for my understanding the general structure and function of gangs.

As a side effect of my therapeutic efforts in these intensive group therapy and psychodrama sessions, I learned a great deal about the participant's family and the causal context of their participation in their gang on a level that was both direct and personal. The data from my therapy sessions also revealed a great deal about the meaning of the gang to the participants and about the structure and function of the gang in the gangster's life. It is from this composite and conglomeration of research data that I have collected over the years that I have developed and constructed my definition of gangs and a basic theory on the structure of violent gangs.

WHAT IS A GANG?

Sociologist Emile Durkheim exhorts the sociologist to be explicit:

> Every scientific investigation is directed toward a limited class of phenomena, included in the same definition. The first step of the sociologist, then, ought to be to define the things he treats, in order that his subject matter may be known. A theory, indeed, can be checked only if we know how to recognize the facts of which it is intended to give an account.[4]

As previously alluded to, the term "gang" has been varyingly used to describe Thrasher's gangs, the Capone-like adult gangs of the Roaring Twenties and the Mafia, Whyte's Norton Street group, Bloch and Niederhoffer's Comanche adolescent groups, Cohen's delinquent boys, Cloward and Ohlin's conflict gangs, and the contemporary Crips and Bloods.

From my perspective, as previously defined, the contemporary violent drug gang incorporates the following basic characteristics and activities:

1. All gangs have a name and a territorial neighborhood base, and they maintain a fierce proprietary interest in their neighborhood. They will

fight for the territory they claim as their own and will attack any interlopers who come into their hood who belong to an enemy gang.

2. Joining a gang often involves a form of jumping in (a ritual that ranges from informal verbal acceptance to a violent initiation rite), and leaving the gang takes many forms.
3. Delinquent and criminal acts involving burglary and theft are important gang activities for achieving a rep and status in the gang.
4. Senseless violence, including drive-by shootings and gangbanging is a basic gang activity.
5. The commerce of drugs, their use, and violent acts for the maintenance of drug territory are part of the gang configuration.
6. Gangs provide a form of social life and camaraderie, involving gambling, getting high, hanging-out, and partying.

GANG STRUCTURE: THE GANG AS A NEAR-GROUP

Many theorists, based on their research perspective, have determined that gangs are very cohesive entities. Others have depicted gangs as very loose structures. My research has led me to perceive the violent gang as somewhere in between being a highly defined group and a loosely organized mob. The gang is what I would term a "near-group."

My viewpoint of the gang as a near-group is illuminated by being more specific and defining a "group" as a sociologist would. A standard group is an identifiable, coherent, and finite entity made up of people who relate to each other on the basis of defined norms and rules for interaction. Membership in a group is clearly defined, involving some form of self-identification and recognition by other group members that the individual belongs to the group. In most groups the role of each member is clearly defined and entails certain rights, duties, and obligations. When all of these factors are clear, the members of bona fide social groups can reciprocally interact with each other in terms of the accepted norms of the group.

Social groups have defined values and the behavioral expression of these values are openly accepted in the larger society. Deviant and illegal groups whose values and behavioral enactments are considered antithetical to the values and goals of the larger society tend to be less clearly defined, partly because they operate outside of the norms and laws of the society. Because the behavior of individuals who participate in deviant groups is often illegal, the rights, duties, and obligations of their participants are apt to be less clearly defined. In brief, in most criminal and deviant groups, including the violent gang, the definition of who is a member, the norms of the group, and the expected behavior of participants in the group are murkier than in groups that are socially acceptable and for the most part conform to the acknowledged norms of the larger society.

For the purpose of a better understanding of the structure and function of violent gangs, I would posit that in terms of structure in the overall social system there are three basic types of collectivities: (1) social groups, (2) mobs or crowds, and (3) what I have termed near-groups. Social groups are coherent entities that have a clarity about their norms, and membership in this type of group is obvious to both the members and their group. At the other end of this continuum of group organization is mob or a crowd. These are spontaneous collectivities that meet sporadically for some event, have limited or no continuity, are not basically interactive, and the people who participate in this type of collectivity have no membership status or clear roles.

On a continuum, in terms of structure and behavioral function, a near-group is somewhere in between a mob or crowd and a defined social group. In a near-group the definition of membership and leadership and the norms and values of the collectivity are not as chaotic as found in a mob, and not as coherent as found in a socially acceptable group. Based on my research and perspective, the violent gang is a near-group.

The violent gang as a near-group has the following characteristics that enable a socially disabled gangster to have a sense (albeit synthetic) of belonging and community:

1. Participants in the near-group violent gang are generally sociopathic personalities. The most sociopathic are core participants or leaders, and the less sociopathic are more marginal members. These individuals belong to the near-group gang essentially because they do not have the social ability to belong to more coherent and demanding social groups.
2. The near-group gang for the socially disabled gangster serves as a socially desirable adjustment pattern that not only accepts but aggrandizes their macho-syndrome behavior.
3. The nondemanding roles that characterize the near-group violent gang structure, because they are imprecise, satisfy the emotional needs of its participants who lack the ability to become members of more socially demanding groups.
4. The behavioral expectations for participating in the gang is diffuse, and it

varies for each participant. Behavior is essentially emotion motivated within loosely defined boundaries. There is a limited consensus of normative expectations for behavior in the near-group gang.

5. In a near-group, cohesiveness decreases as a participant gangster moves from the center of the collectivity to the periphery. Core participants are at the center of the gang, and there are many marginal gangsters who sporadically participate less often and less intensely in the gang's varied activities.

6. Limited responsibility is required for belonging. Leadership is often self-appointed and varies with the activities of the gang at a particular time. There is a shifting and personally defined stratification system. Participation is often in flux, and it is difficult at any point in time to define the exact number of participants who comprise the gang.

7. There is a limited coherent and defined consensus among participants in the collectivity as to the near-group gang's functions or goals.

8. Norms and behavior patterns are generally deviant and, consequently, in conflict with the inclusive social system's prescriptions for behavior.

9. Interaction within the collectivity and toward the outer community is often hostile and aggressive, with spontaneous outbursts of violence to achieve impulsively felt goals. Violent behavior, especially extreme and bizarre violence, is a highly regarded value, and violent behavior contributes enormously to the power and status of gangsters in the near-group violent gang.

A number of researchers have corroborated my viewpoint on the gang as a near-group. Notable among these researchers is Howard and Barbara Myerhoff, who have carried out extensive empirical and theoretical research into gang structures in general and my near-group theory in particular. In their summary in an incisive article on the subject, they state,

> The sociological literature about gangs contains at least two sharply conflicting descriptions of the extent of gang structure and the nature of their values. In the most prevalent view, the gang is seen as a kind of primary group, highly structured, relatively permanent and autonomous, possessing a well-developed delinquent subculture which is transmitted to new members. . . . Cohen has identified the primary needs met by the gang as those of resolving status frustration for lower-class boys, and providing an expression of masculine identification for middle-class boys. Parsons has also emphasized the achievement of sexual identity as a problem dealt with by delinquent behavior in a gang.

Cloward and Ohlin, following Merton's conception, have specified the discrepancy between aspirations toward success goals and opportunities for achieving them as the problem giving rise to gang behavior. Kvaraceus and Miller have stressed the inherent conflict between lower- and middle-class values and the delinquent's predisposition to the former in explaining gang behavior. Eisenstadt and Bloch and Niederhoffer have pointed to the gang as a collective response to the adolescent's striving toward the attainment of adulthood and the frustrations attendant on the transition from one age status to another. These authors identify different components of the gang subculture according to their interpretation of its function, but implicit or explicit in all these positions is the view of the gang as an integrated and relatively cohesive group.

A strikingly different interpretation of the structure of gangs describes them as more informal, short-lived, secondary groups without a clear-cut, stable delinquent structure. Lewis Yablonsky has suggested a conceptualization of the gang as a "near-group," specifying the following definitive characteristics: diffuse role definitions, limited cohesion, impermanence, minimal consensus on norms, shifting membership, emotionally disturbed leaders, and limited definition of membership expectations. On a continuum of the extent of social organization, Yablonsky locates the gang midway between the mob at one end and the group at the other. . . . The supervisor of a large, long-lived detached worker program in Los Angeles, with many years of gang experience there and in Harlem, has given a description much like that of Yablonsky. He observed that delinquent gangs . . . and their antisocial activities are committed in small groups. . . . He found communication between members to be meager and sporadic, reflecting the same limitations in social abilities that Yablonsky identified.[5]

SIGNIFICANT FACTORS THAT DEFINE THE VIOLENT GANG AS A NEAR-GROUP

Many of the following observations have already been discussed in the body of the book; however, it is useful to present these characteristics in one section. The following summarizes what I consider to be the most significant characteristics that define contemporary violent gangs as near-groups.

THE EMOTIONAL CHARACTERISTICS OF GANGSTERS

The gangster's personality is formed in the depressed, deprived, and violent cultural milieu of their hood or barrio. For youngsters growing up under these onerous conditions, which often include a dysfunctional family, the gang becomes for many minority-group youths their only source of identity, status, and emotional satisfaction. Ill-trained to participate with any degree of success in the dominant middle-class world of language and norms foreign to their own, they construct their own community — the gang. In their gang they set goals that are achievable; they build an empire, part reality and part fantasy, that helps them live through the confusion from adolescence into early adulthood. All of these factors impact on their emotional characteristics.

A disproportionate number of gangsters are sociopathic, if not clearly in their basic personality, certainly in their unconscionable behavior. Their sociopathic personality is most manifest in the nature of their senseless violent behavior.

Pathological gang youths have difficulty in functioning in normal, demanding groups. The demands for performance and responsibility in the cultural context of the gang are readily adapted to the personal needs of these youths. The larger society with its foreign values and expectations is not compatible with their perception of the world. From my perspective, the interplay between the sociopathic gangster's pathological personality structure and his gang's organization is the most effective way to understand the phenomenon of contemporary violent gangs.

A primary motivation of the gangster is his continuing quest for respect, reputation, and a sense of personal power, which he feels is lacking because of his low self-esteem. The acquisition of respect and some kind of reputation, even one as a killer, is sought to nourish their underlying feelings of low self-esteem and feeling like a nobody. They put in work in their gang by committing acts of senseless violence in an effort to achieve the respect and personal power they feel is missing in their inner life. Many gangsters are willing to literally die for respect. This drive helps to explain their suicidal tendencies.

A social-psychological perspective that I have found helpful in analyzing the personality issue in a gangs youth's motivation is the concept of existential validation. This syndrome basically involves a gangster's sense of alienation from human feeling or meaning. Most relatively normal people have a sense of identity and existence in their everyday activities. They do not require intense emotional excitement to know that they are alive, that they exist. In contrast, some pathological people, including sociopathic gangsters, need extreme Dyonesion forms of emotional arousal to feel that they are alive.

Their sense of ennui and of being alienated, ahuman, and unfeeling requires increasingly heavier dosages of bizarre and extreme emotional behavior to validate the fact that they really exist. Extreme, violent behavior is one pattern that gives the sociopath a glimmer of being someone. In some respects, in this context, violence is an addiction. Many gangsters have told me that they are addicted to the emotional rush they experience in an act of bizarre and senseless violence.

BELONGING

Because of their personality problems, most participants in the violent gang cannot be clearly or fully defined as members since the values, norms, and expectations for participation in the gang are not clearly defined. If a youth lives in a particular hood or barrio, joining and belonging to most violent gangs is a relatively easy process. Membership has a quality of vagueness.

The ritual of being formally jumped-in to join a gang is often a myth presented by gangsters to demonstrate that their gangs are more defined than they really are. There are no high standards for entrance placed in the way of a Wannabee who wants to do the deviant work associated with becoming a member and rising in the hierarchy. The main criterion for belonging to the gang is a proclivity toward violent and delinquent behavior. There is a mythology built up around joining and initiation rites, such as the requirement that a potential member steal something or assault someone, but these entrance demands are not always fulfilled or really expected to take place. At the whim of his homies, on entry, the individual may run a violent gauntlet, be forced to commit an act of violence, or simply be accepted because he lives in the hood and begins to hang out with the gang.

There is little precise definition of role behavior in the gang. If qualifications and standards for belonging were more precise and definite, most gangsters would be unable to participate since they usually lack the social ability to relate to others in a definitive way, an ability that is necessary for assuming responsibilities and belonging to a socially acceptable group.

The usual overt rationale given by gang boys for joining a gang is related to their need for a family that involve their defense, protection, and a feeling of security. Although this is the surface reason given, deeper analysis reveals that the gang is a malleable vehicle for adjusting the gang boys' personal problems and feelings of inadequacy. A youth's motivation for community and belonging to something has more value for him than the spurious nature of the security and affection that is provided in reality by his associates. He seldom finds the love and caring of a family or community that he seeks in the violent gang; however, this reality is less important than his desire for some form of belonging, even if it is illusory.

Participation in and belonging to the violent gang does provide a sense of power. It also provides a channel for expressing a retaliatory aggression related to other emotions and difficulties, such as a response to discrimination or an acting out of racial prejudice itself. Thus many youths in an effort to cope with a variety of emotional problems act out their personal frustrations and aggression through the gang. The gang provides a feeling of self-protection and defense, albeit a false feeling in a hostile world that the paranoid gangster himself has helped to create.

Unlike a normal group, the expectations for participation in the near-group violent gang's activities is unclear. Leadership and leaders are characterized by megalomania, strong needs to control territory, and an emotionally distorted picture of the gang's organization. The image and size of the gang's membership is often exaggerated and glorified by gang members to enhance their own feelings of power.

A consequence of the sociopathic disorder that exists in many gangsters fuels violent behavior even in their own set. A considerable amount of the gangster's time is spent in a pattern of needling, ridiculing, or fighting with his homies; consequently, a great deal of their social participation and camaraderie is of a negative nature. The underlying theme of these playful, but often violent street-corner activities is an attempt to prove one's self by disparaging others. There is a continual verbal and sometimes physical attack and defense going on. In most of these "playful" but aggressive encounters with his homies is the underlying theme of expressing a hostility and rage that emanates from the gangster's depressed life situation.

There is a myth in many violent gangs that you can never rescind your belonging. In the Chicano gangs the expression "por vida," meaning "for life," is the standard. Yet many youths do separate from the gang in a variety of ways. They don't usually resign from a gang and give up their participation in a formal way. After a sojourn in prison or jail, a gangster can voluntary decide to give up gang life. Most of the time if they are making an effort to go straight, they will not be hassled in their efforts. In fact, in many instances their desire to get a job and change their deviant lifestyle is encouraged by their homies.

It is true that in some cases leaving the gang can result in violent retribution; however, this is often done sporadically, at the whim of other gangsters. There are no hard-and-fast rules about quitting the gang, as when a member resigns or retires from a corporate entity. Gangsters do not receive pink slips, however, on some occasions their pink slip may take the form of an assassination from a homie or from an enemy in a drive-by murder.

And many times, in contradiction of the mythology that an individual is in the gang for life, a gangster can gracefully retire from gang activity without any retribution from his associates. This is most true for veteranos or OGs. They can retire with dignity. As one active OG said about another OG who had retired,

> He's thirty and he put in his work. He was shot eight or nine times fighting for his homies, and he did about ten years in the joint. He's married and has kids. He's got a little job. He just hangs out with us sometimes, gets loaded, and talks about the old days when he was gangbanging. People respect him for what he did, and if a kid wants some advice or a war starts, we might get his opinion on what to do.

In brief, belonging to and leaving a gang is not as clearly or formally defined as it is in more coherent social groups.

LEVELS OF PARTICIPATION: MARGINAL AND CORE GANGSTERS

Gangsters participate in their gangs at different times with different levels of involvement. Some individuals are very marginal gangsters and have a limited participation in a gang, even though they appear to be gangsters by their demeanor and the way they dress. These marginal gang youths may present a gang appearance for the purposes of protection.

The core category includes both the Gs and OG leaders, who are at the center of the gang's structure and are the most dedicated and involved gangsters. Core participants in a gang tend to know each other on a face-to-face, primary-group level. They live in close proximity to each other in the hood, hang around the same location, play together, fight among themselves, worry together, and plan gang strategy for warfare.

The solidarity of the core gangsters is much greater than that of the outer ring of more marginal gang participants. Gang involvement is close to the core gangster's lifeline of activity, and to them, the gang constitutes their primary world. Their ego strength, position in the world, and any status or pleasure they enjoy are tied to gang activity. Their turf and activities, particularly the gang's violence, give meaning to their existence.

LEADERS AND LEADERSHIP

One gangster commented in response to the question on leadership:

> We don't have anyone as a special leader. We certainly don't elect anyone
> as a leader. If a homie puts in a lot of work like hurting or killing some
> enemies or backing up his homies with action rather than bullshit, he is
> looked at as a leader. Also OGs are leaders because they been with the
> gang for a long time, they've earned their stripes, they know our history,
> and people respect them for lots of things they've done to help the gang
> be known.

Most gang leaders are essentially self-appointed and tend to assume a
leadership role in a particular activity of the multipurpose gang. OGs have a
level of leadership status based on their longevity in the gang and the violent
quality of the work they have put in as a gangster. Many gangster leaders
manifest paranoid delusions of persecution and grandeur. In some cases they
are attempting to compensate and adjust serious personality disorders
through acting in the role of powerful but pseudoleaders. Their wild dreams
of glory often serve their personal pathological needs.

THE DRUG FACTOR

Crack-cocaine and heroine are the main drugs of use and commerce for
gangsters. Crack is a commodity for both black and Chicano gangs; however,
heroin in the 1990s remains a part of Chicano gang culture. Crack is a
heavily addicting drug that has dominated hoods and barrios throughout the
United States since about 1985. Gangsters are involved in the distribution
and sale of these drugs at all levels. Some OGs and Gs have direct contact
at the very top of the drug business with manufacturers and distributors on
an international level. Gs and WBs, at the lower rungs of the drug business
ladder, deliver and sell drugs on the street.

The commerce of drugs (especially crack-cocaine) and the use of drugs
by gangsters has an impact on the overall structure of the gang. The gangsters
who are centrally involved in the commerce of drugs tend to form a more
coherent and cohesive structured subgroup in the context of the multipurpose gang. They are in a business that involves the performance of rather
specific roles in the buying and selling of drugs, and this requires some
coherence to their behavior. They have to handle specific amounts of money,
launder the money, and protect their territory from any incursion by dealers

who are not part of their organization. They literally have to call the shots on assaulting anyone who intrudes on their profit-making business. In some cases they have the responsibility of exporting their drug business into new markets.

The entrepreneurial/corporate drug-dealing subgroup of the overall multi-purpose gang has most of the qualities of cohesiveness that exists in most normal coherent groups. However, there are a number of factors that affect this structure. These include the fact that the drug subgroup of the overall gang is involved in an illegal enterprise involving secrecy, due to the constant threat of being arrested, incarcerated, or killed.

Another problem that exists in the commerce of drugs is that some of the purveyors of the commodity get hooked on their product. This usually leads to the abuser being ostracized from the gang. However, even in the harsh world of the violent gang, there is sometimes room for compassionate help. When pressed on the subject, I was told by a number of hard-core gangsters that they would often make an effort to counsel their homies out of using when they were hooked. While smoking a joint, these "drug-counselors" would discuss their "clients" and the difficulties of treating a crackhead. (Although negative attitudes about crack and heroin prevail in the gang, marijuana and alcohol are perceived as harmless drugs that are smoked and drunk on a normal, day-by-day basis.) The evidence is overwhelmingly clear that the persistent use of any mind-altering drug by participants in any group has an abnormal impact on the structure and function of the group, and in this regard many gangs are near-groups because of the drug factor.

VIOLENCE: GANGBANGING AND GANG WARFARE

Illegal violence is a basic characteristic of the violent gang. The use of illegal violence, either rationally or irrationally, necessarily affects the structure of any collectivity. As previously discussed, there are two general types of violence enacted in the near-group violent gang. One has a level of rationality as related to drug territory, the administration of a drug business in an area, or for the punishment of a snitch who violates the gang's code of secrecy. The other form of gang violence, the gangbanging pattern, is senseless and revolves around emotional issues that have no clear purpose or consensus of definition for the participants in this brutal activity.

In most cases, gang wars originate over trivia. A territorial violation, a "bad look," an exaggerated argument over a girl, paranoid revenge, or a remark that is perceived as disrespectful may be the flash point for stirring up a large collection of youths into gang warfare. These absurd reasons are exaggerated and spread through gang networks in distorted ways to inflame many gangsters into battle.

Such surface provocations give disturbed youths a cause célèbre and a legitimate banner under which they can vent hostilities related to other issues in their life situation. The gangsters' emotions are fanned through interaction and produce a kind of group contagion. What starts out as a bad look from one youth can develop into a major battle with a real or imagined enemy. Each youth who becomes involved can project into the battle whatever angers or hostilities he has toward school, his family, the neighborhood, prejudice, or any other anger-provoking problems he may be living with at the time.

In gangbanging that is not involved with the drug business, at an "actual gang-war," or in a drive-by, many participants have little or no idea of why they are there or what they are expected to do, except assault someone who appears to be an enemy. OGs, Gs, citizens, and sometimes the police and the press are often caught up in the fallout contagion of gang-war hysteria. Although violent gangsters may not be clear about their motives, a gang war can result in injury and often homicide. In fact, the confused nature of the near-group gang with its fantasy qualities helps to make it a more highly destructive instrument of violence than it would be if the violence were organized in the more deliberate and coherent fashion of La Cosa Nostra.

As previously described, in the past fifty years, gang warfare has escalated from one-on-one fistfights and knifings, to rat-pack group attacks, to the grand form of the drive-by murder — the dramatic approach to murder that was invented in the adult, organized bootlegging gangs during the Roaring Twenties. These early, adult-gang drive-bys most of the time had a precise target. A contemporary drive-by is sometimes an actual hit on a real enemy who has invaded a gang's drug territory; more often than not, it is a spontaneously organized random hit on an imagined enemy that is fueled by the unspecified rage of gangsters who are high on alcohol or drugs. Gangbanging for some youths is a social narcotic in its own right.

The following description of a typical drive-by by a participant reveals the near-group nature of the violent gang:

We were hangin' out, talkin' shit, and getting loaded. This cat "Little Snowman" — we called him that because he had a cold heart — kept talkin' about how these Bloods had dissed him the day before. My homies had some guns that we had stole out of this house, and we had a car.

Pretty soon we're talkin' about how we had to teach those motherfuckers a lesson they wouldn't forget. Myself, I didn't want to go — but there was no way to back down.

The next thing I remember we're in the car and rolling on our enemies hood. The closer we got to their hood, the higher I got. I remember my homie, OG Willie, who was leading our attack, screaming, "We're going to show those motherfuckers no love!"

I only had a pistol, but my homie with an automatic sprayed these guys on the corner. Like in the movies — they all ducked, and I saw two guys get hit and go down. We split, and for the next week that was all we talked about — who did what and how those motherfuckers deserved it. And how funny it was to watch this one dude get hit and fall into some garbage cans. That week we all watched our backs 'cause we knew they would be coming back at us.

This hysterical drive-by is typical: a spontaneous action, with no special planning or motive, whose targets can include anyone in the line of fire, whose shooters are typically high on some substance and whose participation in the violence provides an even greater emotional high, and the more bizarre a participant's violent act, the greater the status he is accorded in the gang's postviolence dialogues.

The foregoing analysis of the personality of gangsters, their gangs' organization, and their basic behavior indicates that gangs differ significantly from most nondeviant normal social groups. This is why I have characterized the gang as a near-group. The social-psychological lens of the near-group provides a more insightful and reality-based perspective for understanding the contemporary gang.

PARANOID PSEUDOCOMMUNITIES: WHY GANGSTERS JOIN AND BECOME ENMESHED INTO NEAR-GROUP VIOLENT GANGS

Norman Cameron's insightful social-psychological concept of the "paranoid pseudocommunity" provides a theoretical perspective that contributes to my analysis of why gangsters join and become enmeshed in violent gangs, and it further illuminates my viewpoint of the gang as a near-group.[6]

His concept, briefly stated, is that emotionally disordered individuals who are paranoid create a pseudocommunity in their mind, and sometimes these delusions find credence in reality. This concept is useful in analyzing some gangsters who perceive enemy gangs as always out to harm them. In response to this impending violent doom, they organize their lives around the gang in a continuing defensive stance. Of course, there is some reality to this perspective on the hostile world that surrounds them; however, more often than not, their perception of enemy gangs as being out to get them is delusionary.

The creation of this mental pseudocommunity, according to Cameron, results from a series of events that impact an individual. He posits that, in general, a group makes certain demands on its participants, and in the normative pattern of life, the individual gives of himself to group demands. Most normal individuals find their participation in a group a satisfying experience and are willing to adhere to the normative demands of the group. In their daily level of group interaction, their participation is validated by other individuals in the group.

However, under certain circumstances individuals with socially inadequate personality development (like gangsters) fail progressively to adhere to the group's (society's) minimal requirements for behavior. This results in their becoming "socially disarticulated," and very often these individuals have to be set aside from the rest of their community to live under artificially simplified conditions.[7] In my view, derived from Cameron's thesis, the violent gang is a creation that provides these "artificially simplified conditions."

Cameron further posits that some people with socially inadequate personalities become paranoid. He states,

> The paranoid person, because of poorly developed role-taking ability, which may have been derived from defective social learning in earlier life, faces his real or fancied slights and discriminations without adequate give-and-take in his communication with others and without competence in the social interpretation of motives and intentions.[8]

The gangster, whose role-taking skills are impaired in this way, lacks the ability to appropriately assess the behavior of others in their interaction with him. He begins to take everything the wrong way, and because of his social inabilities to think as others do, he becomes increasingly alienated and disassociated from the consensual world of reality that is perceived by most people. In this context, the gangster's delusional fantasies become hardened, and he begins to see and experience things not consensually validated or similarly felt by others. He lives in the context of what Cameron has termed a paranoid pseudocommunity. In his paranoid delusions the actions and attitudes ascribed by him to enemy gangs do not fully exist in reality. Enemy gangs and their imminent danger to him begin to exist mainly in his pathological mind.

Cameron's description of this type of paranoid person fits the personality of the sociopathic gangster. In his paranoid sensitivity, a bad look, or any "dis" (disrespect) becomes a major issue. He too often responds with a level of violence that is out of proportion to the act that he interprets or imagines has been perpetrated on him by another gangster or by people in the larger society. He often feels people are out to get him.

The fact of the real community's response and retaliation to his deviant behavior serves to strengthen the gangster's suspicions and distorted interpretations about the social system and its institutions. He utilizes this as further evidence of the unfair discrimination to which he is being subjected. He comes out into the open with overt action against his real and supposed enemies and manages to bring down further social retaliation. Society's retaliation includes arrest and incarceration. This makes the internal mind-set of the paranoid pseudocommunity more objective and real to him. As Cameron states, "The reactions of the real community in now uniting against him are precisely those which he has been anticipating on the basis of his delusional beliefs." [9] Even though most gangsters are aware that they are locked up because they have violated the law, they tend to perceive society's response to their deviance as unfair. Most incarcerated criminals, gangsters included, see themselves as innocent victims of a discriminatory society.

In summary, adapting Cameron's theory of the paranoid pseudocommunity, I note four main phases in the process of a gangster's becoming enmeshed in the paranoid pseudocommunity of the near-group violent gang:

1. Defective Socialization is the first phase. Most gangsters have been physically, emotionally, or sexually abused. The impact of this negative socialization by their dysfunctional families produces a disproportionate number of sociopathic youths with limited social conscience or ability to relate effectively to other people and groups in society. They are as Cameron indicates in a state of social disarticulation.
2. Because of their paranoid sociopathic tendencies, these youths are alienated from the more consensually real and constructive community of the larger society. Their negative self-feelings of difference, social ineffectiveness, and rejection become reinforced and hardened by society's response to their illegal and violent behavior.
3. The youth's sociopathic personality is articulated in a pathological paranoid reaction to the world around him. Participating in a gang gives the sociopathic youth some illusionary ego strength and contributes to a

reaction formation that takes the form of a "tough-killer" macho-syndrome.

4. The violent gang becomes for this type of youth a convenient paranoid pseudocommunity; it functions by alleviating his personal inadequacies and problems, at least temporarily. The structure of the near-group violent gang, with its flexibility of size, power roles, and delusionary possibilities, make it a most convenient and acceptable collectivity for the sociopathic gangster.

POLICY AND TREATMENT IMPLICATIONS DERIVED FROM PERCEIVING THE GANG AS A NEAR-GROUP

It is axiomatic in any medical model that a correct diagnosis is vital for the solution of a problem. In my view, the same reasoning applies to the effective solution of social problems. The current general perspective on the gang as a cohesive group that is presented by many theorists is not in accord with the drug-dealing, gangbanging, indiscriminately murdering characteristic of contemporary multipurpose gangs. A consequence of this erroneous view is that it leads to ineffectual treatment.

My perspective on violent gangster's as sociopaths in a near-group gang structure correctly characterizes the devastating social problem that currently exists in cities throughout the United States. From my perspective, therefore, it is necessary from a policy and treatment perspective, to accurately diagnose today's gangs as near-groups in order to develop and implement appropriate means for their effective treatment.

The therapeutic community approach, in my view, provides the most promising approach for teaching gangsters how to relate to constructive groups in a positive community. In simplistic terms, the TC approach involves removing the gangster from a destructive gang and integrating him into the positive gang he will find in a TC. A gangster's participation in a TC can modify his sociopathic personality and resocialize him. The following chapter will delineate a projected plan for accomplishing the complex and difficult feat of retraining gangsters in a TC for positive participation as law-abiding citizens in the larger society.

10.

Joining a Positive Gang:
A Plan for Treating Gangsters in a
Therapeutic Community

○ ○ ○ ○ ○ ○ ○ ○ ○ ○

I N GENERAL, ABOUT 65 percent of the 1.6 million prisoners who have been in custody in the United States are rearrested for various crimes within a few years of their release. A summary analysis of a five-year research project built into the Amity Prison Program in California's Donavan Prison reveals that only 35 percent of the prisoners who go through this program are rearrested for crimes in a five-year period after release. In comparison, 65 percent of the control matched group of prisoners in the general prison population were rearrested within five years.[1]

Research data from other TC programs in other states reveal similar positive results. In brief, the Amity TC program in particular, and TC programs in general, have the potential for reversing the recidivism rate and having a profound effect on Americas overall crime and gang problem.

Based on the Amity research and other research results that I have observed over a thirty-year period, I am persuaded that the TC methodology can be an effective approach, in concert with others, for resocializing gangsters. In this context, if instituted, the following detailed projected plan would have a profound impact on controlling and ameliorating America's violent gang problem.

THE PLAN

An effective plan for utilizing the TC approach in resocializing gangsters could have four possible organizational forms:

1. A standard community-based TC that houses and treats the variety of criminals/addicts.
2. A special TC in the community that focuses on the gangster problem.
3. A TC in a cellblock of a prison that deals with the variety of offenders, including violent gangsters.
4. A special cellblock in a prison for core gangsters.

All of these programs would require a combination of a professional staff and staff personnel comprised of ex-gangsters who have themselves successfully been through a TC program.

THE PLACEMENT OF CORE AND MARGINAL GANGSTERS

In the proper placement of gang youths in this variety of possible TC programs, an issue of some significance is differential placement of core and marginal gangsters. Core and marginal gangsters should be placed in different types of TCs. Wannabees and marginal gangsters are more amenable to treatment in community TCs than core gangsters. Peeling off marginal gangsters from the gangsters at the core and reconnecting them to constructive social facilities that exist in the community solves part of the problem.

These youths should be referred by the courts to a community-type TC. Also, in this context, some older residents of a community TC (like Ed) might function as detached gang workers who go out in the community and recruit young Wannabees to voluntarily enter their TC.

The more sociopathic core gangsters, after being arrested and convicted for an offense, should be placed through the courts into a prison TC community, where there is more time to work with them and more control over their behavior.

A prison TC program for the hard-core gang youth is more appropriate because it is necessary to use the power of the law to force them into a custodial TC program. A core gangster like Ed, when forced in court to select between doing his time in the general population of a prison or in a shorter-term TC gang program, will more likely select the latter.

At first he will make this choice because he believes he will be with his homies, and that he will return to gang life as usual in custody. He will be surprised, however, to find himself in an entirely different situation, involving a TC gang-resocialization program. This new situation is directed by both savvy, university-trained professionals and, to his astonishment, some of his former homies, in a program to direct the newcomer's behavioral change through a combination of group methods especially developed for this purpose.

Necessary Groups: Types and Subjects

In all types of TCs, whether in the community or in prison, a number of basic group treatment methods and focused group subjects are required to effect attitude and behavioral change. Those required include (1) a special group early on in the program for the indoctrination of the newcomer into modifying his gangster attitudes and integrating him into the positive gang of the TC community; (2) special TC encounter groups; (3) a general group psychotherapy approach that focuses on self-disclosure — with insights into the participant's socialization process — and on past behavior; (4) psychodrama groups geared toward using role playing for dealing with the variety of gangster problems, especially focused on his past senseless violent behavior; (5) a family focus group that involves discussions with and about the gangster's family, especially his attitude toward his father; (6) an education focus group that emphasizes and stimulates the youths toward a general education about the larger society; and (7) groups focused on occupation selection and training geared toward preparing the youth for life on the outside when he leaves and has to find a job.

These varied groups are basic types that have already been effectively utilized in the several hundred existing TCs. There is evidence that these groups have benefited thousands of former criminals/addicts. There is considerable room for innovation in the further development and actual implementation of these groups for gangsters in a TC program. Given this context, each of these group approaches will be discussed in the following analysis, with some emphasis on how they can be implemented, the processes involved, and the goals that are sought and can be achieved through their implementation.

INDOCTRINATION AND ORIENTATION FOCUS GROUPS

These groups should focus on introducing the client to various phases and ramifications of the TC program that will be encountered in the recovery process. These group sessions analyze the overall structure of the TC organization and the value and purpose of various methods, such as the encounter group and psychodrama. The general goal of these groups is to integrate the newcomer into the therapeutic community he has voluntarily or involuntarily joined.

A necessary early goal involves a series of group discussions directed at redefining the gangster's perception of his gang and past gang life. Discussions in these groups should focus on the nature of gang life and why the youth was motivated to join and participate in gang violence. In this process, for example, it is necessary for him to begin to recognize that his gang is not really a family full of love and to face some of the harsh realities and the deadly future of gang life. A platitude of the gangsters is that "I'll be dead before I'm thirty"; such aggrandizing of his life of suicidal violence needs to be modified. He has to recognize that he has a serious problem as a gangster and that his gang is the vehicle that will put him either in prison for most of his life or in a coffin. One astute gang worker described the gangster as having a virulent form of "AIDS," "gangsters have AIDS, the Addiction to Incarceration and Death Syndrome."

Another attitudinal change involves dealing with his macho-syndrome. He can learn that the macho-syndrome may be a necessity for survival in the gang and prison world, but is a hindrance for him in the real world of employment and in actually relating to a loving family in the larger society.

Basic to the control and treatment of the gangster problem is, therefore, a shift of attitude on their gang and its deadly activities early in the program. The youth needs to make a shift from legitimizing, indirectly institutionalizing, and accepting violent-gang behavior as normal, expected behavior in his hood to perceiving it as a pathological and negative entity. Along with this process is the necessity for the gangster to begin to recognize that there is another more positive way of life for him, and that this can be accomplished if he quits the violent gang and joins the "TC gang."

ENCOUNTER GROUPS

In the early days of Synanon, the first TC for criminals/addicts, Chuck Dederich developed the simple but profound concept that tough guys had to be talked to in a tough way to get them to listen. Kindly cajoling a tough gangster to see a point of view usually does not get through to him. As a result of learning this, an innovative method, the "encounter group" approach for communication, was created for utilization in TC groups. The encounter group (hereafter referred to as EG) is a treatment method that is especially valuable for reaching sociopathic gangsters.

Briefly, the EG format involves ten to fifteen individuals sitting in a circle. One individual at a time is put on the hot seat and talked to by the entire group about some issue related to his negative behavior in his past life or in the TC program. In the process the person being helped is challenged on some aspect of his deviant behavior, past or present, in a relatively harsh way by the group. He, of course, may defend himself on a verbal level. It can be perceived as a verbal and emotional battlefield where an individual's delusions, distorted macho self-image, and negative behaviors are verbally attacked by the group in order to help the person better understand the reality of his life, at least as seen by other group members who have shared an addiction to the gangster lifestyle. The method often at first involves exaggerated statements, ridicule, and analogy; and after the person begins to listen, the situation is discussed in more rational, intellectual, and even philosophical terms.

The EG is a complex approach that is at the core of most group methods in a TC. The basic process involves the group attack on the self-deception that characterizes the resident. For example, his belief that the violence he committed with his homies was a positive activity, necessary for the defense of his turf, could come under the group's scrutiny for its absurdity. Another issue that might be the subject of an EG group is the stupidity of black-on-black or Chicano-on-Chicano violence. A benefit of verbally attacking this behavior is that in defending it, the person on the hot seat will comprehend the ridiculous nature of the violence.

The macho-syndrome is another important subject that can be hammered at in an EG, as in the following example. One youth, a newcomer in the TC, was overheard giving instructions in a secretive form of big-yard prison talk on how to mug a person. Another youth had overheard him and in the EG session brought the subject up. The first youth's behavior was attacked by various members of the group. The encounter was led by Bill, an older ex-gangster in the TC who had been through the criminal wars as a gangster, a heroin addict, and a convict. He was now a staff member in the TC.

In the encounter session Bill belittles the tough-guy gangster attitude as being stupid. And because he himself had a reputation of past behavior as a tough, violent gangster, the group listens to him. Professional university-trained therapists are not in a position to attack the gangster's macho-syndrome in the same way as an ex-gangster like Bill, who has lived the tough-guy role for most of his life, understands the necessity of it in prison and in the gang, and most importantly, has changed his own behavior.

An important consequence of the EG is that it forces the recovering gangster to examine his behavior and lifestyle retrospectively and introspectively. In my view, the EG is a necessary process in all TC work because sociopathic gangsters do not usually respond to the other, more supportive approaches until his basic self-deception devices are vehemently confronted by the group.

A complicated characteristic of the therapeutic community's EG process is an approach that is the reverse of that commonly used in psychotherapy. In most traditional therapeutic practice, the starting point for treatment is usually the internal family dynamics of the patient's early life and how he was raised (or not raised properly) by his parents. Generally, in professional therapy the assumption is made that if a person's inner, early problems are somehow resolved, he will stop acting out his "bad" behavior.

In a TC the starting point is the overt bad behavior of the newcomer. In the EG, and in their life situation in the TC, the group demands positive work habits, truth telling, and nondeviant behavior. If the gangster lives positively and constructively in a TC for one or two years, this will change his inner emotional dynamics in a positive way.

A basic rule that obtains in the EG is that no physical violence is allowed, and surprisingly, this dictum is almost always followed. Consequently, the normal response of violence on the part of a gangster to what he construes as disrespect is transformed into verbal discussion about his behavior and other vital issues in the youth's life. The EG approach is especially relevant to and therapeutic for violent gangsters. As a result of their training in this type of group, they can learn how to channel their rage into verbal discussion rather than their formerly automatic response of physically violent behavior.

The EG process can also help a youth to see himself as relevant others do. The encounter often produces information and valid insights into his problems. If at the conclusion of his turn on the hot seat an individual has been able to hang on to any of his defenses about his behavior, they are probably "valid defenses." In the EG the gangster is forced to examine positive and negative aspects about himself, as well as some dimensions about his behavior he would never have considered on his own. This process often leaves him with a clearer knowledge of his inner and outer world.

It should also be noted that a significant part of the process involves support and "picking up" a person at the end of or after an encounter session. Here the positive aspects of the group are reinforced with care and love. The encounter, paradoxically, is an expression of love. As one gangster told another at the end of a harsh group encounter, "If I didn't care about you and also feel that you could change, I wouldn't tell you the things I do. It would be foolish to attack someone who is hopeless or helpless in improving his behavior."

In this way the encounter group is always supplemented and enriched in a positive way by later informal discussions in a "caring circle" of friends in the TC. All residents in a TC are encouraged to develop a circle of people with whom they can discuss issues brought up forcefully in the EG in a more casual interpretive, analytic, and supportive way. These nurturing, supportive discussions with a caring circle of friends are most significant in the overall group process for changing the gangster's lifestyle in a TC in a positive direction.

SELF-DISCLOSING AND NURTURING GROUPS

In an informal discussion I had with a tough, former Chicano gangster who was now involved in a prison TC program, I asked him, "What is the toughest part of this program for you?" Without missing a beat he said, "The hardest part of this program is talking in front of other guys in groups about my early personal life in my family, and how my father abused me. Mexicans have a kind of rule that you 'don't put your business out in the street.' So for me talking about these personal things is very hard."

In an effective TC for resocializing gangsters, in addition to the encounter groups and other types of groups, self-disclosing and nurturing groups are required. These groups deal with "putting your business out in the street" in the context of standard group therapy methods.

There are special problems in the process of counseling most gang youths, especially sociopaths. They are often manipulative, recalcitrant, and self-deceptive. Consequently, the therapist must often deal with a tough facade and deceptive tactics in order to get through to the youth and his underlying real feelings. Once the therapist gets past the youth's criminal mask and game playing, he can help by counseling the real person behind the facade. This kind of breakthrough often takes place in group therapy in a TC because a youth's peers tend to understand each others personal backgrounds.

For gangsters, in most cases their rage emanates from being physically, emotionally, or sexually abused as children by their parents — most usually their fathers. Mixed into this abuse syndrome is uncaring abandonment. Tough guys find these negative early life experiences difficult to talk about because it reveals an emotional part of themselves that they have kept private in order to maintain their macho face to the world.

In many respects the gangster's rage has not been repressed. In a nurturing group he begins to understand the source of his hostility and how it has been displaced and acted out against the wrong target. This process can explain the senseless black-on-black and Chicano-on-Chicano violence acted out through the gang. Once this is understood by a former gangster, it is one vector in the diminution of his violent motivations because he can see that his early abusive childhood experience was the real enemy and the cause of his violent behavior.

The overall goal of all the types of group approaches delineated here is to help a recovering resident deal more effectively with their emotional problems, and the nurturing group is instrumental in his opening up. In most respects, what I am referring to is a standard form of group therapy. A basic difference between standard group therapy and the type employed in a TC group is that the "group therapists" include his peers and paraprofessional ex-gangsters, in the context of a TC system.

PSYCHODRAMA

In most TCs with which I have been involved or have studied, psychodrama and role training are significant methods utilized for the purpose of group psychotherapy. Psychodrama, as has been described in various sessions with gangsters delineated throughout the book, is a very useful methodology for effectively treating the emotional problems of gangsters.

In a psychodrama group session, beyond simply talking about his problem, a person encounters his conflicts and psychic pain in a dramatic setting that more closely approximates his real-life situation with a stand in for the person(s) with whom he has a problem.

For example, many gangsters have hostility toward their father, who has abused or abandoned them. In one typical psychodrama on this issue, a sociopathic gangster named Tomas who had committed many violent offenses in his criminal career and was now in prison for murder, opened up about his hostility toward his father. At one point in the session, after he had revealed a litany of abuse by his father, I handed him a "battoca" (a rubber bat) and told him to hit a chair with the bat for each abusive offense his father had committed on him. He was told to state the offense and that when he was hitting the chair (that represented his father), it was tantamount to retaliating against his father.

At first his response was one I had heard many times when I invited a protagonist in a psychodrama to act out his feelings of revenge. "Oh no, man, I would never hit my father, he would fuckin' kill me! This comment would typically be followed by a denial of their hatred and rage since many youths try to maintain that their parents are caring people. This youth was encouraged by the group to enact his rage, since many of them knew what was coming from comments he had made in group therapy. As I usually do, I assured Tomas that what he was going to do would be held in strictest confidence in the group and his father would never hear about it.

He began by announcing his father's abuses and then hitting the chair. At first his blows to his father-chair were light ones, however, toward the end of his role playing, in a kind of exorcism, the enactment of his rage became increasingly intense. As he hit the chair, he screamed at his psychodramatic father through clenched teeth:

> This is for all the beatings you gave for no reason when I was a little kid when you came home drunk. *(Bang.)* This is for the times you locked me in the closet. *(Bang.)* This is for all the times you threw me up against the wall. *(Bang.)* This is for the time you punished me by putting my hand on a hot stove for some nothing bullshit thing I had done. *(Bang.)* This is for the time you tied up my arms and hung me like a piece of meat in the cellar. *(Bang)*.

And there was more.

After the session, with the aid of further group discussion, others opened up and shared the abuse that they had received. The source of their enormous rage became manifest to Tomas and many other members of the group. They had a better understanding of the dynamics motivating their senseless acts of rage, that they stemmed from their own abuse and pushed them to commit violence on undeserving victims, including enemy gangs.

A facet of the emotional problems of gangsters that often emerges in psychodrama is that they have committed acts dictated by the gang's norms that conflicts with their underlying emotions. In one memorable psychodrama that I directed, a gangster acted out when he stabbed a homie in prison because his "friend" had snitched on someone in the gang. He tearfully cried his regrets throughout the psychodrama about his violent act. He kept repeating, "I didn't want to hurt him, but I had to do it."

Other gangsters in the group sympathized with his plight, because almost all of them had been involved in violent acts that went against human feelings that they had buried in order to conform to the expectations of their gang and the rules of prison life. The psychodrama triggered an in-depth discussion about the tyranny of the gang's expectations for their violent behavior. One result of the psychodrama was the participants' realization that they had the personal power to stop the violence. This may be an obvious fact to most people, but to the gangsters in the group, the insight that they could control their destiny was a revelation!

In psychodrama, the resolution of a problem does not necessarily require an extensive analysis or discussion because the subject of a session is experiencing the emotions and resolving his problem in action. Often when someone has had a deep psychodramatic experience, there is no need for lengthy group discussion or analysis. The protagonist has unraveled the mystery of his problem in action.

In psychodrama sessions therapeutic benefits accrue to members of the group other than the central protagonist. Group participants other than the main protagonist in the session are encouraged to attempt to understand and identify with aspects of their own lives that are revealed in the session. For group members, it is tantamount to watching a dramatic play that reveals their own problems on the stage in front of them.

Psychodrama is an important method for working with gangsters in a TC because it enables them to examine and analyze situations and scenes in their lives that lead to their self- and other-destructive behaviors. In many psychodrama sessions that I have directed with gangsters, in their enactment of a violent act, I have utilized the soliloquy technique. In this way, the protagonist acts out his violent act in the controlled situation of a psychodrama group and expresses his inner feelings as he is committing the act. There are many gangster Hamlets who don't plan to kill their uncles — their soliloquies do reveal, as in Tomas's psychodrama, that their father is more likely to be the source and target of their homicidal emotions.

The positive consequence of acting out violent or deviant behavior in the controlled setting of a psychodrama often deters the gangster involved in this therapeutic process from the necessity of acting out his violent proclivities in real life. In a psychodrama, under controlled conditions, he can learn more about the underlying familial sources and causes of his violent behavior, and develop skills and strategies to control his impulsive and violent behavior patterns.

Most TCs attempt to have family groups, mainly comprised of the resident's parents, meet on a regular basis. These groups are the counterpart of the AA's Al Anon, and the parents participate after the individual has moved into the TC. It is important to involve the gangster's family in some way into the TC treatment program. Of course, many youths who participate in gangs do not have coherent family situations, and it is difficult to acquire their usually dysfunctional family's cooperation in the therapeutic process.

The Italian TC system (there are over forty TCs in Italy) utilizes a different and perhaps a more effective approach to the family than those used in American TCs. Before someone is accepted into residence, the applicants and their families attend indoctrination groups for a few months, where they learn about various aspects of the TC program. In this way the potential resident gets a head start on becoming involved in the program with the cooperation of his family prior to entering the TC.

Typically in these family groups, work is begun on the potential resident's problems. He may work out a contract with his family for improving his behavior and for becoming drug and crime free as a prelude to entering the TC. These orientation and indoctrination groups facilitate a more effective learning experience when the newcomer finally becomes a full-time resident. This might prove to be a useful approach for some youths entering a gang program. Before entering the TC they might be able to make some progress in disassociating from their homies and becoming more positively involved with their family situation.

Some discussions on family issues involve only residents. Other groups include parents, spouses, siblings, and other relatives. Hovering over every type of family-issue session is the concept that the recovering resident is the nucleus of a familial social atom, and his problem is inextricably bound up with his family system. This concept encompasses J. L. Moreno's admonition that "treatment must always take into account the person's social atom, including family relationships."

A statistic based on a study of Los Angeles high schools (1994) reveals that 39 percent of black youths drop out of high school without graduating. The same statistic is generally true of Chicano and African American youths in urban area schools around the country. This statistic is even higher for youths who participate in gangs. Consequently, gangsters are highly deficient in terms of educational skills and general knowledge.

I have observed that, on their path to social reality in a TC, most residents become enormously motivated to learn to write, read, and acquire the education they missed when they were out on the streets. This hunger for knowledge is fed in educational groups that focus on all kinds of subjects, including philosophical discussions.

In many TCs I have observed residents with a limited educational background enthusiastically participate in educational discussions related to analyzing such philosophers as Emerson, Plato, Kant, and Spinoza; learning about current events related to a range of contemporary social and political issues; social and psychological theories about mental health, including those of Freud, Moreno, Fromm, and Erikson; racism and its roots; studying biological sciences; discussing great literature including Shakespeare; and opening up their minds to classical art and music. There is evidence that youths who participate in the gangster life are as basically intelligent as most other youths and, if presented with the opportunity and properly motivated through a TC educational group, can become involved in intellectual pursuits.

In brief, TC educational groups can cover the range of human subjects and become an important pathway for youths to move out of their alienated life in a gang into intelligently participating in the larger society. In many TCs that I have researched, an educational group process often motivates residents to complete their formal high school or college educations and to better determine the kind of life work they will pursue when they graduate from the TC.

JOB-PLANNING GROUPS

In a discussion I had with a detached gang worker, he told me that one of his most difficult tasks in working with gang youths was related to finding and keeping them in jobs. He said, "Most of these guys, especially core gangsters have never worked a day in their life. And when I do get some of them work, they don't last very long on the job. They get belligerent with their boss, they show up late, or not at all." It is apparent that some effort has to be made to help youths learn how to get a job and to understand the necessity of developing some occupational skills if they are to succeed.

In order for a TC to function, there are a variety of jobs built into the organization that require workers. Many TCs have gas stations, light manufacturing plants, and advertising specialty businesses for the purpose of helping to finance the organization's work. In the TC organization, there are business office jobs, housekeeping and kitchen jobs, and manual labor. These jobs are filled by residents and provide realistic on-the-job training, with the necessary backup of groups where they can discuss problems they confront in the process of their work.

In the occupational group's discussions, each resident's efficacy and inclination toward meaningful work are analyzed based on their work performance. The group's goals are to help residents to learn how to work and to clarify the kind of work they would like to engage in when they graduate and return to their community. These groups foster on-the-job training and clarify occupational goals. A focus in educational groups on how to get a job (perhaps through role playing), how to hold a job, and the necessity of learning some trade is beneficial for residents in their necessary future occupations in society after graduating from the TC program.

Factors Required for the Effective Resocialization of Gangsters

The foregoing group methods have been effective in the general application of the TC approach with criminals/addicts, including former gangsters who have gone through the TC resocialization process. There are some basic social-psychological factors that I believe are necessary for a successful TC program for gangsters. Following is a summary review of these factors and a brief commentary on how this projected TC plan can impact the resocialization of a gangster.

INVOLVEMENT

Initially the TC society of professional therapists, former criminals/addicts, and ex-gangster staff is able to involve and control the newcomer by providing an interesting social setting comprised of understanding associates who will not be outmaneuvered by the newcomer's manipulative behavior. This kind of staff understands the newcomer because many of them were once in his position.

ACHIEVABLE GOALS

Within the context of the TC system, with achievable ex-gangsters as role models, the newcomer can (perhaps for the first time) see a realistic possibility for legitimate and constructive achievement, independence, and prestige. A TC provides a rational opportunity structure for the newcomer. He is not restricted to inmate or patient status since there is no inmate-staff division and all residents are immediately staff members who are required to do some work in the TC. At first they are assigned simple tasks, like cleaning or working in the kitchen, but they can aspire to and achieve higher-status roles occupied by people who they know were once in their position.

SOCIAL GROWTH

In the process of a former gangster experiencing and acquiring legitimate and higher social status in a TC, the resident necessarily, as a side effect, develops the ability to relate, communicate, and work with others. The values of truth, honesty, and industry become necessary means to this goal of status achievement. With enough practice and time, the former gangster socialized in this way reacts according to these newly found values in a natural way. This is a most effective system for people who, upon entrance to the TC, had an egocentric/sociopathic posture toward life.

THE DEVELOPMENT OF EMPATHY AND SELF-ESTEEM

The constant self-assessment required in daily TC life and in the group sessions, especially the nurturing and encounter groups, fosters the consolidation of self-esteem and empathy. The individual's self-estimation is under constant assessment by relevant others, who are sensitive to and concerned about the individual. The process provides the opportunity for a youth almost literally to see himself as others do. The former gangster in this situation is compelled, as part of this process, to develop the ability to identify with and understand others, if only out of a self-interest in acquiring higher status in the system. The side effects are personal growth, greater social awareness, an improved ability to communicate, and a greater facility for being empathic about the needs of others. The development of empathy and better self-esteem can have the impact of changing a gangster with a sociopathic personality into a caring, humanistic person.

SOCIAL CONTROL

The self-control of the former gangster's deviance is a by-product of the individual's participation in the TC organization. Conformity to the norms is necessary for achievement in the TC. Anomie, the dislocation of social goals and the means for acquiring them, is minimized. The norms are valid and adhered to within the social system of the TC since the means are available for legitimate goal attainment in the organization as a prelude to participation in the overall society.

Another form of control is embodied in the threat of ostracism. This, too, becomes a binding force. The relative newcomer in a TC usually does not feel adequate to participate in the larger society. But after a sufficient period of positive social living in a TC, the resident no longer fears banishment and is adequately prepared for life outside (if this is his choice). However, residents may remain voluntarily and assume an ex-gangster paraprofessional role for working with newcomers because they feel a TC is a valid way of life.

A NEW SOCIAL ROLE AS A TC THERAPIST

Changing from a gangster role to a new "TC professional" person has the possibility, as evidenced by Ed and hundreds of other ex-gangsters, of providing these individuals with a new and valuable social role. That role can be, temporarily or indefinitely, the process of social growth and development while in the TC. Upon graduation he has an opportunity to acquire a job as a counselor in the TC that has changed him or work in this capacity in another TC. TC-trained ex-criminals/addicts are increasingly in demand. (The Therapeutic Communities of America organization now provides many job opportunities for TC professionals who qualify as TC counselors.)

The Social Vaccine Theory for Treating "Aids" (Addiction to Incarceration and Death Syndrome)

If the foregoing projected TC plan for a gangster is effective, the combined impact of varied group modification forces in a TC has the impact of providing him with a new identity, insulating him from the need to return to his former gangster lifestyle. If successful, he has developed an antigang attitude and personal identity that enables him to lead a happier, more productive life — and to pass on his newly found antigang attitude to others immersed in their deadly gang-syndrome. Consequently, in addition to his personal success, an ex-gangster TC graduate can be a valuable asset as a role model in society's overall efforts at preventing, controlling, and possibly eliminating violent gangs.

The dynamic process of the TC approach for resocializing gangsters by dealing with their addiction to incarceration and death syndrome suggests a theory that I have developed, defined, and labeled as the "social vaccine theory." I originally developed this for the purpose of analyzing the value of the TC approach for criminals/addicts in general; however, I believe it has an equally appropriate value for the projected TC approach for ameliorating the gang problem.

The theory is derived from the immunization concept and the use of vaccines for diseases that was first introduced by an English physician, Edward Jenner. Webster's New World Dictionary's definition specifies that "a vaccine is a living attenuated organism that is administered to produce or increase immunity to a particular disease." Dr. Jenner demonstrated that inserting a low level of virus into a person's physiological system stimulated antibodies, which would defend and prevent an immunized person from having a more virulent form of the disease.

Transposing this physiological concept to a social sphere, I would assert that the social vaccine concept would involve the insertion of individuals, in this case ex-gangsters with a socially based disease of sociopathic gangster behavior, into a virulent gang community for the purpose of immunizing the community against the continuance of violent gangs. My speculation is that the former gangsters who are properly employed in a TC or simply living in a law-abiding manner in their hood created an "antibody" to the gang disease in the larger society.

In this context I would suggest that paraprofessional ex-gangsters are individuals who, once their problem has been arrested, can in time and in sufficient numbers serve as antibodies to the peculiar "AIDS" gang disease that exists in their community and in the overall society. To some degree the force of antialcoholic AA members has produced this kind of antibody on an international level for helping to prevent and control alcoholism. I believe this same approach would, if properly applied through the TC methodology, prove to be effective in helping to ameliorate the gang problem.

The social vaccine application to the gang problem may be summarized as follows: The individual who has had the gang "AIDS," has gone through the TC process of recovery, and is now functioning effectively "AIDS"-free in a TC for gangsters or in his hood or barrio provides a kind of antibody or social vaccine for his community and the overall social system. In this regard ex-gangsters who have been immunized against the virulent addiction of gang life can become antibodies in the overall social system, and they can be a vital force in preventing and helping others, especially youngsters from their hood, to resist the deadly "AIDS" of violent gang life.

In brief, I perceive the TC plan I have proposed for the gang problem as a vital therapeutic system for immunizing people who have passed through the fires of destructive gang life. The ex-gangsters who successfully emerge from the proposed TC plan can provide valuable research data and an antigang posture that is useful to help prevent others, especially young, vulnerable individuals, from their participation in senseless violent gangs. The projected TC system for treating gangsters can potentially produce thousands of ex-gangster graduates, who in the role of paraprofessionals or as active, concerned citizens in their community, can significantly contribute to the prevention, control, and potentially the eradication of the virulent disease of violent gangs in America.

Notes

○ ○ ○ ○ ○ ○ ○ ○ ○ ○

NOTES TO THE INTRODUCTION

1. Jimmy Cannon, *New York Post*, February 22, 1955.
2. Lewis Yablonsky, *The Violent Gang* (London: Macmillan, 1962; rpt. New York: Penguin Books, 1966; rpt. New York: Irvington Press, 1983).

NOTES TO CHAPTER 1

1. In his interview, "Tookie" made these insightful comments to *Los Angeles Times* reporter Barbara Becnel on why youths participate in gangs and the complex phenomenon of black-on-black gang violence. Barbara Becnel, "An Interview with a Gang Leader," *Los Angeles Times*, August 22, 1993.
2. Elijah Anderson, "The Code of The Streets," *Atlantic Monthly*, May 1994, 64.
3. Selwyn Raab, "A New Breed of Criminal," *New York Times*, March 20, 1988.
4. Ibid.
5. Ibid.
6. "Warring Gangs Keep Residents Fearful," *Los Angeles Times*, July 16, 1995.
7. Kody Scott, *Monster* (New York: Penguin Books, 1994), 78.
8. Richard Cloward and Lloyd Ohlin, *Delinquency and Opportunity* (New York: Free Press, 1960), 54.
9. Kurt Lang and Gladys Lang, *Collective Dynamics* (New York: Crowell, 1961), 35.
10. Gregory Boyle, "Hope Is the Only Antidote," *Los Angeles Times*, January 6, 1995.

11. Henry Louis Gates, Jr., "The Downtown Chronicles: Sudden Def," *New Yorker*, June 19, 1995, 34–38.

NOTES TO CHAPTER 2

1. Herbert Asbury, *Gangs of New York* (Garden City, N.Y.: Garden City Publishing, 1928).
2. Ibid., 112.
3. Lewis Yablonsky, *George Raft* (New York: McGraw-Hill, 1974).
4. Henry D. Sheldon, "The Institutional Activity of Children," *American Journal of Psychology* (March 1898): 37.
5. J. Adam Puffer, "Boys' Gangs," Pedogogical Seminary (1905): 56.
6. Ibid., 3.
7. Frederich Thrasher, *The Gang: A Study of 1,313 Gangs* (Chicago: University of Chicago Press, 1926).
8. Ibid., 62–63.
9. Ibid., 48.
10. Frank Tannenbaum, *Crime and the Community* (New York: Columbia University Press, 1939), 46.
11. Ibid., 12–13.
12. William F. Whyte, *Street Corner Society* (Chicago: University of Chicago Press, 1943).
13. Ibid., 255.
14. *Working with Teenage Gangs* (New York: New York City Youth Board, 1950).

NOTES TO CHAPTER 3

1. "In Brooklyn: A Wolf in $45 Sneakers," *Time*, October 18, 1981, 36.
2. Scott, *Monster*, 12.

NOTES TO CHAPTER 4

1. Diego Vigil, *Barrio Gangs: Street Life and Identity in Southern California* (Austin: University of Texas Press, 1988).
2. Ibid., 45.
3. Joan Moore, *Homeboys: Gangs, Drugs and Prisons in the Barrios of Los Angeles* (Philadelphia: Temple University Press, 1978), 132.
4. John Irwin, *Prisons in Turmoil* (Boston: Little Brown, 1980).
5. Ibid., 36.
6. Ibid., 87.

NOTES TO CHAPTER 5

1. Scott, *Monster*, 57.
2. Hervey Cleckley, *The Mask of Sanity* (St. Louis: Mosby, 1976).
3. Harrison Gough, "A Sociological Theory of Psychopathy," *American Journal of Sociology* (March 1948): 46.
4. Albert Rabin, "Psychopathic Personalities," in *Legal and Criminal Psychology*, ed. Hans Toch (Austin: Holt, Rinehart, and Winston, 1961), 278.
5. George Herbert Mead, *Mind, Self, and Society* (Chicago: University of Chicago Press, 1934), 132.
6. Harry Stack Sullivan, *Conceptions of Psychiatry* (New York: William Alanson White Psychiatric Foundation, 1947), 145.
7. Joan McCord and William McCord, *Origins of Crime* (New York: Columbia University Press, 1959), 5.
8. Edwin Megargee and Roy Golden, "Parental Attitudes of Psychopathic Delinquents," *Journal of Criminology* (February 1973): 56.
9. As told to Alex Haley, *The Autobiography of Malcolm X* (New York: Grove Press, 1965), 189.

NOTES TO CHAPTER 6

1. *Reaching the Unreached* (New York: New York City Youth Board, 1952), 108.
2. Bella Stumbo, "East L.A. Gang: Youth Worker Struggles for Peace in Barrio," *Los Angeles Times*, September 19, 1976.
3. Lewis Yablonsky, *Psychodrama* (New York: Basic Books-HarperCollins, 1976; rpt. New York: Brunner/Mazel, 1992).

NOTES TO CHAPTER 7

1. Lewis Yablonsky, *Synanon: The Tunnel Back* (Toronto: Macmillan, 1965); Lewis Yablonsky, *The Therapeutic Community* (Lake Worth, Fla.: Gardner Press, 1989; rev. ed. 1994).
2. For a fuller analysis of the theory, methods, and evaluations of the TC approach, see George DeLeon, *The Therapeutic Community: Perspectives and Approach* (Springfield, Ill.: Charles C. Thomas, 1986).

NOTES TO CHAPTER 8

1. Albert Cohen, *Delinquent Boys* (New York: Free Press, 1955), 45.
2. Ibid., 31.
3. Ibid., 59.

4. Ibid., 132.

5. Herbert Block and Albert Niederhoffer, *The Gang* (New York: Philosophical Library, 1958), 99.

6. Ibid., 143.

7. Ibid., 136.

8. Walter B. Miller, "Lower Class Culture as a Generating Milieu of Gang Delinquency," *Journal of Social Issues* (March 1959): 86.

9. Ibid., 37.

10. Ibid., 48.

11. Richard Cloward and Lloyd Ohlin, *Delinquency and Opportunity: A Theory of Gangs* (New York: Free Press, 1960), 56.

12. Ibid., 126.

13. Ibid., 132.

14. Ibid., 52.

15. James Short, Jr., and Fred Strodbeck, "Youth Gangs and Society," *Sociological Quarterly* (winter 1974): 48.

16. Ibid., 19.

17. Ibid., 34.

18. Barbara Tomson and Edna R. Fielder, *Gangs: A Response to the Urban World* (Pacific Grove, Calif.: Brooks/Cole, 1975).

19. Ibid., 122.

20. Ibid., 87.

21. Irving A. Spergel, *Racketville, Slumtown, Haulberg* (Chicago: University of Chicago Press, 1964).

22. Ibid., 39.

23. Irving A. Spergel, *The Youth Gang Problem* (Oxford: Oxford University Press, 1995), 37.

24. Ibid., 53.

25. Malcolm W. Klein, Cheryl L. Maxson, and Jody Miller, *The Modern Gang Reader* (Los Angeles: Roxbury, 1995).

26. Malcolm W. Klein, *Street Gangs and Street Workers* (New York: Prentice-Hall, 1971), 58.

27. Ibid., 89.

28. Martin Sanchez Jankowski, *Islands in the Streets* (Berkeley: University of California Press, 1991), 47.

29. Ibid., 56.

30. William B. Sanders, *Gangbangs and Drive-bys* (Hawthorne, N.Y.: Aldine De Gruyter, 1994), 42.

31. Ibid., 5.

32. Jerome H. Skolnick, "Gangs and Crime Old as Time; but Drugs Change Gang Culture," in *Modern Gang Reader*, ed. Malcolm Klein et al. (Los Angeles: Roxbury, 1995), 136.

33. Ibid., 138.

34. John M. Hagedorn "Homeboys, Dope Fiends, Legits, and New Jacks" *Criminology* (May 1994): 24.

35. Ibid., 27.

36. George Knox, *An Introduction to Gangs* (Bristol, Ind.: Wyndham Hall Press, 1995).

37. George Knox, David Laske, and Edward Tromanhauser, *Schools under Siege* (Dubuque, Iowa: Kendall/Hunt, 1992), 132.

38. Ibid., 134.

39. George Knox, *The Economics of Gang Life* (Chicago: National Crime Research Center, 1995).

40. Ibid., 96.

41. Ronald Huff, *Gangs in America* (Thousand Oaks, Calif.: Sage Publishers, 1991).

42. Scott Decker, "Field Studies of Gangs: A Synthesis of The Past and Suggestions for Future Research" (Unpublished, 1995), 10.

NOTES TO CHAPTER 9

1. Robert Merton, *Social Theory and Social Structure* (New York: Free Press, 1957), 131.

2. Sanders, *Gangbangs and Drive-bys*, 24.

3. Jankowski, *Islands in the Streets,* 56.

4. Emile Durkheim, *The Rules of Sociological Method* (New York: Free Press, 1950), 65.

5. Barbara G. Myerhoff and Howard L. Myerhoff, "Field Observations of Gangs," *Social Forces* (March 1964): 348.

6. Norman Cameron, "The Paranoid Pseudocommunity," *American Journal of Sociology* (July 1943).

7. Ibid., 25.

8. Ibid., 32.

9. Ibid., 46.

NOTES TO CHAPTER 10

1. Harry Wexler, *Research Reports on the Therapeutic Community* (La Jolla, Calif.: Center for Therapeutic Community Research, 1995).

Index

○ ○ ○ ○ ○ ○ ○ ○ ○ ○